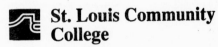

First United States Edition, 1990
First published in France by Éditions du Chêne

Library of Congress Cataloging-in-Publication Data
Bazin, Germain.
  [Paradeisos, ou, L'art du jardin. English]
  Paradeisos, the art of the garden/Germain Bazin.—1st U.S. ed.
    p. cm.
  'A Bulfinch Press Book.'
  Translation of: Paradeisos, ou, L'art du jardin.
  Includes bibliographical references.
  ISBN 0–8212–1794–1
  1. Gardens—History. 2. Gardens—Design—History. I. Title.
SB465.B3913 1990   89–82268
712'.09—dc20   CIP

Bulfinch Press is an imprint and trademark of Little, Brown and Company (Inc.)
Published simultaneously in Canada by Little, Brown & Company (Canada) Limited

PRINTED IN SWITZERLAND

PARADEISOS

The Art of the Garden

Germain Bazin

A Bulfinch Press Book   Little, Brown and Company

BOSTON · TORONTO · LONDON

Preface

One fine summer's day, I had arranged to meet someone in a fashionable shop in the rue du Faubourg-Saint-Honoré. Unfortunately I was kept waiting rather longer than expected. I felt myself getting increasingly uncomfortable; the walls and ceiling seemed to be closing in on me. Noticing my growing depression, the friend who was keeping me company beckoned me towards the lift. Up we rose to the top of the building, where I emerged into a long corridor, separated by a sheet of plate glass from a roof garden. This unexpected island of greenery, surrounded by stone benches, measured scarcely more than 90 square metres, yet it was crammed with all kinds of plants: box, white hawthorn, red hawthorn, santolina, althaea, ceanothus, rosemary, syringa, lavender, magnolia, roses, including climbers, and in the centre an apple tree. Curiously appropriate, too, for as I gazed delightedly at the mass of colour, Eve herself appeared, trimly turned out as a gardener in blue jeans (this was, after all, the neighbourhood of fashion houses) and traditional blue apron – in fact, just like the gardeners of my childhood – with its capacious pocket containing pruning knife, secateurs, two dibbles, one attached to a cord, and the indispensable ball of raffia for tying up any wilting shoots.

Eve (who may well have been sent to divert me) went about her business. She did a little watering, picked up a few fallen leaves or petals, pruned the occasional plant and, just by her presence, frightened away the cheeky Parisian sparrows who were clearly familiar with the tiny oasis. Reflecting on this miniature garden improbably suspended above one of the busiest crossroads in Paris, my thoughts travelled back to the garden of my childhood. This, of course, had been much larger and, as I came to realize later, it combined beauty and utility. For a child, it was a constant source of wonder and surprise – a whole universe where the dreams of a lifetime could be conjured up. There were floral displays and borders, immaculate (and forbidden) lawns, espaliers, laurel and euonymus, trimmed box, laughing Cupids in syringa bushes, a verandah, a kiosk, a conservatory which I converted into the *Nautilus*, a sea of sand where I could build volcanoes, and a maze of pools, rockeries and cascades.

Eventually, of course, my guest arrived to awake me from my dreams and project me brutally back into the real world. Once home, however, I began to look through my library and files, where I found an unexpectedly large number of books, guides, pamphlets, photographs, postcards and notes on the many gardens I had visited in all parts of the world. And so it was that I decided to explore further the theme of the art of the garden, which, although not without historians, has never attracted the attention of the great art theorists. Neither Winckelmann, Burckhardt, Walter Pater, Ruskin, Warburg, Wölfflin, Elfie Faure nor Panofsky showed any interest in this world of rich and complex symbolism. Of the major art historians, only Rudolf Wittkower, at the Warburg Institute, touched on it in his study of the labyrinth. Perhaps Berenson had the best approach of all: he actually created a garden.

I was further encouraged in my project when I was appointed by the Institut de France to be keeper of one of the most prestigious gardens of the age of Louis XIV, that of Chantilly. As I began to explore the enormous variety of gardens through the ages, both in the West and East, I always came back to the same archetype. The garden appeared to me to represent one of the most secret aspirations of the human spirit. This book is the result of my quest and I would propose as a symbol of this preface the bookplate of the Baroque monastery of Vorau in Austria: the physical aspect of the subject is expressed in the illustration of a gardener watering the flowers in the garden of an Italian villa, while its spiritual content is the subject of the motto: *Dirigit et irrigat*.

Germain Bazin
Paris, Chantilly, 1987

IN THE
BEGINNING

9

THE GARDEN
IN CLASSICAL
ANTIQUITY

PAGE

15

THE ISLAMIC
GARDEN

PAGE

31

THE CLASSICAL
GARDEN

PAGE

125

THE BAROQUE
GARDEN

PAGE

163

THE LANDSCAPE
GARDEN

PAGE

193

IN THE BEGINNING

The garden was born from the desert. After countless days of travel across an ocean of sand, dying of thirst, what mirage would the bedouin see in his delirium but a verdant oasis, always unattainable on the horizon? And having abandoned his nomadic life, what more could the man of the desert ask for, in this land of torrid summer heat, than a place of rest and refreshment (*refrigerium*) close to his home, listening only to the murmur of running water and the rustling fronds of the date palm, the providential tree of the oasis?

For the civilizations which have developed on the edge of the desert, along the Nile valley and in Asia Minor, the date palm provides almost everything necessary for the maintenance of life. Firstly, there are the dates themselves, which can be compressed, dried and conserved; and then, too, palm wine which can be fermented to produce an alcoholic drink. At the very top of the tree, moreover, the palm-cabbage provides a succulent dish. The palm can also be used for building; huts fashioned from its branches, or roofing for mud dwellings; it can even be made into brooms for sweeping the house. The kernels when ground supply the camel with one of its favourite foods, while the same kernels provide fuel for the metal worker and the blacksmith. It is hardly surprising, then, that this tree should have been deified; and the Greek geographer Strabo mentions a hymn that celebrates the 36 uses of the tree. As a fertility symbol, the date palm also graced the sacred gardens surrounding the temples to frighten away evil spirits. In this role it often performed the same role as the cypress, symbol of eternity because of its indestructible wood and still bearing a funerary association in our own times: some of the finest cypresses of Italy, mature after more than half a century's growth, stand as guards of honour for those who fell on the battlefields of the First World War.

Fertility is closely related to the image of woman, from whom all life springs. The very name of Eve (*hava*) in Hebrew is probably etymologically linked to the term used to describe life itself. Even as early as the Palaeolithic period, statues with deliberately exaggerated feminine characteristics were held in special esteem; in the Neolithic period, woman appeared as the goddess-protectress of animals, pictured between two wild beasts, sometimes in the process of giving birth, as at Catal-Hüyük in Turkey.

The first gardens must have been cultivated by women. While the men were engaged in the hard and dangerous activity of hunting, the greater delicacy of the woman and the fact that she was permanently in a state of pregnancy made it necessary to take care of herself and led her to specialize in domestic work, notably the upkeep of the hearth (the deity responsible for fire in Classical antiquity, Vesta, was female). She was probably also responsible for the gathering of plants to complement the meat brought home by the hunter. Taking note of flowering and germination patterns, she kept the edible species in a plot of land close to the home. Indeed, the use of the flower as a symbol of beauty must have occurred quite early in the history of civilization, since flowers are found in early tombs. It is tempting to believe that this first *hortus* was rectangular, since the square was the form of the primordial paradise, which has been perpetuated in our own time in the guise of the square and rectangular beds of the kitchen garden. However, we have no accurate knowledge of primitive man's sense of space nor of when he first grasped the rudiments of geometry.

It is probable that the primitive garden was soon surrounded by some kind of enclosure to protect it from wild animals, and so the *hortus conclusus* appeared.

It was certainly the woman who began to domesticate certain animals. Her more intuitive sensibility brought her closer to them, while their own instincts told them that she did not pose a danger since she did not hunt. Once they had been tamed, these animals would be put in grazing land surrounded by an enclosure in the forest; this was the *viridarium* of the Romans. It is worth recalling, incidentally, that the forest was a place of pasture for domestic animals until very recent times.

Early in the the Neolithic period, it is likely that man, whose life until then had been very precarious, was filled with wonder at all these gifts of nature. He both worshipped them and took great pleasure in them, as we can see from the *Song of Songs* where the poet can find no better way of celebrating the beauty of the loved one than by comparing each of her attributes to an element of nature: 'Your hair is like a flock of goats poised on the side of the Mount Gilead.'

We now know that this lyricism in the *Song of Songs* predates Solomon, from the existence of Sumerian texts on the sacred marriage of the goddess of love (Inana) to a mortal (Dimouzi); these become Ishtar and Tammuz for the Assyrians. Ishtar became Astarte for the Phoenicians, while in Greek mythology Aphrodite falls in love with Adonis. The same poem exists among the peoples of the Nile well before Solomon, and the recognition of the affinities between feminine beauty and the natural world can be found in other civilizations. In one Egyptian tale, for instance, a tree praises the beauty of a woman thus: 'My seeds are the image of your teeth, my bearing like that of your breasts.' Such reversal of roles is very much in the spirit of Eastern sensibility, which is much more disposed than that of the West to compare different things, thus making them less separate, less individual: the same universal spirit is seen to flow in all natural phenomena. This disposition towards metaphorical expression was especially notable in the work of the Persian poets. In the West, with its penchant for figurative description, such a tendency produced allegory, which is really a 'figure of art', as a trope is a figure of speech; this same use of allegory, claimed by Winckelmann to be one of the major creative forces in works of art, was to be the dominant element in the humanist

The hanging gardens of Babylon, reconstruction by J. Lacam after Mme M. Rutten from 'The Hanging Gardens of Babylon', Revue Horticole, July–August, 1949, p. 86.

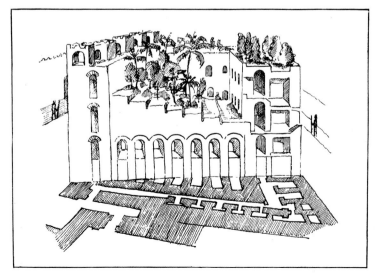

garden created by the Italian Mannerist designers.

The sacred garden became linked to the temple at the beginning of the third millennium BC; the temple itself was made in the image of a mountain as a stepped pyramid – the ziggurat. The famous hanging gardens of Queen Semiramis in Babylon were not unique in Mesopotamia; however, the fact that they were still considered one of the wonders of the ancient world even as that world came to an end means that we have several descriptions of them from Greek and Roman observers – including Diodorus of Sicily, Strabo and Quintus Curtius. These commentators enable us to reconstruct a fairly accurate picture of the gardens, which were not, in fact, devised by Semiramis but by Nebuchadnezzar II. He laid them out close to his palace for the pleasure of his wife Amytis, granddaughter of Astyages, king of the Medes, who evidently yearned for the paradisal landscape of her own country. The gardens consisted of a series of terraces, one above the other; the floor of the terraces was made of baked brick and bitumenized for waterproofing and to contain the earth in which the trees and flowers were planted. What surprised contemporary observers was the ease with which the hydraulic engineers had contrived to raise the water for the plants to the uppermost terrace. In fact, ever since the time of the Sumerians, the people of Mesopotamia had been skilled in irrigation work and had even constructed canal networks which could supply water directly to the individual consumer. The Code of Hammurabi considered it a serious crime to divert water intended for one's neighbour; this was also the case in Egypt, where the Rolls of the Dead from the period of the New Kingdom show the 'suppliant' at the day of the last judgement swearing never to have stolen water from his neighbour. The immense effort

Hunting in a pine forest, bas-relief from the palace of Sargon at Khorsabad, 8th century BC, Musée du Louvre, Paris.

of reclaiming land from the desert by irrigation must have left the countryside of Mesopotamia criss-crossed with irrigation canals and drainage systems from the beginnings of its civilization. It is tempting to believe that this archetype reappeared much later when garden design reached another of its peaks and the canal, sometimes several kilometres in length, became one of the most prestigious ornaments of the French garden.

Sacred gardens also existed outside the temples; an Assyrian bas-relief in the Louvre apparently shows priests using pineapples to scatter purificatory water on a garden in what must have been a spring fertility rite. Records exist of the existence in the first millennium BC of botanical gardens consisting of plant varieties from foreign countries and even of zoological gardens which must have resembled the paradisal visions of the Persian kings.

Towards the end of the 8th century BC Sargon II built a fine botanical garden in his capital of Khorsabad, near Nineveh, replicating the mountains of the Amanus where he planted every imaginable species of plant from the country of the Hittites in Anatolia. All the trees were imported since almost the only plants along the rivers were reeds, though these were of course extremely useful, especially in building. We read of date palms, cedars, cypress, box and myrtles, as well as of more northern trees from Lake Van: planes, willows and poplar, and ebony from the Red Sea. Flowers included the rose and the lily, with pride of place going to the jasmine; there were also irises, tulips, hollyhocks, mallows, anemones, buttercups, daisies, camomiles, immortelles, crocuses (saffron) and poppies.

Ducks frolicking among lotus flowers, painting from the Akhenaton palace, el-Amarna, c.1365 BC.

Throughout the imperial period, Egyptian gardens, large or small, were made to the same plan; the main element was a rectangular pool surrounded by an area of land criss-crossed by paths at right angles to each other. The pool was usually square, though it could also be T-shaped or, more rarely, an oblong. In the time of the Pharaohs the ruling Egyptian classes built their villas outside the towns. The most remarkable surviving plan of such a villa is that discovered by the Italian Egyptologist Ippolito Rossellini in a Theban tomb, which dates from the reign of Amenhotep III. A canal brought the water of the Nile to the garden, which was entered through an imposing gate. The house was set in the depths of the garden close to three pools, two of which were overlooked by small garden pavilions.

The pools were filled with water plants – lotus and papyrus – as well as fish, for the sport of the owners, and ducks. Some of them were extensive enough to allow boat trips. The garden was further embellished by ornamental trees, shrubs, fruit trees (vines, figs, pomegranates and date palms) and flowers (red poppies, corn-flowers and safflower). The rose did not make its appearance until the Graeco-Roman period. Other flowers were cultivated for their scent. Sometimes the owners of the gardens would have ornate tombs constructed to indicate their position in the social hierarchy. The gardens were evidently tended by numerous workmen, while the flowers were gathered by girls.

In addition there were the sacred gardens attached to the temples; Rameses II boasted that he had planted 514 such gardens in honour of Amon. An essentially well adjusted society, which partly explains its long duration, the Egypt of the period was also fascinated by the exotic, attaching considerable importance to produce from Syria, Arabia and Abyssinia. Queen Hatshepsut, for instance, sent an expedition to the land of Punt to obtain essences then unknown in Egypt; her ambassadors returned with 32 varieties. By the time the ancient world was nearing its

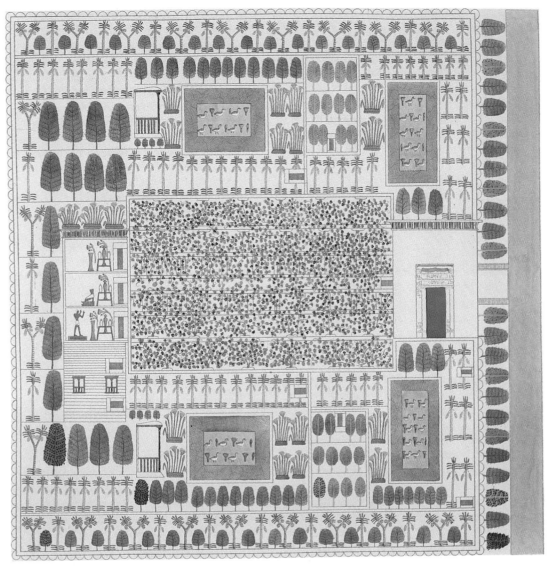

end, Egyptian gardeners were recognized as experts in the cultivation of plants and were in demand in every corner of the Roman empire. They originated the practice of growing vines along trellis and over pergolas; they also introduced the idea of suspended vines as garlands among higher trees, a system which was eventually exported to the western Mediterranean and is still in use in Campania in Italy, lending a particularly luxuriant aspect to the vineyards of that province.

The prevailing civilization in Persia from the 9th to the 4th century BC was that of the Medes and Achaemenians and it was here that a type of garden made its appearance which was to have a mythical significance in the human imagination: paradise. The word is derived from the Greek *paradeisos*, which in turn comes from the Persian *pairidaeza*, meaning 'enclosed place'. Such enclosures would be surrounded by walls and contain a great abundance of plant and animal life. In addition to the fully grown trees, carefully tended, would be well watered orchards and lawns,

where large and small game could roam freely. Shooting hides would be located in the trees, in pavilions or in towers. Other pavilions, dotted here and there in the garden, took various forms from tents to open kiosks, and served as places of rest. The various types of plants were set out in regular plots, presumably corresponding to some ritual significance.

The earliest information we have about such a Persian paradise dates from the 4th century BC: Xenophon's account of the garden of Cyrus at Sardis. There were, however, many other throughout the Persian empire and we also know that the Great King specifically ordered his provincial governors to maintain these gardens carefully.

In spite of the political turmoil in the Eastern world which followed the death of Alexander, the tradition of the paradise garden was continued and taken up by the Sassanid dynasty which established itself in Persia in AD 226. This dynasty was in turn overthrown by the Arabs under whom entire

Garden of a high Egyptian dignitary, from Monumenti del Egypto and della Nubbia, *Fo 69 1834, by Ippolito Rossellini.*

regions of the country reverted to desert. The irrigation canals silted up and the paradise gardens disappeared under the sand. Yet the memory of paradise lived on in men's imaginations, both in the East and the West. The religious significance of the paradise garden becomes much clearer in the Sassanid period. The garden, in which animal life and plant life were equally important, was divided into four quarters by two median axes meeting at right angles; thus it constituted an image of the universe which was itself divided into four parts. In winter, the king would still retain in his palace an image of the gardens in the form of a carpet decorated with precious stones. The monarch, who possessed the gift of fertility, could thereby ensure the preservation of the natural world during the winter and its rebirth each spring. This image of paradise eventually reached the West in the form of Persian garden carpets which continued to be woven until quite recently, and, for a shorter period, in the guise of Persian miniatures.

This belief in the magical properties of an imitation was one of the basic concepts of Egyptian civilization. The image bears the same characteristics as the original that it reproduces, and the artist, however humble his position, thus becomes a creator of godlike proportions. Thanks to the artist, the carpet preserves the creative forces of the spring during the winter, and their sacred character is emphasized by the addition of precious stones.

The cultural fall-out of the Persian paradise garden was of incalculable significance: it gave its name to the ideal garden which lies at heart of Jewish and Judaeo-Christian religion – the terrestrial paradise. Indeed, the first translators of the Bible into Greek rendered the Hebrew word *gan-eden*, meaning 'garden of delights', by the word *paradeisos*. Mircea Eliade, however, has pointed out that the Sumerian world *eden* means 'steppe' and that the text of Genesis actually tells how God decided to create a 'garden', which is after all not far removed from the afore-mentioned origins of the garden in the desert. But perhaps such an interpretation of the symbolism of the garden falls a little too neatly into place; the Hebrew scholars I have consulted are agreed that it is impossible to dissociate *gan-eden* from the root *e'den* which means 'sweetness' or 'delight'.

The belief in the existence at the beginning of time of a 'paradise' from which man has been banished is common to many civilizations, even relatively primitive ones (except, apparently, in Africa). This belief is certainly present in the Graeco-Roman system and is the origin of the Golden Age described in such idyllic terms by the poet Lucretius. The same mythology also incorporates the idea of a punishment handed out to man for having presumed to rise above his allotted condition. Jupiter, for instance, despatches Pandora to expose mankind to every possible evil for having received the gift of fire from Prometheus.

According to the text of Genesis, the terrestrial paradise was divided into four equal quarters by four rivers which had their source there: the Tigris, the Pishon, the Gihon and the Euphrates. God created man in his own image, blissful and immortal; then he fashioned woman from the side of man. In this garden populated with animals (like the Persian version) to which man gave names, the first couple could do as they wished except taste the fruit of a tree planted in the centre of the garden, the tree of knowledge of good and evil, to which only God could have access. But once Adam and Eve had disobeyed this order, they were banished from paradise to exist henceforth in a state of sin, forced to work for a living and now mortal.

As centre of the world, the terrestrial paradise is complete in itself and reflects the completeness of the world. Each garden made by man was to be the mirror in some way of this completeness and sense of wholeness which God had wished to create.

Nowadays, our search for paradise may take other forms; for example, each summer individuals and families from northern climes journey to the Mediterranean – the paradise of the south. Perhaps this annual migration is motivated by a desire to return to our origins, to those shores which are synonymous with warmth and happiness. And for those conscious of our literary heritage, the Mediterranean is the sea of the gods.

To wander in a garden, to gaze on this image of nature reshaped and subdivided by man, is perhaps to feel a breath of the universal harmony which urban life has made us forget. This may be a quest for paradise lost or the search for the Golden Age, but whatever the precise religious or mythological context, the garden is born of nostalgia and is a refuge for our deepest dreams.

In the East, this dreamlike quality has been preserved, since the art of gardening is pursued with such loving care and refinement that the garden itself still seems wild and untouched by human hand. In the West, however, we have tried to tame nature, seeking to revive the past with a clutter of 'civilized' bric-a-brac, and ending up by creating not a garden but a theatre.

THE GARDEN IN CLASSICAL ANTIQUITY

GREECE

Socrates claimed that he had only ventured outside the city boundary of Athens twice in his life – doubtless a complaint rather than a boast, since he had been legally forbidden to leave the city. As a philosopher, Socrates' world was bounded by what his mind was capable of understanding. In the following century, however, another Athenian – the poet Menander – recommended a life in the country only to those who earned so little that they could not afford to live in the city. His comedy *Dyskolos* features a spendthrift whose unsociability drives him into the country; he takes up residence in a distant province where, as the god Pan says in the prologue, 'the inhabitants need all their courage to cultivate a land of pebbles'[1].

The democratic Greeks of the Classical period do not seem to have been much attracted by the countryside. Admittedly, as in all pagan societies, nature for them was far from lifeless. Louis Hautecoeur[2] has described in his book *Les Jardins des dieux et des hommes* how every mountain, every tree, rock and flower concealed a god or demi-god; the entire universe was alive with the murmur of voices from the beyond. The Greeks, however, regarded nature in a very different way from the peoples of the Orient, who had always felt themselves to be an integral part of the natural world. The habit of philosophical reflection had encouraged the Greeks to develop feelings of superiority towards nature; man was considered to be the only creature in the universe capable of comprehending the idea of a world outside himself and, in objectifying it, he separated himself from it. Judging himself greater than a tree or the heavens, he saw the exterior world as something to be made in his own image. His gods, for instance, were stripped of the attributes which, even during the most advanced periods of Asian and Egyptian culture, had produced hybrid

beings who could very easily share their sacred character with an animal. The concept of human independence, however, was central to Greek thought; and this autonomy was expressed more perfectly than ever before or since by the Greek vision of the human body. Whereas the sculptures of previous civilizations had either formed part of a wall, of which they were a sort of extension, or else a block of masonry to which they remained firmly attached, Greek sculptors were the first to create isolated, free-standing figures.

This sense of man distanced from nature remained firmly embedded in the Greek consciousness, and by the 2nd century AD it even emerged as a philosophical standpoint of the Stoics. Zeno, the founder of the school, railed against peacocks and nightingales: 'The wise man,' he said, 'grants no place to these things in the city.' His pupil Chrysippus went so far as to write, 'There are people who embellish their properties with climbing vines and myrtle bushes; they raise peacocks, pigeons, partridges and nightingales to sing for them. Soon we shall be painting muck-heaps.' How better to reject the natural world than by dismissing the nightingale as so much rubbish! It is perhaps worth noting that, while Plato, Aristotle and Epicurus reflected on life in a garden, the Stoics felt more at ease in a portico (*stoa*) from which the name of the school was derived. There were of course gardens in ancient Greece and there is some mention of them in Homer. These, however, like the famous orchard of Alcinous, were horticultural gardens, although it was permissible to stroll in them and even, if you were rich enough, to tend them. These gardens, then, were essentially utilitarian, unless they were designated sacred places, such as the grotto dedicated to the nymph Calypso. This is a feature which was to become very important in the Roman garden and, much later, in the gardens of the Renaissance.

In towns and cities, shade was to be found under porticoes and also in the promenades (Latin *ambulationes*) planted near the gymnasiums or palestras or sometimes in an old, sacred wood. There were many of these, dedi-

A sacred landscape. painting of the Villa Boscoreale at the time of Tiberius, now in the Museo Archeologico Nazionale, Naples.

[1] P. Grimal, *Les Jardins romains*, 2nd ed., 1969, p. 81.
[2] L. Hautecoeur, *Les Jardins des dieux et des hommes*, 1959, p. 29

cated to some divinity, in Greece; entry to them was forbidden to anyone who did not belong to the cult of the god or goddess of the wood. At the beginning of *Oedipus at Colonus*, Sophocles shows the aged Oedipus, blind and tired, wishing to rest in a wood. But Antigone warns him: 'We are treading on sacred ground, if I understand aright the laurel and the vine which grow there and the voices of the nightingales echoing from every tree.' And the inhabitants of the nearest settlement refuse to let Oedipus stay there. In a forest of oaks at Dodona, Zeus was the god worshipped and the priests made predictions about the future according to the wind in the branches. The oak, of course, was the tree dedicated to Zeus.

The history of the gardens of Academia in Athens shows the transition from sacred wood to public promenade. Academus was a divine king from some legendary epoch to whom an area of olive trees had been dedicated; the area also contained a number of altars to other gods. In the 6th century BC, Hipparchus, the son of Pisistratus, built a gymnasium there, which he surrounded with a wall. During the following century, Cimon built a stadium on the site, to which he brought water and planted different varieties of trees. It was in this new quarter of Athens that Plato bought the garden which he dedicated to the Muses, and from 388 he held his school of philosophy in the gymnasium. Aristotle followed the example of his master when he went to teach in Athens and started to give lessons in the quarter of the city known as the Lyceum near the temple of Apollo Lyceus. He delivered his lesson while strolling with his followers, who as a result became known as 'peripatetics'. The habit of associating the act of walking with the spoken word or thought lasted until the Middle Ages and even later. It was one of the functions of the monastery cloister to provide a place for such activity. The library of Attalus at Pergamus had a portico running along one of its sides which allowed students to pace up and down, breaking off from their reading to meditate

from time to time. And around the library of the Collège de la Sorbonne in the university of Paris, there ran a portico, constructed in 1480 for exactly the same purpose.

The philosophical centre of the world from the 6th century until the end of Classical antiquity, Athens was also the home of the movement known as Epicureanism or the 'Garden School', but this was significant in quite a different way. It referred to a kitchen garden which Epicurus cultivated himself, thus giving practical expression to his philosophy which sought serenity for the soul in a modest life free of all strong emotion.

Outside the democratic city states, there were parks intended for pleasure, but these were built by various autocrats for their own use. Hero of Syracuse had a garden built around 500 BC; its principal feature was the 'horn of Amalthaea', which must have been a grotto or rather a 'nymphaeum', dedicated to Zeus. This *amaltheion* was a reminder of the childhood in Crete of the god Zeus whom Rhea, his mother, placed in the care of the nymph Amalthaea; there he was obliged to take on the form of a goat to avoid discovery by his father Cronos, who devoured all his children after being warned by an oracle that one of them would overthrow him.

During the period which Droysen has termed 'Hellenistic', following the death of Alexander and lasting until the conquest of Egypt by Rome (AD 31), the diverse parts of the Empire were ruled by various sovereigns who would have come into contact with the Persian paradise garden and helped to popularize them. These monarchs, particularly those of the Ptolemaic line, donated sanctuaries, porticoes, basilicas (as meeting places), assembly rooms, libraries, theatres, gymnasiums and gardens to the cities.

The garden now made its appearance in literature. In *The Golden Ass* by Apuleius, which tells the story of the loves of Eros and Psyche, the garden which surrounds the palace of Love was inspired by the paradise Garden of the Orient. This story remained of largely literary significance during Classical antiquity; in the paintings of Pompeii, Cupids and Psyches can be seen fluttering about on butterfly wings, while the figure of Psyche in the Catacombs symbolizes the soul. By the 16th century, however, under the influence of Platonic thought, the fable of *The Golden Ass* was to become one of the themes used in villas and châteaux.

Did the Hellenistic period, then, with its proud architectural achievements, contribute some specific innovation to the art of garden design? The answer to this question lies to some extent in the Roman garden.

ROMAN GARDENS

The Greeks were deeply shocked by the transformation of the infernal divinities into celestial gods; the latter, in fact, consigned them back to the underworld. Things were different in Italy, where the Etruscans and the Latins remained faithful to their earth deities which incarnated the various forces of nature; it was some time before Priapus, the Roman god of garden produce, gave way to Dionysus. Priapus had to settle for being part of the retinue of Dionysus, the Thracian god of vegetation, who was identified with the old Italic god Liber Pater. The Greeks were essentially sailors, whose most familiar horizons were the heavens themselves, which never looked more immense than when they were resting on the waves. The Romans, those conquerors of the world, on the other hand, were peasants. Whether the Roman was on the frontiers of the Empire in Asia or on the Elbe, the home country – some corner of the Sabine lands or Latium or, later, Cisalpine Gaul – was always present in his memory. Unless the legionary received a plot of land to cultivate on his retirement from the army, he would be obliged to return to the family *heredium*, where he would be welcomed by the two Lares gods of the hearth. The victorious general, his moment of glory past, would go back to his ancestral lands. Cincinnatus is remembered by posterity for returning to the plough, after being consul and twice dictator. Two centuries later, the puritanical Cato, in his *De agri cultura*, elaborated the idea of an estate given up to intensive cultivation (and even envisaged workshops) to produce everything necessary for an independent existence. This was the *villa rustica*, a self-contained agricultural unit; aerial photography has since shown the presence of numerous examples in the province of Gaul.

By the end of the republican period, several centuries later, all the smallholdings and smaller farms of Latium had disappeared; corn now came from Sicily or Africa. Gradually, Rome was surrounded by a band of sumptuous villas built for the pleasure of their owners, and there were others within the city walls. The Roman countryside was still a place for the gods but, instead of the crude idols of the past, the skills of Greek immigrants brought statues carved in marble or cast in bronze. These new images now decorated sanctuaries, porticoes, hippodromes, grottoes or nymphaeums in the villas of the ruling class. The gods kept company with the master of the house, who could retreat into his own home together with the Olympians, leaving Rome to the lower orders and exposing himself to them only on the occasion of some official function. The pleasure villa would often be complemented by a *villa rustica* – a combination especially recommended by Varro – where the master could watch his peasants at work and envy the simple quality of their life.

Villa, painting from Stabies, Museo Archeologico Nazionale, Naples.

By this time, the city of Rome had grown enormously to become, in the terms of the period, a megapolis or the 'megamachine' whose shortcomings have been so comprehensively criticized by Lewis Mumford. Many citizens must certainly have been assailed by feelings of disgust and frustration, a sense of being imprisoned and a vague longing for the country life. Such yearnings provided a subject for the writers of the period, particularly in the beautifully cadenced verses of Virgil.

One of the qualities of such a life, which enabled Pliny the Younger to enjoy the delights of his villa and to indulge his curiosity about the natural world, was *otium*, which may be inadequately translated by 'leisure'. The word nevertheless possessed a complexity of meanings which shifted and changed from the time of ancient Rome to the end of the Republic and the beginning of the Empire. In the earlier period, every citizen had an obligation to his *gene* and the common good; *otium* was therefore seen as a detestable concept, leading to vulgar displays of wealth, extravagance, idleness, the pursuit of sensual pleasures and lechery, and all the misfortunes conferred by the irrationality of love. But by the time of the Romans who had undergone the hellenizing influences of Stoicism and Epicureanism, such as Cicero, Sallust, Pliny or Horace, *otium* had come to be considered as the golden rule of moral philosophy, the object of which was to make oneself master of one's own destiny. This, Pliny tells us, is the path to the true and pure life which cannot be achieved amid the uproar and moral laxity of the city; only nature offers us true 'leisure' in surroundings improved by literature and the arts, the privileged domain of the Muses.

Unlike the gardens of Greece, of which we still know very little, the Roman garden is sufficiently well documented for us to paint a reasonably accurate picture of it. Our information comes from two sources: literary and archaeological.

The literary sources in this case are numerous. Varro (on agriculture), Vitruvius (on architecture), the orator and politician Cicero, the poets Lucretius, Catullus, Virgil, Horace, Propertius, Tibullus and Ovid have all written of the garden with greater or lesser exactitude and enthusiasm. The most informative texts are those by Pliny the Younger in which he describes his two villas: a pleasure villa near Ostia and a *villa rustica* in Tuscany.

The archaeological documentation comes from excavations spread pretty well throughout Italy. There is an especial wealth of information from the excavations which have continued for more than 200 years in the two cities of Campania, Pompeii and Herculaneum, and in a neighbouring area of coastal villas; both these sites were buried in AD 79 by lava from an eruption of Mount Vesuvius. It was on the beach at Stabiae that Pliny the Elder, uncle of Pliny the Younger, met his death. He was at the time commander of the fleet stationed close by at the naval base of Cape Misenum and had gone to the beach to get a better view of the eruption until, according to his nephew, he was overcome by the fumes.

The archaeological evidence is all the more interesting in that it reveals art forms which were still close to those of Greek civilization.

Villas by the sea, painting from the house of Marius Lucretius in Pompeii, Museo Archeologico Nazionale, Naples.

the foreground there are often pitchers from which birds can be seen drinking; beyond is a trellis or balustrade bordering a veritable thicket of trees of all varieties, where fruit-bearing species can be seen mingling with flowering kinds. The most remarkable painting of this type of arrangement does not, in fact, come from Pompeii but from Prima Porta and the family villa of Livia, the wife of Augustus Caesar. The four walls of an underground room were painted in the manner described above; these paintings have been detached and are today conserved in the National Museum in Rome. More recent excavations at Pompeii have yielded fragmentary representations of this type of garden, which bears a certain resemblance to the enclosed garden of the Middle Ages.

The interpretation of the other type of garden, often referred to as the 'sacred garden', is more difficult. The Latin term for gardener was *topiarus*. In a letter to his brother, Cicero speaks of *ars topiara* when describing the villa of a friend. *Topia* is a Greek word and in the lost art of Greek easel painting *topiagraph* (which should not be confused with topography) referred to the specific art of painting the landscape. Inevitably this raises the question as to where the 'sacred landscape' paintings of Pompeii originated. Could they be, in some measure, a sort of anthology of motifs borrowed from Greek paintings by the *graeculi* who worked for the Romans? Later, of course, the word 'topiary' came to mean the trimming of plants in specific shapes

At Herculaneum, which was a seaside resort, the villas were ranged along the seafront. The excavations at Pompeii have yielded several gardens belonging to private residences which it has been possible to reconstruct, in addition to two large villas on the edge of the city – those of Diomedes and the Mysteries. The villa of the Papyri at Herculaneum has made possible the reconstruction of a complete living complex.

Of particular interest among these archaeological remains are the numerous paintings, especially in Pompeii, which are inspired by the theme of the garden. They fall into two categories: those representing real gardens and those representing imaginary ones.

The real gardens are all of the same type; in

View of a garden (detail), painting from Livia's house at Prima Porta. National Roman Museum, Rome.

– an art which was already practised by the Romans.

In the plan of the Pompeiian villa, the designated site of the garden was in the centre of the peristyle; this architectural feature originated in Greece and was incorporated into the Roman house. It occurs frequently in the villas of Pompeii. A number of gardens, such as those of the house of the Faun, of the Vettii, or of the Golden Cupids, have been sufficiently well preserved for us to reconstitute the groupings of the flowers and the shape of the trees from the evidence of paintings; the statuary and water ornament either remained in place or could be discovered by excavation. Where there was no peristyle, the garden tended to be sited wherever some free space existed in the house. And when no space at all was available, the garden could be simulated in a wall painting, sometimes even behind an illusory portico with columns.

The sheer size of the villa of Diomedes and the villa of the Papyri at Herculaneum (a reconstruction of which houses the Paul Getty Museum at Malibu) gives them a special importance. In addition to a peristyle of considerable size in the complex of the house itself, another enormous peristyle surrounding the main garden is positioned at the back of the building.

Any house of importance in Pompeii was covered with painting. Like his Italian counterpart of the 16th century, the Roman seems to have had an aversion to empty space, so that no available area in his home could be left bare of some form of decoration. It is now possible to understand how Lucretius, having fled from his town house, very likely full of figurative art, to his villa, perhaps similarly decorated with paintings, and feeling hemmed in by this multitude of people and gods, should have described perfect happiness as the meeting of a group of friends (philosophers and poets, of course) stretched out on the grass beneath a high tree, surrounded by summer flowers. Speculative though this may be, it conforms to the famous Epicurean image of the first of Virgil's eclogues which shows the shepherd Tityrus under a beech tree close to a spring. It

House of the Amorini dorati, Pompeii: the garden in the peristyle.

Pergola at the house of L. Tiburtinus, Pompeii.

Pergola at the house of L. Tiburtinus, Pompeii.

expresses the eternal dream of the earthly paradise which the Mediterranean lands inspire in their inhabitants, as they did in the barbarians from the north who were to discover them later.

It is surprisingly difficult, nevertheless, to get an accurate picture of the overall plan of the Roman garden. Even Pliny the Younger, in his descriptions of his villas at Ostia and in Tuscany, seems unclear about the exact arrangement of the various garden elements. For the last couple of centuries, therefore, departments of archaeology and architecture throughout the world have vied with one another to present architectonic reconstructions of these villas, based on available descriptions. The variations in their conclusions show what a difficult task this is.

We can, however, learn quite a lot from Pliny's own description of his Tuscan villa, which he preferred to the one in Ostia for the clemency of the local climate, the freshness of the air and the rustic charms of the villa itself. The arrangement of the villa would have met with the approval of Varro in that a farm was attached to the villa. The various parts were ranged on a hillside in terraces, an arrangement which corresponded to the usual method of dealing with the steep slopes of the Mediterranean landscape, whereby low walls were erected at each change of level to hold the earth in place during heavy rain. In the plan, the residential quarters of this villa are situated between the garden and the farm. Pliny does not say exactly where these were in relation to the slope, but the presence of a large, flat, open space suggests they lay at the foot of the hill. The pleasure garden would, therefore, have been on level ground. Its main feature was the hippodrome which, unlike the great peristyle of the Papyri villa in Herculaneum, was not surrounded by a portico; instead, the colonnades were replaced by lines of plane trees covered with ivy which also formed connecting garlands from one tree to the next. Laurels and box trees were ranged in front of the planes, and the centre of the hippodrome was planted with roses and other flowers. Pliny also mentions box clipped in such a manner as to spell out the name of the master of the house and that of the gardener. In another corner of the garden was a rustic retreat comprising a vine trellis supported on four pillars of Carystian marble; the table and benches were in white marble. When a meal was served in this arbour, the main courses were placed around the edge of the central pool, but the side dishes, in the form of boats and waterfowl, were sent to float on the water, so that presumably the guests could launch these vessels, containing spices or bread, from one side of the pool to another. A similar eating space has been preserved at Hadrian's Villa at Tivoli (formerly Tibur). Unlike the villa at Ostia, Pliny supervised the building of the one in Tuscany himself, and he describes his beloved house with boundless enthusiasm, ending with a remark that typifies the philosophy of his time, deploring life in the cities and extolling the delights of the country: 'No need to wear a toga, no unwanted client seeking protection.' (Such clients – plebeians who placed themselves under the protection of some noble – were equally detested by Virgil, who described them as 'thieves' and 'beggars' institutionalized by custom.) And Pliny adds a note of Arcadian hedonism: 'Everything suggests ease and repose – a healthy climate, open skies, balmy air – everything helps to make a healthy body and spirit, the latter by study and the former by hunting.' Here again is the essence of the Epicurean philosophy: *Mens sana in corpore sano*.

The preferred sites for villas around Rome were, to the west, the countryside around Ostia, which was within easy reach of the sea, Tusculum (now Frascati) to the south, and

*H*adrian's Villa,
*Tivoli: the
crocodile of the
Canope.*

Tibur (Tivoli) to the east. In Rome itself during the imperial period, some 70 villas have been recorded; to that figure should be added the public promenades, planted with trees, given to the city by various nobles. The entire right bank of the Tiber as it flowed through Rome was covered with villas built next to one another – a Roman could almost believe that he was in the country. Another favoured area was the Pincian hill which overlooked the Field of Mars and the valley of the Tiber. The villas there were so numerous that it came to be known as the 'hill of gardens'. One of the most important of these belonged to Lucullus, the conqueror of Mithridates (*Horti Lucullani*), the very name of which evoked the image of epicurean pleasure.

No less famous were the gardens belonging to the poet Sallust, which were especially notable for their collection of Greek sculptures. These included the Niobedes group, now in Florence and formerly at the Villa Medicis.

The huge extent of Hadrian's Villa at Tibur (at the foot of Tivoli) almost bears comparison with that of Chinese gardens which stretched over a whole province. It was essentially the realization of the dream of an emperor-philosopher who wished to surround himself with reminders of the principal sites and monuments of his empire on the eve of its decline. This immense garden, therefore, was in a sense inspired by an incipient feeling of nostalgia for a pagan civilization which extended the entire length of the Mediterranean and which had seemed destined to endure for ever; as in the creation of every garden, desire and regret were intermingled. Pillaged for centuries, Hadrian's Villa has provided the world's museums with priceless works of art. The most recent excavations have revealed the colonnade of Canopus, indicating how harmoniously the various monuments and artefacts were sited in this, one of the most splendid gardens of all time.

Since the villas were to some extent intended to reflect the social position of their owners, precious materials were often used in their construction; there were many varieties of marble available, for instance, especially in Campania, where the finest types from Sicily were imported. The column, the central feature in the architectural language of antiquity, was often of marble in the house itself, but of brick covered with stucco in the garden where its function was to carry the weight of the porticoes. The simplicity of the Tuscan order made it especially suitable for use with the natural form of plants. Wood was also extensively used in the garden to build arches, pergolas (often vaulted) and arbours, or on walls to provide a frame for climbing plants,

*H*adrian's Villa,
*Tivoli: general
view of the Canope,
(opposite and overleaf).*

especially vines, grown for the insulating qualities of the thick foliage and for the refreshing sweetness of the grape. Kiosks were also constructed of wood and a whole range of designs existed which would eventually be revived in the Middle Ages. Roman gardens were notable for a wide range of specially constructed features: exedras equipped with a bench for conversation, baths for swimming, as well as complete thermal baths, *cubicula*, which were a sort of small kiosk furnished with a couch for relaxation. There were also tree houses which have become in popular imagination one of the archetypal expressions of rural life; occasionally, they were even equipped with a complete dining room. The gardens could be further divided by sunken porticoes or cryptoporticoes.

Certain nobles had themselves buried in their own gardens, but this was very rare since the ancient world looked on the corpse as being impure and therefore needing to be interred outside the town walls. This attitude towards the dead body was to change in the Christian Middle Ages when the promise of resurrection after death implied that the body was no longer unclean and church burial became a favour extended to the most privileged.

The garden rooms designated for repose were sometimes built as 'cool rooms' amid the undergrowth or in a bank of earth or outcrop of rock. In the latter case, the room would be converted into a grotto and decorated with pebbles. Pliny mentions that pumice-stone, common in volcanic regions, was often used for this purpose. It is likely that the natural ruggedness of the stone was enhanced by chipping, as it was later from the 16th to the 18th century.

The most frequent use of the grotto, though, was for religious purposes. Recalling the era of the underworld deities, these caves provided an opportunity to commune with divinity. For Freud the cult of the grotto reflected the subconscious memory of the womb and evoked a sense of contentment deriving from the total satisfaction of the needs of the embryo prior to birth. The idea that the grotto is in some way a symbol of human origins has led to its being associated frequently with the birth of Jesus (as in the painting by Leonardo of the *Virgin of the Rocks* in the Louvre). According to one Christian tradition, Christ was actually born in a grotto; and the notion of such a subterranean place does serve to focus attention on the mystery surrounding our origins. I well remember as a child, long before I had any knowledge of mythology, my own feelings of fear, mixed with vague expectation, which accompanied visits to the pebbled grotto at the entrance to my grandparents' orangery on the estate where I was brought up; this grotto, I remember, glistened with water underneath the bracken and ferns.

Grottoes, complete with green vegetation and trickling streams, were the last vestige of the sacred garden still extant in the latter part of the 19th century; they were a feature of private gardens and could also be found in suburban cafés, where Parisians went to get a taste of country pleasures and to drink the local wine. These cafés were often located near a river where it was possible to go boating, as at Suresnes, near Paris, where there was a grotto called 'La Belle Gabrielle' (recalling the visit of Henri IV) and where, until the First World War, customers could imbibe locally produced wines. All these grottoes eventually fell victim to the property developers and even 'La Belle Gabrielle' was recently demolished. As a place of amusement, the grotto had a long ancestry; in one poem, *Copa*, attributed to Virgil, a Syrian dancer and inn-keeper boasts of the charms of her inn, which include a grotto.

For the Romans, however, underground grottoes inspired a sense of closeness with the divine. Such places were initially considered to be the homes of nymphs, the spirits of nature; indeed, a sacred grotto, especially one of considerable size, was often known as a 'nymphaeum'. The oldest nymphaeum mentioned in literature is the grotto of the nymph Calypso who fell in love with Ulysses and kept him a prisoner there. This grotto contained several rooms which opened on to naturally formed gardens, a sacred wood with tall trees and springs from which the water flowed over the mossy ground. Calypso lived there in the company of other nymphs whose main occupations were singing and spinning. This grotto, then, signifies for Homer an entire sacred landscape. As already noted, Hero of Syracuse build an *amaltheion* to the nymph Amalthaea, who tended the infant Zeus in a grotto on Mount Ida in Crete; this doubtless inspired Atticus to build an *amalthaeum* in his own garden – a nymphaeum which was rented by his friend Cicero. Some of these sanctuaries were also associated with episodes in mythology involving a number of figures – for example, the nymphaeum in the garden of Sallust featured a group depicting the 'Punishment of the Nionides'. Such a setting would also be very suitable for such scenes as the 'Hunt of Meleager'. The most extraordinary nymphaeum which has ever been excavated is the grotto of Sperlonga, near Mount Circeo on the Tyrrhenian Sea, where there was a famous sanctuary dedicated to Jupiter. This enormous natural grotto, discovered in 1957–8, was situated on a spur of rock which had been transformed into the shape of the prow of a ship. It contained a colossal group of figures which must have been broken up deliberately since it could only be reassembled in approximate fashion from some 5,000 marble fragments; the original sculpture showed Ulysses struggling with the giant Scylla after the latter had unleashed a storm. One of the most astonishing facts about the group is that it bears the signature of the three sculptors from Rhodes of the 1st century AD who, according to Pliny, were responsible for the 'Laocoön' group in the Vatican.

The beds in which the shrubs and flowers were planted assumed a wide variety of shapes, unlike the monotonous rectangles which were common in the Middle Ages and right up to the Renaissance. One favourite form was that of the hippodrome, derived from the gymnasium which had been put to especially picturesque use by the Greeks. The Romans preferred the form which they had derived from it and made very much their own: the circus. Such gymnasiums or hippodromes were very rarely used as sporting arenas and it was much more common for them to be cultivated.

The plane tree was favoured for laying out avenues, while the cypress was used to add decorative effects. Some idea of Roman tree planting can be gained from the discovery at Torre del Greco of the burnt stumps of planes in a state of perfect preservation.

The feature that really brought the garden to life was, of course, water, and this was used in innumerable ways. A shady pool epitomized rural tranquillity; alternatively, it flowed in channels to irrigate the garden, glistened in the grottoes and spurted from fountains. The jet was not normally very high and the water which splashed back into the basin beneath was encouraged to overflow.

Canals, as already mentioned, played an important role in the development of the world's civilizations. The Romans made fre-

Stump of a plane tree in the garden of an ancient villa, in Torre del Greco.

quent use of them and, drawing on their collective memory, so rich in mythology, history and geography, applied the name 'Euripus' to such a stretch of water, after the narrow strait of Euripus which separated the island of Euboea from the mainland and through which the current could flow in either direction, according to the tides. This hydraulic curiosity could be reproduced elsewhere by constructing sluice-gates.

The writings of Pliny extol the plane tree: its beauty, the coolness of its shade, the majesty of its smooth trunk, suggesting an architectural column. This tree, which is no longer so common in the Italian peninsula, originally came from the Orient to Greece and then from Greece to Italy. It makes its appearance in a Babylonian botanical garden, and is reported to have grown while in the Lake Van region (to the north). The woodland (Norway) pine is a native, but the umbrella pine (*Pinus pinea*) which adds so much beauty to the countryside around Rome and in Tuscany, is probably an import, as is the laurel (the tree of Apollo) which, in ancient Greece, graced the vale of Tempe. The box-tree variety which can be clipped into different shapes came from Phrygia. Very little use was made of the yew whose leaves were believed to be poisonous. The aranthus and the oleander, which blooms from May to October, were indigenous. Ferns were used for the embellishment of grottoes, while borders were marked out with periwinkle. Myrtle, the plant dedicated to Venus, came from the Orient. The plants used for spices would be very familiar to us: basil, marjoram, origanum, savory and thyme. The lemon tree was introduced in Greece during the time of Alexander, though the orange only came much later. Very few varieties were native.

The favourite flowers of the Romans were the iris, hyacinth, marguerite, pansy, narcissus, anemone, carnation, foxglove, violet, gladiolus, jasmine and rose.

By the time of the fall of the Roman Empire, Italy resembled an immense garden; the countryside was assiduously cultivated by methods which were often based on agronomic theory, although the private buying of land was already leading to the establishment of vast estates (*latifundia*) which resulted in serious agricultural impoverishment. From north to south, this glorious landscape took on the guise of that world of fantasy and imagination dreamt up by scholars and patricians as well as by the poets.

In the 5th century all this was to disappear under a wave of invasions. Large areas of Italy reverted to the wild, the few local inhabitants often starving and reduced to rags. It was Saint Benedict who founded a monastic discipline which helped to rebuild those 'fortresses of the spirit' against the barbarians and to give a fresh impetus to civilization by preserving its literary works, both sacred and secular, and reclaiming the land. The monks' concerns were study, prayer and outdoor work. They had little time, however, for the pleasure garden, which now declined in importance. Water could not now be wasted, because the aqueducts were no longer maintained. The civilization of the ancient world had begun with the canal and came to an end with the aqueduct.

The house of L. Tiburtinus at Pompeii.

THE ISLAMIC GARDEN

In discussing the Islamic garden, it is worth remembering that the semitic word *arab* was originally used to designate all land which was arid and sterile – in other words, the desert; the term later became associated with the nomadic peoples who travelled the desert from one oasis to the next. In the Koran the expression *el-arab* is only applied to the Arabs of the desert and does not even include the inhabitants of Mecca and Medina. In those places, clearly, water was always regarded as a major element in life and everything was done to make the most of its beauty and benefits. No one has expressed this division better than the Arabist Louis Massignon who, in old age, became converted to Christianity after discovering the Sufi mystic and martyr Hal-Halladj.

His description of the gardens of the Generalife in Granada is especially evocative: '...this pavilion, where a man sits dreaming, melancholy yet perhaps not sad. And the man's dream hangs by a thread, which is almost literally true, since the waters of the garden fall in threadlike streams. Does he really understand what it is to be a descendant of a race or at least a culture which was founded on the experiences centuries ago of thirsty men who were occasionally obliged to drink the brackish mud of desert wells lying flat on their stomachs?'

Water was therefore a common feature both of the gardens and the house. This sense of unity between interior and exterior is an essential aspect of Islamic culture, in contrast to the West, where such cohesion is never perfectly realized. The garden designers of the West use water to achieve various effects; to ensure that these effects contain the appropriate element of surprise the canalization of the water is usually hidden from sight. This custom of concealing water would be incomprehensible to a Muslim. In any palace of Islam water would travel from one fountain or basin to another through an open gutter or channel, perhaps decorated with multi-coloured mosaics to enhance its attractiveness. Yet even more important than the fact that the water can be seen flowing in and out of the palace is that its gentle, soothing murmur can always be heard. The curious interior vaulting, resembling stalactite formations, is more reminiscent of a grotto than of a man-made dwelling. A portico leads out to the gardens so that there is a hardly noticeable transition from indoors to outdoors, an impression enhanced by the reduction of all the natural elements of the garden to their essentials, except for the water. But in this simplicity lies refinement. The curb-stones of the pools are very elaborate; the basins of the fountains and the ponds are in the form of multifoil or quadrilobate circles, forms common in Muslim art. The pressure of the water is very carefully controlled, so that very often only a slight ripple is visible in a pool or basin, a sudden gleam amid the vegetation.

Each side of the main axial pool is planted with myrtle bushes which join their subtle perfume to the murmur of the water, so that the water itself almost seems to be scented. This is the archetypal garden, as we can still

The Patio de la Reja in the Generalife, Granada.

The Court of the Myrtles, the Alhambra, Granada.

find it in the Court of the Myrtles of the Alhambra in Granada.

In Spanish, the 'court' is the *patio*, which is another essential element in the Islamic garden, although its importance extends well beyond Islam to the entire Mediterranean. In countries subject to intense heat it is an essential part of the home, however modest. Today, as in the past, a visitor from northern Europe can find a little touch of paradise in the simplest of Mediterranean settings – maybe just a shady patio attached to some café in Rome, Naples, Piraeus or Crete, complete with a pergola overgrown with vines, an ilex or an olive tree, a few flower pots resting on the uneven paving stones, and somewhere the sound of running water. The extraordinary light of the countries around the Mediterranean gives their inhabitants the sense of being at the very centre of things. In Greece or in Apulia, somewhere the traveller will find, perhaps far from the main road, a white wall and four columns, which will just about sum up human experience.

Despite its simplicity, or perhaps because of

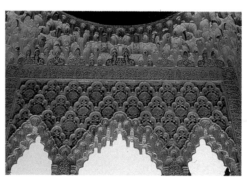

it, the Islamic garden does make certain demands. It is not obvious or blatant; it needs to be taken in slowly; it requires solitude and silence, which the tourist culture is bent on destroying. The gardens of the Generalife are now invaded by visitors from all over the world who are disgorged from coaches which converge on Granada. The Western garden can cope with such crowds more easily; after all it is already populated with figures in marble, stone and bronze.

Belonging to a generation which grew up before the tourist invasion, when there were no security precautions to restrict free movement, I was able to visit the gardens of the Generalife twice, once alone and once accompanied by another person. On one of these occasions I stayed long enough to watch the light of day gradually decline until night spread a veil over those mirror-like stretches of water.

If the Generalife are not the most beautiful of gardens, then they are certainly the most

Decor of one of the pavilions of the Court of Lions, the Alhambra, Granada.

Lion on the fountain of the Court of Lions, the Alhambra, Granada.

The Court of Lions seen from the inside of the Palace, the Alhambra, Granada.

34

enchanting, truly meriting the description of 'paradise' or 'eden', which means 'place of delights'. It is hardly surprising that so many legends surround their conception and creation. The Generalife was originally the summer residence of the sultans of Granada, the first parts of which were probably built towards the middle part of the 13th century on a hill which overlooks the town, the Alhambra, the Albaicim and the Sierra Nevada. The garden comprises a series of patios which are ranged asymmetrically along a hillside. The principal one, the Patio de la Reja, has two pavilions at either end, which afford a view over the surrounding countryside. Beyond the gateway which gives access to the garden is a multifoil basin, like the head of some flower, which overflows with water fed to it by a canal lined with clay tiles. The canal is 48 m in length, but only 60 cm across; halfway along it is punctuated by a second multifoil basin and yet another of similar design is positioned at the end. The canal edges are lined with mixed borders: roses, carnations, dahlias, delphiniums, snapdragons, asters, marigolds, campanulas, white tobacco, etc. Behind is planted a row of myrtle bushes. Very fine jets of water spring from the curb-stones of the canal; these are set at an angle, so that they form a kind of tracery above the canal before splashing to the surface in a myriad of silvery droplets. Other patios of varying size are situated on either side of the axial Patio de la Reja. The luxuriance of the vegetation, the consummate art with which the flowers are arranged, and the simplicity of the materials used in the construction of the paved walks and the walls lend an air of complete naturalness to the whole garden. At the highest point of the garden is the Mirador, and the site of the reservoir where all the water for the various jets and fountains is collected. Forming what the Italians term *bolli*, this water then tumbles in short cascades down a channel let into the parapets of a staircase, which is further ornamented with three basins: water is indeed everywhere in the garden.

Celebrated by poets and novelists, from Chateaubriand to Maurice Barrès, the gardens of the Generalife tend to be regarded by Westerners as the archetypal Arab garden. But is it a purely Islamic garden? After the last of the Moors had left, the garden came under Italian ownership and several changes were made to its original design. The famous water tracery of the Patio de la Reja dates from this period. In fact, the gardens of the Alhambra, in all their austerity, are more genuinely Arab than this jewel of garden design, where so much art has been deployed to conceal all

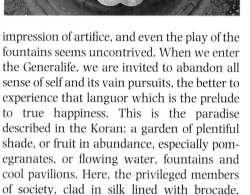

impression of artifice, and even the play of the fountains seems uncontrived. When we enter the Generalife, we are invited to abandon all sense of self and its vain pursuits, the better to experience that languor which is the prelude to true happiness. This is the paradise described in the Koran: a garden of plentiful shade, or fruit in abundance, especially pomegranates, or flowing water, fountains and cool pavilions. Here, the privileged members of society, clad in silk lined with brocade, could lie on sofas attended by compliant houris (whose virginity is constantly renewed) and by delectable ephebes, young men who played an indispensable role in the

Fountain basin in the Patio de la Reja of the Generalife, Granada.

The Patio de la Reja, the Generalife, Granada

pleasures of the world of Islam. After all, the proverb says: 'The goat is useful, a woman is a pleasure, and an ephebe is a delicacy.'

This is very much a male paradise, very different from that painted by Jean Fouquet, in which pious souls in white robes sing the praises of the Lord with the nine choirs of angels. However, it does bear a superficial resemblance to the *Paradisgartlein*, the *hortus conclusus* which celebrated the grace of Mary. There is nevertheless an obvious difference; the evocation of the senses in the *Paradisgartlein* was purely symbolic, whereas that of the promised paradise of Islam was wholly and palpably real.

For a sultan, dressed in silk and wearing a diamond-crested turban, doubtless accompanied by some favourite from his harem festooned with jewels, the gardens of the Generalife must have been a place of sensual delights. Yet the impression these gardens make on a European is quite different – hardly surprising, since the Western method of creating a garden is to plan every feature carefully, leaving nothing to the imagination. Here, everything is so refined, so subtle, so harmonious. Each single element of the garden falls inevitably into place, yet, at the same time, this perfection seems to owe nothing to the intervention of the conventional garden tools – dibble, billhook or shears. Although there is an air of informality, with no obvious indication of a strict geometrical plan, the garden nevertheless seems to be responding to some hidden principle; everything is so exactly right as to seem less the work of human minds and hands than some spontaneous act of creation. We need only stroll through this exquisite labyrinth of scents and soft sounds, caressed by a gentle breeze as daylight fades, to realize just how mundane are the charms of our own traditional gardens.

*P*atio de Daraxa, the Alhambra, Granada.

*P*atio of the Sultana
in the Generalife,
Granada.

The Arab style of garden is more common than any other, for it exists wherever Islam prevails or once made its mark. Its finest examples are to be seen in Andalusia, the territories previously included in Safavid Persia and the parts of India which were occupied by the Mughals for three centuries. The *riâdh*, or enclosed garden, often surrounded by galleries, has survived to the present day in the Maghreb (Algeria, Tunisia and Morocco).

One of the first countries to be submerged under the tidal wave of Islam was Persia, which corresponded to the present-day countries of Iran, Iraq and part of Turkestan. Total devastation followed in its wake; the ingenious irrigation system was destroyed and cultivated land became desert once again. However, the invaders were very much in the minority and tended to adopt the customs and traditions of the people they had conquered. Efforts were eventually made once more to conserve water, and, under the caliphs, the archetypal garden made its appearance. This was the classical Persian garden, with its area for game, its summer house, and division into four equal parts by canals (or channels, according to the size of the garden). These were built at right angles to one another in the form of a cross and represented the four rivers of the earthly paradise, which was also a reflection of the four quarters of the universe. Here were concentrated all the delights afforded by running water, shady nooks and airborne scents, the soothing sounds of fountains and the song of birds in the aviaries. Fruit grew within easy reach for picking – even gluttony could be satisfied in this garden of all the senses. The mosaics in the court of the mosque of Omar in Damascus are probably a fair reflection of how this luxuriant paradise garden looked. The prince himself would not, however, deign to walk in his garden but would be carried, stopping his bearers at points of interest, which would often be marked by a pavilion for resting (*chabutra*). There he would give himself up to dreamy reflection, a mental process which is very hard for people in the West to understand, unaccustomed as they normally are to non-objective thought. Sometimes his dream would focus on spiritual concerns, but more frequently he would simply surrender to the cloudy reaches of the imagination, especially if his meditation was accompanied by the sound of music or human song from a hidden part of the garden, or by the appearance of some courtesan adding her beauty to that of the flowers: narcissi, tulips, hyacinths, lilacs, jasmine, carnations, primulas, violets, lilies, anemones, pellitories, cyclamen, poppies, hollyhocks, fritillaries and, of course, roses. The rose was venerated by

Persian princess resting in a garden, painting from the palace of Chehel Sutun, Isfahan.

*T*he picnic in the garden, fresco from the palace of Chehel Sutun at Isfahan, end of 16th century – beginning of 17th century.

the Persians as the queen of flowers and they raised numerous varieties. The blooming of the rose was celebrated by fêtes, as the blossoming of the cherry trees would later be in Japan.

Yet these delights were not only restricted to the natural world. Converted into precious stones, they could transport the garden lover into a world of metamorphoses.

In the 9th century, the Abbasid Caliph al-Ma'mun made a number of additions to his palace of Dja Far on the banks of the Tigris, including a hippodrome in the Roman style and a multitude of other refinements to compete with those of the Sacred Palace at Constantinople. A description of the palace was made by Porphyrogenitus, the ambassador sent by the Byzantine emperor Constantine to the caliph of Baghdad. In one room of the palace stood a tree of silver in the centre of a basin; it was surrounded by mechanical horsemen, while singing birds perched on its branches. In an outside pool in the garden was another silver tree with many widespreading branches on which were perched all kinds of gilded and silvered birds which sang or cooed at the slightest suggestion of a breeze. These birds were, in fact, automata, activated pneumatically by a wind or hydraulic mechanism; the possibilities of such a mechanism had been studied in ancient Alexandria and writings on the subject have been preserved in the Arab translations of Banou-Mouza and Al-Djazani. The West was only later to discover the wonders of such automata.

The Arab influence in garden design eventually spread westward, eventually reaching Tunisia. In Cairo, Khumaruya, the son of Ahmad ibn Tulun, built the garden of Al-Kataï, where visitors were invited to admire the automata and a pool of quicksilver, while drops of water fell from the trunks of gold-covered palms. The sultan passed his nights on an inflated leather mattress which rocked gently on the pool of mercury in the reflected light of the moon. He also installed a

A 17th- or 18th-century garden rug decorated with the four rivers of paradise, with a central pavilion and a cypress and fruit tree border. Victoria and Albert Museum, London.

menagerie at Al-Kataï which contained examples of all the known animals of Africa.

Under the Timurid and Safavid dynasties from the 15th to the 17th century, the Persian miniaturists showed the princely life in the garden in the context of the legends which they were called upon to illustrate. The miniatures depict pools, canals in the form of a cross, domestic animals as well as game, and various trees, and they show the sovereign being carried by slaves around his garden, dining, hunting and holding outdoor audiences.

The art of the Oriental carpet, never surpassed, was born from the pavings and mosaics of the Persian palace, which provided welcome refuge from the outside heat in summer, but which would have been icy cold in winter had it not been for the woollen floor coverings. The Safavids adopted a fashion begun by the Sassanids (for whom it had magical significance) of depicting, in the carpets they made for winter use, themes redolent of spring or summer. The garden was an obvious subject for such representation, but in a stylized form; for instance, the cypress, with its tip bent by the wind, gave rise to a particular ornamental form, the *boteh-miri*, which has been used constantly in textile design ever since, perhaps also because it was traditionally a good-luck charm. The cypress, representing death, and the almond tree, the first flowering fruit tree, symbolizing life, are often found in conjunction.

The gardens of Isfahan, much simpler, have been preserved and maintained from a Safavid period; these include those of Ali Qapu, Maidan, Chehel Sutun and the patios of

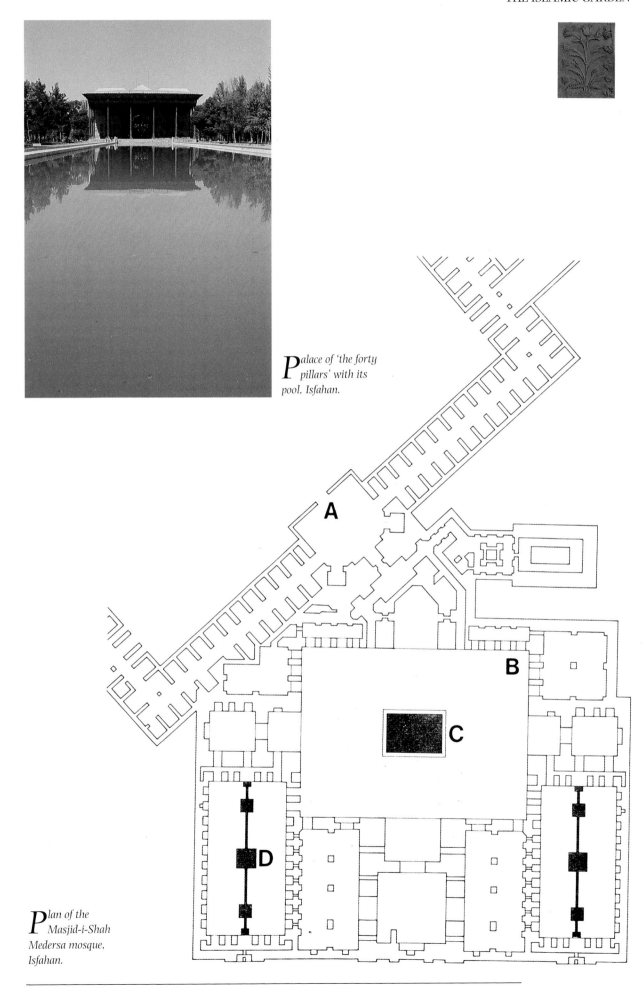

*P*alace of 'the forty pillars' with its pool, Isfahan.

*P*lan of the Masjid-i-Shah Medersa mosque, Isfahan.

the mosques, such as Masjid-i-Jami. One of the most striking characteristics of these secular gardens are the pavilions with their high columns of cedar wood, from which all parts of the garden can be surveyed. The gardens of the mosques are always a pleasant discovery within the plan of the building. Sometimes the patio pool is big enough to reflect the mosque's iwan, as it is at the Masjid-i-Shah Medersa at Isfahan, where the shade provides a marvellous contrast to the light-saturated façades. In a number of gardens in Shiraz, the pool is positioned to serve as a mirror to the central pavilion.

When they first arrived on the plain of Granada, the Moors were captivated by the charms of the country; indeed, it must have appeared almost magical to them, with its abundant supplies of water, constantly renewed by the mountain snows, and its evergreen fields. Having been warriors, they now became poets. Mohammed ben Alhamar, the most literary of the sultans of Granada, succeeded in bringing water up from the river Darro to the fortress of the Alhambra (the red castle, *el-Hamra*), which he transformed into a palace. The Alhambra comprises several palaces together, of which the most important is the Patio de los Arrayanes, the Court of the Myrtles. The central element is a pool in which are reflected the tower of Comares and, formerly, the porticoes of the patio. The principal theme of the Court of Lions is water, which spurts from the mouths of the carved beasts; the stalactite-like columns of the four facing pavilions in the court create something of the impression of a natural forest which has

been frozen by some magician in marble and stucco. The Ladies' Patio or the Garden of Lindajara (which belonged to the women's harem) is lined along one side by an arcade which is reflected in the largest pool of the Alhambra. The great pool of the Partal is decorated by two massive stone statues of lions seated on the edge. In the charming little Patio of Daraxa, which is just big enough to accommodate its exquisite fountain and a few cypresses, is a moving memorial to the mother of Boabdil, the last king of Granada. Scarcely larger is the Patio de la Reja, or Court of the Grille, where Joan of Castile, the deranged mother of Charles V, was imprisoned.

The Court of Lions, the Alhambra, Granada.

To appreciate the value of these patios as gardens, it is really essential to walk through the palace, moving from room to patio and then back inside again. The grotto-like rooms with their stalactite pillars induce a feeling of oppression and slight dizziness, evoking the imagery of the Muslim poets. Theirs was a world in a constant state of metamorphosis, where each thing in nature lent its attributes to something else to serve as an allegorical disguise, where the world of actuality was recognized as a perpetual mirage, where the ancient Bedouin traditions had mingled with Persian refinement and elements of Greek philosophy and science. Theirs was a language which could become art virtually on demand, where everything resisted exact definition and where there were 200 synonyms for a serpent, 500 for a lion and 1,000 for an eagle. Emerging from the palace apartments into an airy patio produces a great sense of calm, intensified by the friendly murmur of water or the reflection in a pool of the dreamlike image of an ancient wall.

At Cordoba, the palms are arranged fanwise in the great entry patio of the mosque and seem a continuation of the famous forest of treelike pillars within the place of worship itself.

In Seville, the old patio of the mosque still exists at the foot of the Giralda, the minaret of the sanctuary, which has become the bell tower of the cathedral. During the Christian period which, in Seville, preceded the fall of Cordoba by two centuries, the Arab pattern of garden design was given a further lease of life by the Mudejar style. In the 14th century, Peter the Cruel, king of Castile, initiated the rebuilding of an old 12th-century Arab palace, the Alcázar, which was to be carried out by Moorish architects and workmen. The garden was then modified to bring it up to the

*G*arden of the Great Mosque, Cordoba.

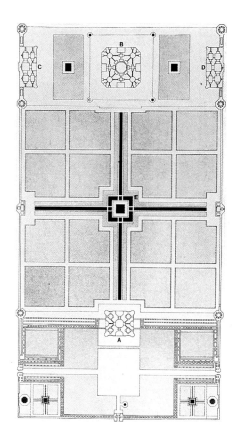

level of other major European gardens. It is interesting to see there a pavilion for Charles V in the Mudejar style dating from the time he was destroying part of the Alhambra to accommodate a circular palace in the romanesque style, built by Pedro Machuca, whose brutal lines and sharp edges look completely out of keeping with the soft and subtle designs of the Arab palace. Two gateways in the same style emphasize the mixed lineage of the Alcázar garden. In the 15th century, a labyrinth was built there, but this has since disappeared, although references to it can still be found on the tiles of Charles V's pavilion. It was later replaced.

One of the most paradoxical meetings in history was that of Islam and India, of a religion deeply committed to a single deity and a country where everything is god. This symbiosis was successful partly because of the religious tolerance of Islam and partly because, like the early Arabs, the Mongol peoples who created the Mughal empire were still very primitive and learned much from the countries they had conquered. Islam's delight in sensuality was thus to mingle with a similar tradition in India.

Babur (1483–1530), a descendant of Tamerlane, invaded northern India in 1526 and made his capital at Agra. His grandson, Akbar (1542–1605), a gifted administrator, increased and consolidated the Mughal empire. Akbar's son, Jahangir (1569–1627), took over his father's mantle. All these rulers had a notable passion for building; this was especially the case with Jahangir's son, Shah Jahan (1593–1666) who was responsible for the building of Delhi, Agra and the Taj Mahal. The Mughal emperors were particularly attracted by the valley of Kashmir, at the foot of the Himalayas, where, in the climate that was excellent in both summer and winter, trees and flowers grew in abundance, and they established gardens in three areas of the empire: in the region of Delhi-Agra, on the road to Kashmir and in the Kashmir valley itself.

The Mughal garden (charbah) took up the traditional design of the Arab garden, and notably of dividing the garden into four equivalent zones by means of canals arranged in the form of a cross, reflecting the four divisions of the primordial paradise. It is interesting to note that, whereas the individual designs of the Islamic gardens in the Maghreb or in Asia generally differed from one another, the Mughal garden was constructed according to a rigorous geometrical plan, which may well reflect the carefully structured administration which was one of the most notable characteristics of the dynasty.

It is in Kashmir that the Islamic garden

found its supreme expression. The garden was laid out on three levels, but on uneven ground; at the first, the emperor would give his public audiences seated on a throne of black marble; the third was the *zenana* or 'cradle of love' and was reserved for the harem. There was a pavilion on each terrace, either positioned centrally or to one side. But perhaps the most characteristic element in the Mughal garden was the abundance of water, gleaming mirror-like in pools and canals, or – in complete contrast to the tradition of the Muslim gardens of Persia, the Maghreb or Andalusia – flowing swiftly in cascades and staircase torrents. To achieve these effects, immense reservoirs were needed to collect the precious water. The garden was surrounded by thick, high walls. These vast gardens were frequently used for court ceremonies, in contrast to the gardens of Islam which were mainly reserved for private occasions.

Another motif of these gardens is the tomb, often built initially as a reception room and then transformed into a mausoleum on the death of the owner. The garden then became a funerary park.

The mausoleum of Itimad-ud-Daula at Agra, graced with four minarets at each corner, is in the centre of a rectangular garden, resembling that of Humayun in Delhi. This position had a symbolic significance, although the Taj Mahal at Agra is situated in the northern section of its garden. The Taj

The Taj-Mahal, 17th century, Agra.

Plan of the mausoleum and garden, Taj Mahal, Agra.

Mahal was built by the emperor Shah Jahan for his Persian wife Mumtaz Mahal, who was 22 when she became his second favourite and who died in childbirth in 1631. The emperor wished her mausoleum to be worthy of her beauty. Some 20,000 men worked on its construction, using marble, sandstone and semiprecious stones.

With a minaret at each corner, the mausoleum in pure marble is flanked by two mosques built of sandstone, from which it is separated by lawns; in the centre of each of these is a small pool. The garden proper, lying south of the mausoleum, is strictly rectangular in design and divided into four smaller rectangles. These are further subdivided by four canals in the form of a cross which join together in a rectangular canal surrounding a central pool. The pool is fed from marble spouts inside the basin, which project the water in a fan of tiny drops. Despite its small area, the central pool reflects the tomb perfectly. The presence of this immense 'paradise' in front of the tomb is obviously intentional. Access to the garden is gained through a monumental gateway.

The elegance of this building has rarely if ever been surpassed. Built to perpetuate the beauty of a mortal, the ethereal character of the architecture has made her immortal. Perhaps the love of Jahangir for his wife Nar Jahan was the inspiration of Shalamar-Bagh

(royal garden) in Kashmir, on the north-west bank of Lake Dal, which is surrounded by gardens remarkable for large pools which reflect the mountains and their snowy peaks. Their names have a poetic ring: Baghi-Vafa (garden of beauty), Nishat-Bagh (garden of delight), Nashim-Bagh (garden of breezes). This last, the most grandiose, is composed of a series of planted terraces, linked by majestic staircases, the lowest of which looks over the 120 m-long lake. This vantage point affords some extraordinary mirage-like effects produced by the reflection of light on the water.

Although they were much more extensive and thus less intimate than the gardens of Persia or of the Maghreb, these Mughal gardens nevertheless offered a sanctuary for lovers, whose acts were often depicted by the Indian miniaturists in a manner reflecting the all-pervading sensuality of the culture. The legendary loves of Krishna were portrayed against the background of such gardens – a remarkable example of the syncretism of two civilizations. Every summer, the emperor Jahangir took his entire court, his harem and his servants, by elephant, by carriage, on horseback or in palanquins, to enjoy the delights of his garden of Shalamar-Bagh in Kashmir. At the entrance to the gardens, he wrote, with justification: 'If there is paradise on earth, then it must be here, it must surely be here.'

Mughal garden: prince with a favourite on the terrace of a palace, gouache on paper, school of Murshidabad, c.1760. Bibliothèque Nationale, Cabinet des Estampes, Paris.

Garden of Shalamar, Srinagar.

THE DECLINE OF THE GARDEN
IN THE MIDDLE AGES

Charlemagne's cartulary, *De Villis vel curtis imperialis* of 812, tells us a great deal about the state of garden design at that period. Garden design as an art had effectively disappeared by the 9th century and even the utilitarian garden must have fallen into neglect for the emperor to be obliged to remind the stewards of his agricultural holdings to gather in peas and chervil. The cartulary listed all the species to be cultivated, either for their utility or for their ornamental value. It names 73 plants and is thus invaluable for botanists although, unfortunately, many of the plants have not been identified. We know that the Merovingian king Childebert liked to cultivate his garden near the Seine himself; in this garden were roses which an astute courtier, Fortunat, bishop of Poitiers, compared to the roses of paradise.

Anyone looking for information on the art of the garden during the succession of centuries we know as the Dark Ages will find little help in the *Liber de cultura hortorum* of Walafried Strabo, abbot of the monastery of Reichenau in the 9th century. Although the poem is pastoral in inspiration, it is really one of those literary exercises in which the more scholarly monks of the Carolingian era indulged themselves. However, it does contain a very exact statement as to what kinds of medicinal plants – simples – should be grown. It is interesting to read the learned abbot's expressions of nostalgia for the rustic life – sentiments which place him firmly in the bucolic tradition.

For the Middle Ages the garden was more a literary theme than an actual place – a realm of fable in the *chansons de geste* or the Arthurian romances, in which any knight venturing there might be entrapped by the spells of fairies or magicians. This was the enchanted but deceitful garden, full of snares into which a victim could be tempted by illusions and thus fall prey to evil. In this world, the hero undergoes a series of initiation tests which, if he is successful in them, lead him to his goal; glory or love. The tradition of the enchanted garden, in which love is seen as something to be pursued by way of all kinds of unforeseen obstacles, was continued by Ariosto and Tasso and later by d'Urfé in *L'Astrée*. Through them the tradition was handed down to the humanists of the 16th century and was thus the inspiration of one great garden, that of the Villa Orsini at Bomarzo. Rather more pleasant is the 'Vergier de Deduit' described by Guillaume de Lorris in the 13th century *Roman de la Rose*, where the lord passes his time in a pavilion built of greenery amidst laurels, pines, olives and cypresses, all Mediterranean trees. This garden is a dreamlike place; in it is the very fountain in which Narcissus fell in love with his own reflection. The narrator sees the reflection of a rose in the same fountain and falls in love with it; but the rose is in an enclosed garden and the hero will only be able to obtain it after overcoming many obstacles. He is just about to reach his goal when the story comes to an end.

The Italian Petrus Crescentius wrote his *Opus Ruralium Commodorum* ('Book of Rural Profits') in Latin between 1304 and 1309; it was translated into Tuscan about 1350, into French around 1373 and then into a number of other languages. This agricultural treatise enjoyed great success and its eighth book is devoted to 'gardens and delectable things,

Paradise, miniature from the Chants royaux sur la conception, *surmounted by the Puy de Rouen 1519–28. Bibliothèque Nationale, Paris, Ms. fr. 1537, Fo 87.*

Carol singing in the garden, miniature from the Roman de la Rose *by Guillaume de Lorris and Jan de Meung, c.1460. The paintings in this manuscript were executed by the Master of Jouvenel, possibly helped by a pupil. Bibliothèque Nationale, Paris, Ms. Fr. 19153, Fo 7.*

small trees and herbs, and their fruits which are to be arranged with care'; he is referring, then, to a garden cultivated for pleasure.

According to Petrus Crescentius, there are three types of garden: 'small, medium and grand'. The last two categories concern us here. At the top of the list the author puts the 'royal gardens and those belonging to other nobles and rich lords'. For such gardens, aesthetic considerations must come first; what is needed is 'the art of science of putting all the parts in order'. The site chosen for the garden must have flat ground; the garden itself should be rectangular, surrounded by walls, along which would be espaliers, with pergolas here and there. The garden would be divided by straight pathways, some shaded by pergolas, others flanked by hedges.

A central area of closely mown grass would be planted with a variety of flowers and surrounded by orange and citron trees, palms, pomegranates and cypress. A few trees could also be dotted here and there in the grass. The form of the garden is, then, distinctly Mediterranean. There would be a fountain in the centre of the lawn, which could either take the form of an octagonal pool with steps round it, a column surmounted by a statue or a basin on a pedestal.

Water for the irrigation of the flower beds (*aiole*) was to be channelled through various canals. One area would be designated for the *erbaio*, where fragrant herbs for the kitchen would be grown: mint, thyme, rosemary, sage, basil and rue. Medicinal plants could also be cultivated there. Another bed is described by the author as being of flowers: roses, lilies, gladioli and violets, and also those blooms which trade or war had brought from the East, such as the hyacinth or lilac.

The various beds were separated by narrow pathways, along which ran fences made of trellis work; the beds themselves were lined with hedges. The lower hedges were made up of roses, and the higher ones of pomegranate, hazel or laurel. In another part of the garden was the *pomario*, the area devoted to fruit trees. The term *viridarium* was applied by Petrus Crescentius to denote a wood consisting entirely of evergreens: pine, cypress, citron, fir, laurel and olive. This part of the garden was also the refuge of wild animals such as rabbits, hares, roe deer and birds. The pheasants and partridges would be kept in special reserves. Indeed, this *viridarium* is really another version of the paradise garden of the Persian kings.

The covered arbours were generally made of vines supported by wooden frames covered with a flat roof, with vaulting or even with small domes. Pavilions were to be sited here

and there throughout the garden. Room also had to be found for a fishpond (*peschiera*) and a bird-cage for song birds. In addition there would be a pool for bathing.

Such a garden was conceived essentially for the leisure and delight of the lord and his lady. Exactly how they were to enjoy this garden, at least in Italy, we know from the description by Boccaccio. In 1348 the author, together with a number of other well-born young people, fled the plague-ridden city of Florence to take refuge in his father's garden some distance away. In the *Decameron* the group takes up residence in the beautiful and richly appointed palace of the Albizzi, 'set on a small hill', which is then described in detail. To the

Fishing, 14th-century fresco in the tower of the Wardrobe of the Palais des Papes, Avignon.

We also have a very good description of the garden laid out at Hesdin in Artois from 1295 onwards. This was effectively an amusement park – full of little jokes and hydraulically driven automata, which had been brought back home by a Crusader, Robert II of Artois. Returning from Tunis with the mortal remains of his uncle, St Louis, Robert had travelled via Palermo, where he had seen the oriental gardens left by the Muslims who had occupied Sicily. Robert later returned to be regent of the island from 1283 to 1289; but once back in Artois he began the construction of the park which was continued by the Countess Mahaut of Artois after his death in 1302.

Most of the practical jokes in the garden were located in the gallery of 'playful devices'. The visitor was inevitably splashed with water, and also showered with flour. There was a missal which, when opened, gave off a cloud of black smoke; there was a bridge which collapsed as soon as anyone set foot on it; and there were machines producing thunder and storm effects. Visitors were liable to be attacked with a stick by an automaton dressed as a hermit, dropped on to a bed of feathers and subjected to other humiliations.

Gathering fruit, from the Heures de la duchesse de Bourgogne, *15th-century, Musée Condé, Chantilly.*

side of the palace is an enclosed garden divided by a number of attractive paths which run quite straight and are covered with pergolas over which grow vines or white and red roses; in the centre of the garden is a lawn of closely cropped grass of such dark green as to appear almost black, contrasting with the many different varieties of flowers. Further areas of grass are surrounded by lemon trees and other citrus trees valued more for their scent than for their fruit. In the centre is a fountain of whitest marble 'with marvellous sculptures', attesting to the fact that statuary already played a part in garden design in Italy. The garden is also full of animals, including rabbits, hares and fawns.

Such was the fame of this park that the dukes of Burgundy maintained it until 1553 when it was destroyed by the armies of Charles V.

The park of Hesdin, however, was very much an individual enterprise and not too much importance should be attached to it. Of far greater interest are the surviving descriptions of the gardens of the Hôtel Saint Paul which belonged to Charles V of France, who termed it 'a house devoted to marvellous diversions'. This garden closely resembled those which can be seen in many of the miniatures of the period, with fish-ponds, court-yards, pergolas, arbours and a bathing pavilion. There was also a menagerie with lions – a feature which must also have been borrowed from Sicily. The crowning glory was a labyrinth or 'daedalus'. The garden of the Hôtel Saint Paul continued to be maintained after the death of the king, but was finally destroyed in 1431 by the Duke of Bedford, then resident in Paris as the representative of the English court. Charles V owned other pleasure houses outside Paris, including the manor of Beauté. These country houses were known as 'follies' because they were partly sheltered by 'foliage' and were close to the fields. In the 18th century the word 'folly' was to take on a completely different sense.

The rose, symbol of the virgin, was the favourite flower of the period, and Albert the Great (1193–1280) could already list 54 species in his *De vegetalibus*. The famous rose of Provins, which is still cultivated in that town, was perhaps introduced from the East by Count Thibaut of Champagne.

References to the labyrinth of the Hôtel Saint Paul are the earliest certain mention of this feature in any French garden, though such devices are frequently represented in pavement mosaics dating from Classical antiquity; in the centre were portrayed such motifs as the Minotaur, its struggle with Theseus, Daedalus, an imprisoned man or, in contrast, a bird suggesting deliverance. One piece of Roman intaglio work shows a centaur, symbol of the hybrid. As always in the ancient world, the myth is simply stated, not explained. It retains its sense of mystery, referring to a fabled past where men, gods and monsters merge into one another. The Christian era brought a distinct change when dogma had to be concealed under pagan images when they had to be interpreted symbolically. The labyrinth at the entrance of Santa Reparata of Orléansville (El Asnam) in Algeria (4th century BC) could hardly be more self-effacing. In a square at the centre of the labyrinth is a palindrome, where the words 'Sancta Ecclesia' are repeated in every direction, vertical and horizontal, with the 'A' of Sancta positioned in the centre. The correct way through the maze is indicated by Ariadne's thread which lies in the entrance gallery. It is hardly surprising that there were a number of labyrinths with Christian significance in the province of Africa where the Manichean heresy was especially prevalent. To the faithful who enter, the maze makes visible the correct way to their goal. Later, the labyrinth was to be seen on a much greater scale on the pavement of Gothic churches, usually in the nave. In France, the churches of Saint Quentin, Saint Bertin in Saint Omer, the cathedrals of Bayeux, Poitiers, Arras, Chartres, Rheims and Amiens once had or still have representations of labyrinths. These mazes are either true or false labyrinths – the latter are those consisting of simple spirals, in which it is impossible to get lost and where the return to the outside follows exactly the same path. They thus symbolize the whole concept of pilgrimage, a function indicated by the name formerly used for the one at Chartres: the 'league of Jerusalem'.

There are only two examples of pavement labyrinths in English churches, but smaller ones, with a purely symbolic function, are to be found.

Several chroniclers, including one contemporary, have told how Henry II of England (1130–89) shielded the beautiful Rosamund Clifford, with whom he had fallen in love, from the jealousy of his wife Eleanor of Aquitaine by shutting her in a labyrinth which he had had built in the park of Woodstock. But the queen discovered the secret and the beautiful Rosamund was given the choice of death by poison or the knife. This is the earliest reference to a garden labyrinth or maze, but it must have been built of stone. During the Tudor period, the tragic story of Rosamund became the inspiration for popular ballads and it is possible that the tale was responsible for the great success of the maze as a feature of English gardens, where several remarkable examples can still be found. Mazes traced in turf were a popular form, but these differed from the true garden maze in that they were always circular. It is unlikely that this device, the source of popular games at festivals in England, was derived from the Roman labyrinth, although there are several examples of the latter. The origins of the turf maze may perhaps be found in those prehistoric labyrinths which seemed to express man's desire to return to the womb. The Troy game consisted of a competition between horsemen to see who could arrive at the centre of the turf maze without the horse ever stepping outside the lines marked on the grass. Even up to the 19th century, Welsh

Turf maze at Hilton Manor, Huntingdonshire. The inscription on the central column states that it was laid out in 1660 by William Sparrow, a boy of nineteen.

54

shepherds still marked out turf mazes which they termed *caerdria* or 'the walls of the castle of Troy'. The legend of Troy and the disembarkation of Aeneas in Italy has influenced a number of local legends. After all, according to Virgil, the Trojans came from Crete.

Perhaps these English folk games should be seen in relation to deambulation customs in which the sun's movement was re-enacted in spiral form, mentioned by authors at the beginning of the 19th century and which may have been associated with rituals for averting evil.

N.H. Matthews[1] has collected examples of about 50 turf mazes, some of which are more or less preserved while others are mentioned in written documents.

The board game of goose, played with counters, which also has folk origins, is likewise related to the concept of the labyrinth; the maximum score in it is 42 which is the double of the 21 tarot cards and which represents the cosmos.

The labyrinth is one of the oldest archetypal forms known to man and numerous examples exist from prehistory; in the garden, that universe of symbols, it has been revived.

The Duc de Berry, brother of Charles V, took great care of his gardens, but the French prince who displayed most enthusiasm for this form of leisure was René, titular King of Naples; he owned a number of magnificent gardens on the estates which he lost one after the other, eventually retiring to Gardanne in Provence where he promptly laid out yet another garden.

In most cases, the medieval garden had a fountain which assumed a variety of forms: water would shoot up from a column to fall back into basins or cisterns with high curbs. Several paintings from the region of the middle Rhine incorporate such curbed fountains in which the water rises from a well, and which evidently bore a symbolic meaning. The inspiration for such works of art was provided by the mystical speculations of the local monks; in them, the Virgin is shown standing in the *hortus conclusus* of the *Song of Songs*. She is accompanied by two or three male or female saints, one of whom is teaching the infant Jesus to play the dulcimer. There is also a table with a light meal set out on it; a green meadow is embellished with fruit trees, lilies and roses; the enclosure may also be castellated to increase the impression that its contents are inviolable. This is, in effect, the little paradise garden, the garden of mystical

The Hortus conclusus *(enclosed garden), miniature from the* Tableaux et chants royaux de la confrérie du Puy-Notre-Dame d'Amiens, *a book given to Louise de Savoie in 1517. Bibliothèque Nationale, Paris. Ms. Fr. 145.*

[1]N.H. Matthews, *Mazes and Labyrinths. Account of their History and Development*, London, 1922.

la mozt Mais atant se tayst listoure des puens qui
sen Retourneient en esdauome et parle de ceulx de
rodxeflour et dit Coment maulgis lessa oriande
la belle pour ce quelle lui dist quil estoit

Il dist listoure que moult firent chiere joieu
se les ypiens quant ilz vorent les sarrasins

*M*augis and
Orlando in a
garden, miniature
from the Manuscrit
de Renaud de
Montauban,
*Bruges, 1462–70.
Bibliothèque de
l'Arsenal, Paris, Ms.
5072.*

*T*he Master of the
Gardens of Love:
'the Great Garden of
Love.' Engraving
(burin). Bibliothèque
Nationale, Cabinet
des Estampes, Paris.

delights (*Paradisgartlein*). Often one of the sides of the garden is raised to form a bank, a vantage point from which the garden may be contemplated; the bank is sometimes shaded by a pergola planted with a vine or roses.

The enclosed garden, symbol of the purity of the Virgin, was very often used by the illuminators of the manuscripts of medieval *romans* to depict the sport of lovers or other aspects of gallantry. One engraver from the Rhine region became such a specialist in this type of representation that he is known to art historians as the Master of the Gardens of Love. The lovers are surrounded by the same gentler manifestations of nature which accompanied the image of the Virgin: swans, small dogs and rabbits. It is possible that the rabbits were intended to indicate a forthcoming marriage, since this animal also symbolized fertility. In the *Virgin with Rabbit* by Titian (in the Louvre), the little rabbit held by the Virgin is certainly a symbol of the Incarnation.

The basic element of the medieval garden was the quadrangle which could also be turfed to form a lawn. This rectangular area is always shown as enclosed, either by a low or high wall or a fence in wood or metal, which was sometimes gilded. The lawn is decorated with flowers.

So far as can be judged from the fairly fragmentary evidence which has survived in the form of miniatures or paintings, no garden ever deviated from this original model. If the garden had to be made larger, this was done by the simple addition of further quadrangles to the existing one to form a chessboard effect. This 'additive' system of building up a garden remained current practice until the 16th century in the countries of northern Europe. The garden envisaged as a series of rectangular plots is a throwback to the primitive utilitarian garden, perpetuated in the collective memory of the West. Present-day gardeners, whether amateur or professional, still tend to sow or plant leeks, cabbages and other vegetables in rectangular beds, no matter what the overall shape of the garden.

Enclosed and self-contained, the medieval monastery was also isolated from the natural world, even though it had played such a significant role in the development of husbandry; only the open space of the cloister, with running water for washing before and after meals, gave some restricted access to the world outside.

In the early Middle Ages, there was a decline in the art of the garden as the practical fulfilment of a dream, a place to evoke memories of a primeval Eden, a Golden Age or a terrestrial paradise. Such nostalgia was alien to medieval man; indeed, the concept of paradise on earth was rather distasteful. His imagination was not nourished by nostalgia but by hope – the celestial paradise to which he could aspire, as he was constantly told, by his behaviour on earth. Thus he looked forward, not backward. The eventual direction of garden design in the 15th century confirms this thesis. In the 13th century, when the medieval spirit held sway and all human life was governed by faith, reclining figures on tombs were left with their eyes open to gaze towards the Light in a state of beatitude. Later, such figures would be shown almost frozen – weighed down by the fear of death and last rites. At this turning point in history a decline in the absolute power of faith conjured up doubts and anxieties, to avert which man turned his imagination away from the Christian world to come and in the direction of the more tangible pagan world, now to be rediscovered by the humanists of quattrocento Tuscany.

Wash basin and fountain in the Cistercian abbey of Fossanova, Italy, consecrated in 1208.

POGGIO

THE RENAISSANCE GARDEN

*T*he Medici Villa Poggio a Caiano, as it was in 1599 according to the painting by Giusto Utens. Museo Topografico, Florence.

The revival of art and learning which is loosely described by the term 'Renaissance' was initiated by a relatively small number of men who were, by happy coincidence, alive at the same time in two Italian cities: Florence and Rome. After the great schism, and before it lost its way under Alexander VI, who simply used it to satisfy his taste for luxury and power, the Catholic church had two humanist popes. Nicholas V, pope from 1447 to 1455, was in fact the former librarian of Cosimo the Elder in Florence. The second, Aeneas Silvius Piccolomini, was a noble of Siena who became pope under the name of Pius II; his private library formed the basis of the Libreria Piccolomini in the city's cathedral, founded by his nephew Francesco, later Pius III. At about the same time in Rome, Cardinal Prospero Colonna founded his Academia Vitruviana in his own residence; the most notable member of the academy was the polymath Leon Battista Alberti, illegitimate son of a Florentine noble living in Genoa. By the age of twenty he had already written a comedy called *Philodoxus*, in a Latin so pure that he was able to pass it off as dating from the Classical period. This was considered a supreme achievement during the early Renaissance and even Michelangelo misled a cardinal in the same way with a Cupid which he had carved himself.

The academy was, however, short-lived; Pope Paul II (1464–71) an enemy of the new thinking, started to campaign against its supporters in 1468. After losing his job as abbreviator, (drafting papal briefs), which entitled him to live in the curia, Alberti took note of the change of atmosphere and sought refuge with the Medicis of Florence, where he was to have considerable influence.

In Florence, the new humanism depended very much on the prestige and power of one man, who managed to govern the Florentine state for 30 years without any obvious abuse of authority; this was Cosimo the Elder, one of the most complete men to have ever lived. A ruler of great political dexterity, a businessman and great patron of the arts, Cosimo was exceptionally learned in the humanities, knowing Latin and Greek and speaking French, English and Arabic. He was responsible for the founding of the Platonic Academy, which was directed by Marsilio Ficino. The members of the academy usually met in the Villa Careggi, close to the villa that Cosimo had granted its director as a permanent residence. The principal aim of the academicians was to collect and translate all the works of Plato, Plotinus and other Neoplatonists. A number of the members also published works under their own name, outlining their philosophical positions which seem to have been inspired more by the Neoplatonists than by Plato.

Neoplatonism was to inspire a rather curious allegorical romance written in 1467. The *Hypnerotomachia Poliphili* ('The Dream of Poliphilus') was written by Franciso Colonna (*c.*1453–1538), a Dominican monk from Treviso and lord of Praeneste, but was not published until 1499 when it appeared under the imprint of Aldus Manutius in Venice. According to Emmanuela Kretzulesco-Quaranta, a true story underlies the romance – that of the unfortunate loves of Lorenzo the Magnificent and Lucrezia Donati. Polyphilus sees himself as in a dream, travelling through forests, temples and ruins, where he meets such strange creatures as a winged horse, an

*V*illa Careggi, 14th–15th century.

elephant bearing a obelisk, a dragon, and chariots carrying the four elements. Finally, Polyphilus meets the nymph Polia. In this world of allegory, the two lovers are constantly confronted by ancient monuments, many of which seem to have been inspired by the Roman ruins of Latium, especially the temple of Fortuna Primigenia at Praeneste. They find themselves present at many pagan ceremonies, including a sacrifice to Priapus; these ceremonies are only pagan in appearance, and it is left to the reader to decipher the deepest meaning of the story. After refreshing themselves at the Fountain of Youth which washes them clean of sin, the lovers finally take a miraculous boat which brings them to the island of Cythera. There, Venus and her attendant Cupids await them. According to the Neoplatonist interpretation of the story, Venus is a pagan transformation of the Order which governs the world. The island of Cythera is described as a perfectly circular garden, thus indicating its divine origin (the only circular garden ever built was the botanical garden of Padua). The garden is bordered by a line of tall cypresses and divided into twenty equal sections, making up a series of enclosures marked out by porticoes covered with climbing plants. A great circular canal flows between banks of marble, on which groups of orange trees form bowers. There are numerous fountains and monuments dedicated to strange and ancient cults. In imitation of the ornamental style of the Roman gardens, lavish use is made of what was later called the art of topiary, in which a human, animal or other kind of form is given to plants by pruning.

Although the general drift of the *Hypnerotomachia* was really the outcome of 15th-century philosophical speculation, it was only to have widespread influence during the following century in causing the garden to be viewed as a representation of a superworld, a symbolic universe which leads the soul to delight in an antiquity stripped of its historical significance and made real in dreams. The engravings which accompanied the *Hypnerotomachia* certainly appealed to the creative imagination, and the illustrations of parterres in the book were used by later garden designers.

The quattrocento gardens, however, did not resemble those described in the *Hypnerotomachia*, although pleasure gardens were now becoming common in Italy; these were generally attached to a *delizia* or country pleasure house. At Ferrara, the d'Este family liked to give such gardens names which reflected a dominant characteristic: *Consolando* (a garden for relaxation), *Schifanoia* (where anxieties could be forgotten), *Belriguardo* (reflecting a location) and *Belfiore* (expressing the beauty of the garden).

It is interesting to read what Alberti has to say in his *De re aedificatoria* about the pleasure garden, so many examples of which were now being created throughout the Italian peninsula. Taking his cue from Classical antiquity, he reserved particular praise for grottoes covered with pebbles and stone urns. He recommends that a garden should be planned in the same manner as a building, attaching much importance to the choice of site, which must offer fine views over town, sea or countryside. He also proposes the positioning of a sort of amphitheatre in front of the villa and supports the practice of displaying the name of the master of the house in box or other fragrant plants.

From the 15th century onward the design of gardens was entrusted to architects. Important consideration was given to the relationship between the house and the garden, between the mass of the building and the mass of plant growth. The garden was now the setting of a much greater range of forms, expressed in topiary or constructions such as mazes, pools and fountains. And, finally, a new significance was attached to the sculptural elements of the garden, especially the busts of Classical heroes, either genuinely antique or commissioned from contemporary artists. Particular concern was given to harmonizing the interior decoration of the villa and that of the garden.

It is tempting to see the influence of the Classical era in the frequently stated notion that urban man finds relaxation in contact with nature. Petrarch had already expressed the elegiac aspect of the country life. But life at that time in Florence must have been very trying indeed. This was a city stretched to its limits, with complex and confusing organs of government and various mutually suspicious factions, with many of its leading figures in exile (this being the price of internal peace) but still plotting the overthrow of those who held power.

Marsilio Ficino recommended walks in the hills as a cure for melancholia and as a stimulant to good health and thought. The life of the wild animals, the murmur of springs and the rustling of the trees, he claimed, help to calm the soul. This relationship between the countryside and the inner life is the theme of Lorenzo the Magnificent's poem 'Altercation', which is set at Careggi.

Such a conjunction fulfilled a deeply felt need, as may be deduced from the first Tuscan villas whose gardens are sufficiently familiar to us either from description or from illustra-

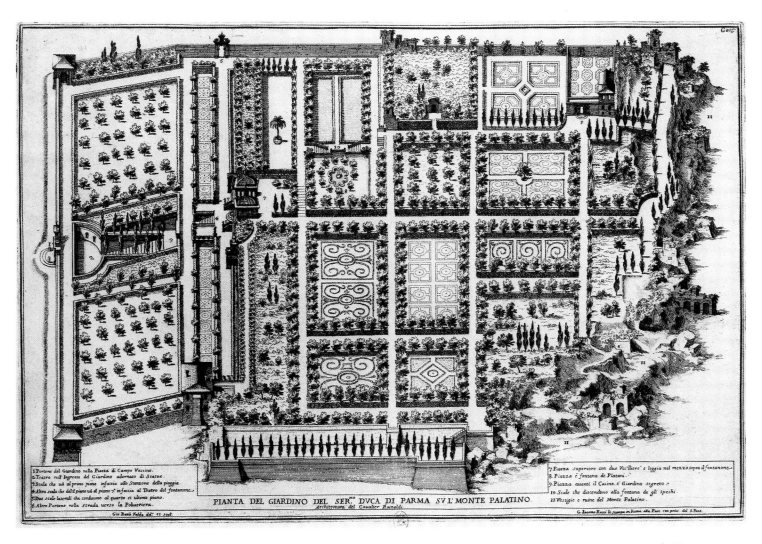

1. Portone del Giardino nella Piazza di Campo Vaccino.
2. Teatro nel'Ingresso del Giardino adornato di Statue.
3. Scala che và al primo piano infaccia allo Stanzone della pioggia
4. Altra scala che dal 2º piano và al piano 3º infaccia al Teatro del fontanone.
5. Due scale laterali che conducono al quarto et ultimo piano.
6. Altro Portone nella strada verso la Poluieriera.

PIANTA DEL GIARDINO DEL SER.ᴹᴼ DVCA DI PARMA SV L'MONTE PALATINO.
Architettura del Caualier Raineldi.

7. Piazza superiore con due Vccelliere' e loggia nel mezzo sopra il fontanone.
8. Piazza è fontana de Platani.
9. Piazza auanti il Casino. e' Giardino segreto.
10. Scale che discendono alla fontana de gli specchi.
11. Vestigie e ruine del Monte Palatino.

Gio. Batta Falda ded. et scul.

G. Iacomo Rossi le stampa in Roma alla Pace. con priu. del S. Pont.

*T*he Farnese
gardens on the
Palatine Hill.
Engraving from
Giardini di Roma, *by*
G.B. Falda, Rome,
1683.

*T*he Fountain of
the Charities (the
Three Graces),
engraving from the
Hypnerotomachia
Poliphili, *Venice,*
1499.

tion. Indeed, these 15th-century gardens remained very close to nature and thus did not differ greatly from those of the previous century. The new world of the imagination still looked inward, remaining within philosophical confines and not projecting itself into external forms. The gardens of Florence were created for philosophers who preferred the truly rural world, 'where feelings are true', to a neat and regulated enclosure. The humanists of the quattrocento did not experience any longing for a paradise lost. For them, paradise existed in the perfectly natural synthesis between the thinking of the pagan philosophers and the faith of the church fathers; the temple of ancient wisdom was also the court of the sanctuary enshining the Truth that Christ had brought to the world. The model for such thinkers was Saint Augustine who was a convert to Christianity and had therefore worshipped the ancient gods before coming to believe in a single deity.

Classical literature was therefore considered to be as great a repository of wisdom as Christian belief. According to the Florentine philosophers, the thinkers of the pagan era could have experienced their own Revelation, just as the idolatrous Hebrew peoples had experienced it through their prophets. In any case, the pagans also had their prophets; indeed, one of these sibyls, of Tibur, honoured at the Villa d'Este, had foretold the coming of Christ to Augustus.

Consideration also had to be given to those other inspired figures of the ancient world: the poets. The poet had, after all, been traditionally considered as *vates*, a seer. In the opinion of the Florentine philosophers and poets, the Classical poets had formulated a *theologica poetica* – an idea already expressed in

Boccaccio's *Genealogia deorum gentilium*, especially in books 14 and 15. And Dante chose to take Virgil as his guide to the world beyond.

The whole question was debated with great energy, which finally degenerated into open disagreement between 1490 and 1500. In 1486, Angelo Poliziano wrote a long poem in Latin (*Sylvae*) as an introduction to one of his courses; this poem celebrated the role of poetry as the wet-nurse of all branches of learning, a claim he repeated in 1490 in a study entitled *Panepistemon*. At this point, a Dominican monk named Savonarola delivered a sermon of apocalyptic intensity on the first Sunday of Advent in 1490. This sermon invoked heavenly wrath against the philosophers, condemning poetry, the *theologica poetica*, Neoplatonism and humanism. It declared the representation of gods to be a sin and invited any artists guilty of it to come and burn their works on a 'bonfire of vanities'. The outcome, of course, was the death of the fanatical monk himself on another bonfire.

Other philosophers adopted an even more extreme position. The writings relating to this body of thought were collected by Cosimo under the title of *Hermetica*; they originated with the Greek scholars of the Council of Florence and were eventually given to Marsilio Ficino to translate. Hermetism considered the philosophy and mythology of the pagan world to be still alive and saw the guiding principles of the world in terms of immanence rather than the transcendence of the scholastics. This sense of the oneness of things could be realized within the self, permitting the resolution of all apparent contradictions (which were after all contradictory only in appearance) and access to the true realities of the universe. Through such forms of syncretism the hermetic philosophers achieved another

*T*he Villa Trebbio, 14th–15th centuries, as it was in 1599, detail from the painting by Giusto Utens. Museo Topografico, Florence.

form of peace for the soul; as Gemisthus Pletho said, 'Religions are only splinters from the broken mirror of Aphrodite.'

The humanists of Florence found themselves living out a unique moment of perfect equilibrium in thought which would lead, by one path or another, to the reconciliation of all things and their opposites. There was no need for them to dream of a world to come since they had already found the true way from the Golden Age to paradise. Indeed, the most appropriate kind of garden for them was one which did not divert their flow of thought, offering such produce from the earth as flowers and fruit, for which they could thank the Creator. It was, in one aspect, very much a philosophy of happiness, which resembles that of Rabelais, although the motto written on the entrance of the abbey of Thélème in *Gargantua*, 'Do what you will', has been much misunderstood, because it also implied an addition, '...since you can do no evil, having acquired wisdom'. In a century when visions of Utopia occupied a central position in discussion, to read Rabelais in a literal sense was to read him the wrong way round.

We have only to look at the villas owned by the Medici, from Cafaggiolo to Poggio a Caiano, to follow the evolution of the garden in Tuscany during the 15th century. The first Medici villas were old family fortresses, such as Cafaggiolo or Trebbio, which had been 'improved' to turn them into pleasure villas. The gardens were remodelled by the architect Michelozzo but were actually mere enclosures

for flowers and vegetables, with a pergola from which the original pillars remain at Trebbio. Nothing now exists of the carefully tended garden and numerous fountains at Careggi, although the villa is still there. It was bought by Lorenzo Bicci de' Medici from Tommaso Lippi in 1417 and inherited in 1440 by his son Piero Lorenzo; seventeen years later it passed by inheritance into the possession of Lorenzo's brother Cosimo. The latter commissioned Michelozzo to modernize the building. It retained its battlements and machicolations and its sloping base wall; the windows, however, were enlarged, and an interior courtyard with Corinthian columns was added, very much in the 'modern' style. Careggi was Cosimo's favourite residence, where he assembled the leading thinkers of the time, often for banquets, as in the age of Plato. They included Pico della Mirandola, Angelo Poliziano, Marsilio Ficino, Cristoforo Landini and the artists Donatello, Michelozzo, Brunelleschi, Alberti and, later, Michelangelo. The future pope Leo X, Cosimo's nephew, was brought up there. On 7 November Careggi was the scene of a reunion to commemorate the death of Plato. It was there, too, that Cosimo quietly died one fine morning , on 1 August 1464. Lorenzo the Magnificent, having survived the massacre of the Pazzi conspiracy, also died there in 1492, followed seven years later by Marsilio Ficino. This villa and its garden, then, preserved an atmosphere of the sanctuary, an aspect which was not, alas, respected by Francis Sloane, an

Sandro Botticelli's Spring, like his Birth of Venus, *originally hung in the Villa Castello. The Uffizi, Florence.*

Englishman who acquired the property in 1848. At that time the garden still existed, but Sloane caused it to be completely demolished to create an English garden in its place. The projecting loggia over a room with an open portico was added later.

The garden at Careggi was famous throughout Italy. In a letter written by Alessandro Brocetti to Pietro Bembo are listed the species which were planted there, from the pale olive tree dedicated to warlike Minerva, to the myrtle of Venus, the oak of Jupiter, the poplar, the plane, the pine and the ilex. There were also a number of trees then considered exotic: cedar, fir, larch and beech. Careful study of Botticelli's *Primavera* has enabled us to identify the flowers which were planted in the Florentine gardens of the time.

All these villas were, however, essentially older houses which had been modified. Another villa, of a completely different type, was now to be built from scratch by Michelozzo on the steep slopes of the hill of Fiesole for Giovanni de' Medici, the son of Cosimo, a lover of books and music. Less forbidding than the previous Medici villas, it included a loggia on three levels; Michelozzo also incorporated a library and a music room. Because of the lie of the land, the villa needed considerable work on its foundations, although the architect failed to take full advantage of the position, contenting himself with superimposed planes connected by rather ordinary staircases. After the death of Cosimo's son, his nephew Lorenzo used the villa as a meeting place for the humanist thinkers, Angelo Poliziano, Pico della Mirandola and Cristoforo Landini.

There is a lack of ostentation in these villas, but the scholars who met there were, after all, hardly concerned with external show. The only luxurious building which Cosimo commissioned was his palace in the Via Larga, which had a small but much admired garden; the expenditure lavished on this building was a source of problem to the owner.

A villa designed by Michelozzo for Giovanni de' Medici in Fiesole.

Garden of the palace at Pienza of Pope Pius II.

In his wish to ensure the future fame of his birthplace, the village of Carignano near Siena, the humanist pope Pius II had it transformed into a town which he called Pienza. The Gothic appearance of the Duomo, recalling the *hallenkirschen* which the pope would have seen in Germany, may or may not have been deliberate. For his palace, however, he chose the most contemporary style available, thus consigning the church very obviously to the past. On three sides the palace follows the straight lines of the conventional square Tuscan dwelling, but the fourth is opened up by means of four superimposed galleries, affording attractive views of the Elsa valley. Positioned close to the galleries is the ideal philosopher's garden laid out as a square; there are a number of benches, vines and some fruit trees, while the water gurgles from the central fountain. The less important that the natural world is seen to be, the smaller the space which needs to be devoted to it; instead, the true meaning of the outside world will be found through an inner process of meditation involving a conscious stripping away of the ego.

Cosimo's nephew, Lorenzo the Magnificent, so called because of the fêtes, games and tournaments which he held, planned a villa much more modern in style than Careggi or Cafaggiolo. It would have been very much his personal creation had he lived to see it finished. His intention was to build a villa in the Classical manner, an *otium philosophicum*. For this purpose he purchased an old manor from the Ruccellai family at Poggio a Caiano on the river Ombrone. Michelozzo having died in 1472, work finally began in about 1480 by Giuliano da Sangallo, a much more progressive architect. Sangallo, however, did not use the hill to create different levels in the garden – a practice that was to become so popular around Rome in the following century and proved irresistible for Tribolo at the villa of Castello. Instead, the architect laid out an area of horizontal ground and, in order to

extend the garden northwards, was obliged to divert the Ombrone, a tributary of the Arno. Sangallo's design for the house was indeed original, the whole of the first storey of the rectangular building, the *piano nobile*, was made up of a porticoed terrace, which could be reached in the centre by two straight staircases.

Lorenzo only lived to see this first storey completed and the building was finished by Giovanni de' Medici, the future Pope Leo X, who added a magnificent entry in the form of a temple façade. In the 17th century the building was modified; the mullions were removed from Sangallo's windows, the straight staircases were replaced by curved ones with half-landings, and the rather incongruous clock was added on the roof. The blue and white terracotta frieze on the temple entrance is especially interesting, since it depicts a number of unusual scenes from mythology – evidence of Neoplatonist influence. We know the form of the garden in 1599 from the painting by Utens, which shows it to be much less original than the interior and exterior decoration of the villa itself. Surprisingly, there is no sign of overall planning or design other than the monoto-

The gardens of the Belvedere and the Vatican from a painting by Hendrik Van Cleve. Musée Royal des Beaux-arts, Brussels.

nous rectangular arrangement of beds in the traditional square. Yet, symmetry in planting is neglected to such a point that, behind the casino, there are firs on one side and grassy areas bordered by fruit trees on the other. There is evidence of planting here and there on the terraces, probably of flowers, while two dove-cotes are placed at each corner. To the extreme right is a secret garden, which looks as though it has been more carefully thought out; this is arranged around an octagonal centrepiece which must be a bed for the planting of fruit trees. Twin bastions, each terminating in a loggia, frame the drive which leads to the entrance, recalling the defensive towers of feudal times.

Finding his palace in the Vatican dark and depressing, Pope Innocent VIII (1484–92) decided to build himself a villa about 300 m to the north, from which he would be able to see the most dramatic panorama: the countryside around Rome, Monte Mario, the city of Rome itself and, in the background, the mountains of Latium, dominated by the Soracte. The square building which the pontiff commissioned from an obscure Roman mason was still sufficiently old-fashioned to be decorated with crenellations and machicolations, but the finely positioned loggias, although perhaps a little severe, wholly justify the name which the pope gave to the building – Belvedere. A garden was planted in the court formed by the buildings of the Belvedere, the southern gallery of which was only to be completed in the 17th century, and the wall in the background of Bramante's plan. It was in this garden that the popes established their open-air museum of antiquities; this we can easily picture from the paintings and drawings left by various northern European artists. The

statues in the garden included those of the 'Nile' and the 'Tiber' (now in the Louvre), a reclining 'Ariadne' which was known as 'Cleopatra', and the 'Apollo Belvedere', the famous torso found in the ruins of the theatre of Pompeii, which was so much admired by Michelangelo that, according to legend, he would still touch it lovingly although almost blind. Finally, there was the famous group of the 'Laocoön', which had been excavated in a vineyard in 1506 and bought for 600 golden écus by the pope, who then had it transported to the Belvedere, accompanied by salvoes of artillery and a day's holiday for all Romans. This garden survived until the major changes which were made to this part of the Vatican from 1772 to 1775 by Simonetti, who was commissioned to build the Pio-Clementino Antiquarium where all the antiquities could be exhibited under cover.

The Villa of Trastevere, which became famous under its later name of La Farnesina, was originally built for the Sienese banker Agostini Chigi, the richest merchant in the whole of Italy at the time of Julius II, but was purchased by Cardinal Alessandro Farnese, who was able to complete the masterpiece of Classicism which in a sense summarized the entire artistic endeavour of the quattrocento. It was built by a Sienese architect, Baldassare Peruzzi, between 1509 and 1521; a number of frescoes were painted by Peruzzi himself, while others were added some years later by Sodoma and Raphael. The present-day garden is separated from the banks of the Tiber and has been considerably damaged. We know very little about its original condition, except from a document dating from 1520 which mentions an *amoenissimum pomerium seu viridaium*, indicating the existence of a kitchen garden and fruit trees in the traditional

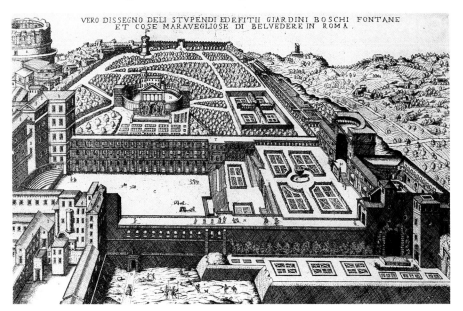

The gardens of the Belvedere and the Vatican in 1571, engraving by C. Duchetti. Bibliothèque Nationale, Paris.

Loggia of the Villa Farnesina, Rome: Cupid bearing away Jupiter's thunderbolts, by Raphael. Floral decoration by Giovanni di Udine.

Tuscan manner. The U-shaped casino has fortunately been preserved, with virtually the whole of its painted decoration. Peruzzi painted two frescoes here, representing the Roman countryside between two columns painted in trompe-l'oeil, thus reflecting the environment. More important, however, are the paintings by Raphael, depicting the story of Eros and Psyche, which decorate the five-arched loggia (nowadays protected by glass) which formed a kind of cool room and was thus a veritable extension of the garden. Indeed, the juxtaposition of loggia and garden is much more naturalistic than that of the heavy festoons and garlands of flowers, fruit and vegetables, attributed without proof to Giovanni da Udine, a form of decor comparable with that in the house of Livia on the Palatine Hill. Raphael was clearly inspired here by antiquity, but the Platonic significance of the Eros and Psyche myth warrants our examining it in a little more detail, especially since it is informed by the thinking which was, in some measure, formulated in the gardens of Florence. Let us look back for a moment to the main themes of *The Golden Ass* of Apuleius, already discussed in the context of Pompeii. Venus, jealous of Psyche, has sworn her destruction. Eros, however, has fallen in love with her and takes her to a palace, where he pays her nightly visits, but on condition that she will never try to discover his identity. She ignores the warning, encouraged by her sisters who persuade her that her nocturnal visitor must be a monster. Psyche finally observes Eros while he is sleeping, but a drop of oil from her lamp awakes him and he flees. She then suffers a thousand torments which are only ended by the merciful intervention of Jupiter, protector of lovers. Obtaining Venus's pardon, he gives Psyche a potion of ambrosia to drink and admits her as goddess of youth to Olympus, where she celebrates her marriage to Eros.

This is not the only Classical fable in which the transgression of an order forbidding the acquisition of greater knowledge is severely punished. Of more importance in this context,

however, is the suggestion of the theme of paradise lost and, indeed the Platonist significance of the story, which can be more readily understood when we recall that Psyche, in Greek, means 'soul'. The full implication of this may be appreciated when we read Marsilio Ficino's commentaries on the *Symposium* of Plato, written in 1464 and published in 1484.

The Florentine Neoplatonists of the 15th century, in their synthesis of Christianity and Platonism, considered the world as a dark abyss, in which man could easily fall prey to his passions. The magical formula which enables him to escape from their tyranny lies in Platonism which offers to the soul (Psyche) the true path whereby it can attain the beauty which is the central secret of the universe. The soul is led along this path by love, an irresistible emotion, provoked as much by beauty of the body as of the soul. Venus is the incarnation of that peace-giving force which reunites what has been separated and reconciles the soul with the universe. Far from being imprisoned in the world of the senses, which would be the Christian view, love is seen here as the means of detaching the soul from its earthbound state and elevating it to the angelic. It is

Mercury sent by Jupiter to bring Psyche to Olympia, by Raphael, loggia of the Villa Farnesina, Rome. Floral decorated by Giovanni da Udine.

for this reason that in the painting by Titian in the Borghese Gallery, Rome, sacred love is represented naked, illuminated by that pure beauty which can only have a divine source, while profane love is represented clothed, as it struggles towards that supreme light which must always remain obscured by the veil of appearances. It is in the mouth of a woman, Diotima, that Plato puts the words expressing the way of true knowledge from the world of senses to that of the spiritual: 'This is the right way of approaching or being initiated into the mysteries of love, to begin with examples of beauty in this world, and using them as steps to ascend continually with the absolute beauty as one's aim, from one instance of physical beauty to two and from two to all, then from physical beauty to moral beauty, and from moral beauty to the beauty of knowledge, until from knowledge of various kinds one arrives at the supreme knowledge whose sole object is that absolute beauty, and knows at last what absolute beauty is.' (Plato: *The Symposium*, trans. W. Hamilton, Penguin Classics, p.94). Such, then, was the concept of love held by the Platonist academy. This Venus is the *Venus Humanitas* venerated by the sages of Careggio. It is also the Venus born in the sea-spray of Botticelli's painting, which Vasari saw at Castello with the *Primavera*. And similarly it is the *Anadyomene* of Petraia, likewise from Castello.

The story written in Latin by Lucius Apuleius in the 2nd century BC was only one episode of his great poem, *The Golden Ass*. In its feeling for the miraculous and its treatment of the natural world – that marvellous theatre of birth and rebirth through reproduction – it was a theme more suited to the decoration of villas than of city palaces.

The frescoes painted by Raphael are among his later works; he was especially attracted by their subject matter and took a greater personal interest in their execution than in those of the Vatican, where he was influenced by Michelangelo. In these frescoes, his sense of Classicism and humanism are once again evident, as is his taste for beauty, evoking wonderfully the Platonic ideal of love. But the later decoration of the Palazzo del Tè, Mantua, was another story. The banquet of the gods depicted in these frescoes is a veritable bacchanalia; indeed, it is Bacchus who is just as much fêted as Venus, since much drink is clearly being consumed, and not only ambrosia! All the guests at the gargantuan feast seem to have an overwhelming desire to grasp hold of their neighbour, as though the painter of these scenes has envisaged the fable of Psyche as more demonstrative of erotic impulses than of pure love. Yet, at the same

*L*abyrinth at the centre of the floor paving in the Sala di Psyche in the Palazzo del Tè, Mantua.

*P*reparation for the
wedding feast of
Psyche and Love, by
Jules Romain and
assistants. Palazzo
del Tè, Mantua.

time, the orgiastic rhythm of these frenzied scenes does somehow give a cosmic dimension to love, which could be more justly described as dionysiac than erotic. There is something here, too, of the Classical villas of Naples: the appetite of the gods is so vast that the peasants rush from all sides to bring them food, while the fishermen are desperate to catch more fish in the rivers to supply the monstrous banquet. This is the Mannerist version of the fable of Apuleius, just as the frescoes of La Farnesina are its Classical expression.

The Villa Madama in Rome, which is discussed in the following chapter, had a direct influence on another villa, the Villa Imperiale near Pesaro, so called because it had received a visit from the Emperor Frederick III in the preceding century. The villa was severely damaged during the wars of the early 16th century, but in 1522 Francesco Maria della Rovere, Duke of the Metaurian States, began to plan its restoration. With this in mind, he wrote to the humanist scholar Baldassare Castiglione, his representative in Rome, asking him to send a copy of a letter written by Raphael, in which the painter describes the villa in Mantua that he was then decorating. The duke, however, was obliged to return to the wars and it was therefore his wife Leonora who completed the project while her husband did battle on distant fields, as indicated by a surviving inscription composed by Cardinal Bembo. The work on the villa was carried out by the decorator-architect Girolamo Genga and the painter Raffaello del Colle and was completed around 1534. The new pleasure villa is linked by a bridge to the old family residence, restored and redecorated with frescoes on themes of family history. The porticoed buildings of the new villa surround a courtyard on three sides, while a spiral staircase leads to the promenade terraces and two belvederes which command a view over the surrounding countryside and a group of tall umbrella pines. This vantage point also allowed the observer to discover the 'secret' of the villa, a marvellous walled garden seemingly suspended in the sky. To stand here today in this little paradise, at treetop level, listening to the twitter of birds in the foliage, is truly a delightful experience. The recollection of the allegories painted indoors in which historical themes receive free imaginative treatment, and the feeling of peace conveyed by the surrounding countryside, combine to give this villa a sense of total harmony, of complete self-sufficiency. The charm of the villa was very evident even in its earliest years, when it was referred to as 'La Farnesina of Pesaro'. More than anywhere else, it is the Villa

Imperiale at Pesaro which most closely suggests the *otium*, the place of peaceful contemplation of the Romans, which was also the ideal of the quattrocento humanists. This idyllic vision brings to a fitting conclusion our survey of the true Renaissance garden in Italy. As we shall see in the following chapter, the Renaissance proper gave way to another set of preoccupations which we know as Mannerism, in about 1530. It was about this time that the foundations of European civilization began to appear less strong and secure; the serenity of the Renaissance was replaced by a sense of doubt, which evoked its own imaginary world. This new world was reflected emphatically in garden design, which, as a result, was to assume a more important place in the history of artistic forms than ever before, even in the Roman times. But while the new surge of creativity and ingenuity engendered by the Renaissance was going on in Italy, the rest of Europe was to take almost a century to assimilate the new ideas, and that time lapse is especially evident in garden design. The forms and practices established in the Renaissance continued to be emulated – in some countries until the 17th century. It is almost as though a different concept of space existed outside Italy than in the country where perspective had first been discovered – a concept which was more concerned with the rational, step-by-step management of space with its creative applications.

OUTSIDE ITALY

The study of the Renaissance garden outside Italy presents considerable difficulties since, in a sense, we are dealing with a dead language: very few examples have survived. Nothing is as fragile or as subject to fashion as a garden. There may be some hesitation about destroying a palace or church, to replace them with a building much more to contemporary taste, but far less trouble is involved in destroying a garden. For once it is changed or modified, it becomes something entirely different. The gardens of Fontainebleau, for

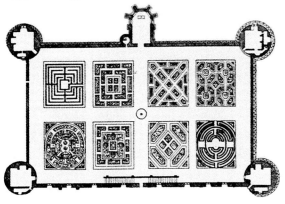

The garden of the Château de Beauregard, after Androuet du Cerceau (Les Plus Excellens Bastimens de France).

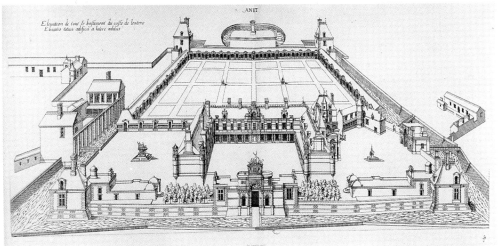

ANET

Elevation de tout le bastiment du cosse de lentree
Elevatio totius ædificii a latere additus

instance, were remade four times. The main reason for this destruction of older gardens was the fashion for the English style of garden and no country suffered more from this than England itself. In France, admittedly, such modifications began to appear after 1660 due to the hankering for gardens 'in the French style'; the fashion for the English garden only came later, but wrought just as much havoc. The French Revolution then brought about the ruin of many châteaux and gardens and caused others to be abandoned, perhaps to be replanted later in a different style. Only Italy escaped this subsequent vandalism, which explains why many of its gardens, which probably reached their apogee at the end of the 16th century, can still be seen today. In France and England, however, it is as difficult to consider the gardens of that period as it is to study the gardens of the Romans. As regards France, we still possess a wonderful record of the gardens of that time in the splendid engravings made by Jacques Androuet du Cerceau in his *Plus Excellens Bastimens de France*, which was published in 1576 and

1579. The influence of the Renaissance can be seen as a shock wave gradually spreading outwards from Florence during the 15th century, first enveloping Italy (although it only reached Naples at the end of the century) and then the whole of Europe, initially affecting France and subsequently the countries of northern Europe. Thus France often played a kind of mediating role between Italy and the lands of the north. Not until the end of the 16th century had these countries that were culturally dependent on Italy fully digested the new ideas and brought their own individual interpretation to them.

Around 1550 a new type of garden design began to appear in Tuscany and in the country around Rome, which I have termed the Mannerist garden. In northern Europe, however, traditional garden design held sway much longer. Yet, in both England and France, certain experiments were initiated in the second half of the 16th century which are only partially known to us because of the almost total destruction of the gardens of the period.

FRANCE

A principal feature of these experiments was an attempt to achieve a sense of unity between the château and the garden. For the first half of the century the various beds were laid out in a fairly straightforward fashion, although sometimes their shape was varied or they were interspersed with elements of the kitchen garden; this was the case at Blois, Gaillon, Bury – (where the symmetry of the château was also imposed on the garden), Chantilly, Ecouen – residence of the Conné-table de Montmorency – and at the royal château of Fontainebleau. At Montargis, which is a circular fortress, the garden beds were laid out fanwise around the château.

A new element in design, which was later to enjoy great success, made its appearance at Le Lydieu; this was a retreat in the park of Gaillon at some distance from the château itself. The retreat consisted of a hermitage with a completely equipped house, a chapel, a garden for cultivation by the hermit (who had to be a Carthusian) and a curious rock surrounded by water, symbolic of his retreat. The whole complex was enclosed by walls and further protected from intruders by a draw-bridge. Later, this hermitage was to be linked by canals to a building in the Mannerist style, covered with fantastic decoration, which must have been a bath house.

At Chenonceaux, Diane de Poitiers desig-nated a large area at some remove from the château to be divided into garden beds; the modern restoration by Duchêne of the beds of *broderie* is completely anachronistic. The res-toration of the gardens at Villandry by Dr J. Carvalho and the reconstitution of the beds divided by clipped box has been much more successful. At Maulne in Burgundy, the Duke of Uzès had the highly individual idea of diverting a watercourse from his garden into the château, where it gushes out from a fountain-head underneath the staircase. In the gardens of the Tuileries in Paris, the rec-tangular divisions are positioned monoto-nously one after the other for a considerable distance; the garden was not even on the same axis as the building.

It was very much a French fashion to add a moat to the garden of a château in recollec-

The grand canal in the park of the Château de Fontainebleau.

tion of the medieval past; this was a feature which was to have a long life and can be found, notably, at Ancy-le-Franc, Anet, Vallery and Bury.

There was, however, one innovatory ornamental element in the French gardens of the period which was completely indigenous and did not come from Italy; this was the canal, which appeared in various forms and was perhaps appropriate to a country of great rivers. Some notable examples were at Dampierre, Verneuil and Courance. Henri IV had the first great canal, as broad as a river and 1,200 m in length, dug at Fontainebleau. It was the ambition of François I to have copies for Fontainebleau of the antiquities recently discovered in Rome, and Primaticcio was despatched to the eternal city to take the moulds. Henri IV considered that the marble statue of Diana and the doe was too fragile to be left in the open and Barthélemy Prieur was commissioned to reproduce it in bronze as an ornament for the fountain designed by the Italian Tommaso Francini, who had already incorporated water displays with the statue of the Tiber.

Grottoes now became fashionable. A number of them, notably at the Tuileries and Ecouen, were decorated with polychromatic ceramics by Bernard Palissy; along with the gods and goddesses, these depicted various animals such as reptiles, fish, frogs and centipedes, and even the moss of the grottoes was represented in ceramics.

ENGLAND

In England, the first gardens of the Tudor period did little more than prolong the designs of the medieval garden, with some elaborations added; such a garden would be located along several sides of the house, enclosed and divided into rectangular areas in the form of beds or parterres. After Henry VIII's break with the Catholic church, England became separated from Italy, source of all innovation in garden design. So there was a tendency to turn towards France for inspiration, although little original work was being attempted there. The French gardeners of the time tended to retain the traditional forms of the garden but to extend them over as large an area as possible so that they could easily be used for fêtes, recreation, masquerades and other forms of amusement. The Dukes of Burgundy had made fashionable the ostentatious display of family wealth and achievements. François I of France and Henry VIII of England vied with each other as to who could put on the most opulent displays; this dynastic pride had a curious effect on garden design. The parterres in the gardens of the great royal houses of Hampton Court and Whitehall were decorated with the colours of the new dynasty, white and green, while inspiring use was made of the Tudor rose. Images of the heraldic beasts of the family's arms were draped from poles of painted and gilded wood; other banners bore the colours of the royal house

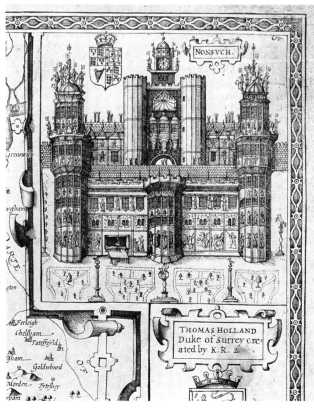

The palace of Nonsuch, Surrey. On the entrance court, to either side of the fountain of Diana, are heraldic columns bearing the emblem of the Falcon. To the far right are columns with the emblem of a horse sautant.

amidst richly decorated tents.

The beds were laid out with plants in the form of 'knots', modelled on those in the *Hypnerotomachia Poliphili*; the plants in these beds were trimmed to different heights to give the impression of intertwining elements. The intricate design of parterres was of especial interest to the English gardeners of the time, as we learn from Thomas Hill's *The Profitable Art of Gardening* (1568), and notably of the labyrinth motif which became one of their favourite designs. In 1571 appeared an anthology of designs for mazes, Didymus Mountain's *The Gardener's Labyrinth*. We know there was a labyrinth at Nonsuch, with hedges which were allowed to grow so high that it really was possible to lose oneself in it.

When the son of Lord Burghley received Queen Elizabeth at Theobalds in 1591, she would have found the garden divided into four sections, in the first of which was a maze. The others were planted with flowers symbolizing the Virtues, the Graces and the Muses: roses for the first, pansies for the second and various for the third. A delicate touch was the reception of the queen in an arbour of eglantines, a flower which contemporary literature often attributed to her as an emblem and which can sometimes be found in portraits of her. Even at that period, the English were already demonstrating their passion for flowers.

Wollaton Hall is of crucial importance in the history of the English garden, since it is the first example in the country of a garden being planned to form an entity with the house. The manor house and the garden, built around 1580 for Sir Francis Willoughby, form a perfect square, divided into nine parts of roughly equal area. The house is approached from a central court lined by two galleries, to which are joined two subsidiary courts; the manor itself stands between two further courts at the extremities of which are two service buildings (the right-hand one housed the stables and gave on to an area planted with trees). On the other side of the house the garden was laid out in three squares, of which only the plan of the central one is known to us; in the centre of it the roof of a building seems to be indicated. At the further side of the central square is another service building similar to those already mentioned. The whole plan, then, is rigorously symmetrical and aesthetically very satisfying; it banishes all memories of the piecemeal, asymmetrical development of the medieval garden, which had remained current in England almost until the end of the 16th century.

The ornamental garden at Wimbledon House was divided into four rectangular areas; the focal point of the garden was a 'piller' (pillar), which Roy Strong believes to have been a symbol of homage to the queen,

Topiary at Longwood.

who visited Wimbledon four times from 1592 to 1602. Elizabeth had adopted the pillar as a device, following the example of the Emperor Charles V; she is sometimes associated with the emblem of a crowned pillar enlaced with eglantines – also her emblem – and the pillar, single or double, occasionally appears in portraits of her.

It is unlikely, though, that the motifs of heraldic pride which had so much effect on English garden design at this period, could ever have been carried further than at Nonsuch Palace. This great house had been sold by Mary I to the Earl of Arundel, eventually becoming the property of his son-in-law Lord Lumley, a Catholic. Lumley had travelled to Italy in 1566, where he had the opportunity to observe the use of large amounts of statuary in the gardens. The house itself was substantially taken up with a collection of family portraits in the manner of the collection of worthies assembled by Paolo Giovio, with imaginative treatments of his ancestors where no evidence of the appearance of the original existed.

In addition to fountains in the Italianate style, the garden also included pillars, columns and obelisks incorporating images of the heraldic beasts of the Lumley family. Topiary also played a large part in shaping the appearance of the garden, populating it with horses, rabbits and deer in imitation of a hunt. On one column was a statue of a nymph or Venus. Several features were devoted to Diana as a form of homage to the Virgin Queen. In one of the fountains, the water flowed from the breasts of the goddess; in another, more Mannerist in style, a woman's torso rises above the heads of lions from which water spurts, while the head is surmounted by a mushroom shape on which there is a crown topped by a crescent moon. In a grotto, hidden in a thicket, Diana and three nymphs bathed under the complacent gaze of Actaeon; all these statues were polychrome. Indeed the cult of Diana was a way of imagining the praises of Gloriana. The garden was also equipped with a labyrinth, the hedges of which were sufficiently high to make it truly effective. There were also three pyramids bearing respectively an eagle, a pelican and a phoenix, the last two being emblems of the Tudors. The emblematic or symbolic aspect of this astonishing garden, then, was not only a celebration of Lumley's own family, but also of the Tudor dynasty and the glory of Queen Elizabeth I. In this, it was a true reflection of the country's situation in Europe at the time and a demonstration of the rather insular character of English garden design. It was left to Salomon de Caus, that international artist, to open up the English garden to Mannerism.

A picnic being served at the centre of a labyrinth, engraving by Hieronymus Sperling, 16th century.

THE MANNERIST GARDEN

The Renaissance, as defined by Burckhardt in 1860, lasted for about two centuries and was followed directly by the Baroque period. Since this definition was made, art historians have increasingly inclined to view the two periods as being divided by a third, Mannerism; even so, within the history of the great movements in art, the Renaissance can still be envisaged as a unified period extending from around 1400 to about 1580. In the world of forms, however, which is the one that concerns us here, this apparent unity is seen to be artificial. The true Renaissance was a patient and long elaboration of Classicism, which took place in Italy during the 15th century and reached its zenith in the geniuses of Bramante, Leonardo, Raphael and Michelangelo, during the pontificates of Julius II, Leo X and Clement VII. Taking nature as its point of departure and a certain concept of beauty as its objective, the Classical aesthetic proved incapable of advancing further, once its goals had been achieved; in the Ancient World, this stagnation lasted for several centuries. But in Renaissance Italy, the creative vitality was such that no similar paralysis occurred. If there was any temptation to lapse into conformity, it only existed at the conceptual stages of artistic achievement; in practice, the evolution of style continued with the modification of Classical forms, which is already discernible in the later works of Raphael and which made the works of the second part of Michelangelo's long career so deeply individual. In its modification of traditional forms, this new aesthetic was inevitably characterized by ambiguity; it is this new mood which present-day art historians know by the name of Mannerism.

Classicism had always been the expression of a profound sense of balance and equilibrium, based on a reasoned and thoughtful application of the human faculties – the ideal of the quattrocento humanists; in contrast, the twisted and contorted lines of Mannerism suggested powerful feelings of anxiety. And we do not have to search very far in the history of events and ideas to understand why the marvellous spirit of optimism which marked the Renaissance came to be abandoned. One obvious factor was the discovery that the Earth is round, rendering the Italian city states only too conscious of their small size in relation to this newly apparent global immensity; in any case, a certain process of decay had set in as the states passed from republic into principality. Moreover, most of the geographical discoveries were being achieved by other bodies politic whose vital interests were not necessarily concentrated on the traditional centres of the Mediterranean. It was disturbing enough for Renaissance man to discover that he was not the centre of the universe, but any lingering illusions he may still have harboured about his status were completely wiped out by the discovery of Copernicus that the Earth revolved round the Sun. No doubt these discoveries provoked some heady thoughts about the possibilities of exploration, both on Earth and in the heavens. At the same time, they must have prompted a deep self-questioning, reinforced by the preaching first of Savonarola and then of Luther, which put an end to the spirit of celebration by forcing man to contemplate his state of sin; the Catholic faith, which had for so long been a received orthodoxy in human affairs, was now being contested. The problems of Erasmus in throwing off this orthodoxy bear witness to the crisis of conscience felt by the greatest thinkers of the time. On the surface, the new thinking proposed a simpler form of religious belief than in the past but, in depriving man of the multitude of practices which had acted as an intermediary layer between him and the fundamental principles of his religion, it also left him face to face with a God as inflexible as the Yahweh of the Old Testament. Against this disquieting background, we must also set the uncertain political climate of Italy, towards which certain northern European powers were already looking covetously. In 1527 the city of the popes suffered the supreme desecration when it was sacked by an army of German protestants, a reminder for the historically informed of the sack of the city in 451 by Alaric, which heralded the end of the Roman empire. Alaric's pillaging lasted only six days; the Lutherans ravaged the city for three months. The year 1527 in fact marks the true starting point of Mannerism, although the work of a number of the more advanced Florentine artists had already shown signs of the style before 1520.

There were many reasons, then, for the climate of anxiety which existed in Italy at that period. To escape this shifting world, the Italians invented an imaginary one, a place of refuge and stability: the Mannerist garden.

Taking the example of Uccello, there has been a tendency on the part of art historians to see the art of the quattrocento very much in terms of its exploration of perspective; in fact, few bodies of painting, apart from that of the Middle Ages, have been so little concerned with the effects of distance. Indeed, it would be more accurate to talk of foreshortening than of perspective; Berenson was probably much nearer the mark when he described the work of the Renaissance painters in terms of their search for tactile values. Both Paolo Uccello and Masaccio created a three-dimensional effect in the human figures they painted. In this they were strongly influenced by contemporary sculpture, which had revived the art of statuary in its imitation of Classical models. Space in the paintings of Masaccio is treated cursorily, as though the observer were expected to fill in the details himself. Piero della Francesca reduced the distant mountains in the backgrounds of his portraits of the Montefeltro family of Urbino to a few small heaps of sand. In the work of Baldovinetti or Pollaiuolo a river may be seen winding around the foot of a mountain, a convention which reached its high point in the background of Leonardo's *Gioconda*. Perspective, indeed, as a means of linking foreground to background, interested the painters of the Renaissance so little that they left its practice to the craftsmen of a minor art, marquetry (*tarsia*).

The heavy physical structure of the buildings of the period was not particularly conducive to the creation of effects of perspective in architecture. The form of the Renaissance villa was often a direct response to the lie of the land, frequently a slope, which allowed the architect to explore the effects of perspective through the use of right and oblique angles within a given space.

The first major characteristic of the Mannerist garden is its architectural quality. It no longer consisted simply of the rectangular area, the basic bed, which claimed direct line of descent from the garden of the Ancient World, itself really an integral part of the main dwelling which happened to be exposed to the open air. By contrast, the dwelling was now to become part of the garden, remaining of modest size while the area of the garden was extended considerably – a reasonable solution if the object of living in such an environment was to relax in countrified surroundings. This was the origin of the casino (little house) which could either serve as the point of departure or as the ultimate focus for the lines of perspective in the garden, according to the position of the entrance.

The landscape architects of the period found themselves compelled to take account of two significant models which had a bearing on their art; one of these was never to take the form of a garden, while the other remained incomplete. The first was Bramante's plan for the Vatican, and the second Raphael's design for the Villa Madama.

We have already seen how at the end of the 15th century Innocent III created a 'country' residence, the Belvedere, at some distance from the official papal palace, from where he could overlook the whole city. Julius II asked Bramante to connect the Belvedere to the palace of the Vatican by means of two long galleries, while the sloping land between them was to be arranged on three levels: an open space (on which jousts were later held after the removal of the great fountain), a monumental staircase, and finally a formal garden which led up to a simple apse or nymphaeum. This was later replaced by a huge recess inspired by that in the Stadium of the Flavians on the Palatine Hill. The grand design of Julius II and Bramante was later spoilt by the construction of two transversal buildings, the 16th-century library and the 19th-century Braccio Nuovo. The grandiose effect achieved by the gradually rising plan of the court may have been inspired by the temple of Fortuna Primigenia at Praeneste. But whatever its origin, this layout was to have far-reaching influence on the arrangement of space in the Mannerist garden.

The Villa Madama in Rome was commissioned from Raphael around 1517 by Giulio de' Medici, later Pope Clement VII. On his death in 1534, the house passed to the condottiere Giovanni de' Medici and then, after he was assassinated, to his widow; she was the daughter of Charles V, Madama Margaret of Austria, hence the name of the villa. The Uffizi Gallery in Florence possesses no less than sixteen designs for the villa, the majority by Antonio da Sangallo the Younger or by Battista da Sangallo, who worked under Raphael's directions and then carried on with the building of the villa after his death, at which point no doubt Antonio introduced a number of his own ideas.

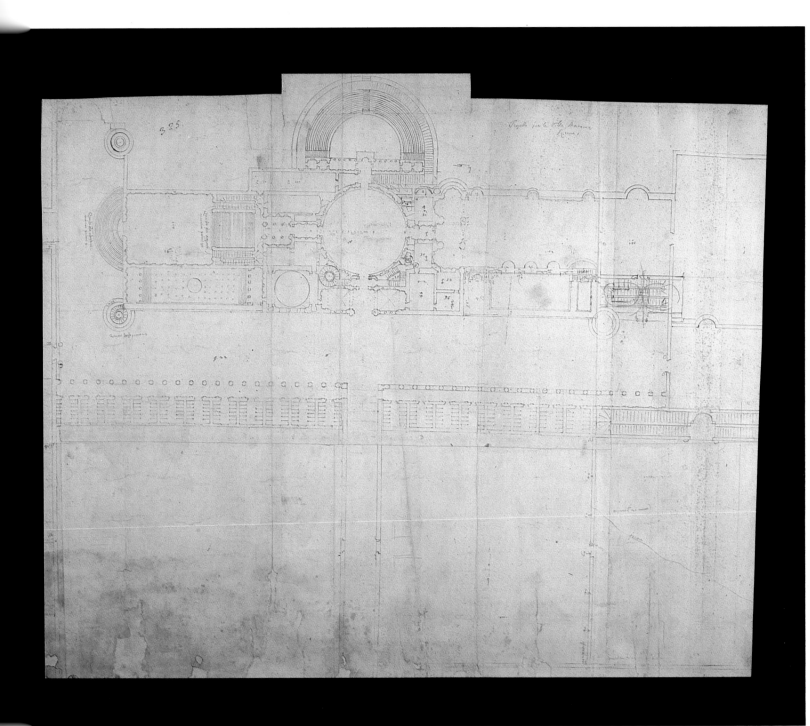

*P*lans for the Villa
Madama, Rome,
plan drawn
by Antonio da
Sangallo for
Raphael. The Uffizi,
Florence.

Villa d'Este, Tivoli: the Oval Fountain.

The villa, as we see it today, consists of a semi-circular court giving on to a casino which leads by way of a loggia to a secret garden ornamented with a fountain; the whole is terraced, following the natural curves and levels of the land. The existing building is only half of what was actually planned for that part of the garden which was to form the furthest point of the total design. The semi-circular court should in fact have been a complete circle and the building to the west would have been exactly reproduced to the east. The furthest point was also to have been completed by a kind of amphitheatre partly let into the hillside; the circular court would have been reached by a staircase following the contours of the land, the final element in a design of several terraces on the slope of Monte Mario; there was also to have been a hippodrome in the antique style, a large fishpond and stables for 78 horses. This massive scheme of terraces was to have been reached by a great avenue of cypresses. Although it was only partly completed, the plan has all the fundamental characteristics of the Mannerist garden.

The walls of the casino are covered with Giovanni da Udine's famous works of 1527; the motifs derived from imperial Roman models and the elegance and quality of workmanship of the decorations place them among the most perfect works of the period to have been inspired by the Classical aesthetic. The four Seasons and the four Elements, which often figured in the adornment of villas, here take on the guise of ancient gods. It was here that Clement came to escape from the cares of governing the church, to a place where he could imagine himself surrounded by the gods of pagan times.

Any amateur enthusiast – philosopher, poet or even gardener – could have laid out a Renaissance garden; the designer of the Mannerist garden would not only have needed to be an architect, but also a hydraulic engineer. The garden artist still had the task of planning and directing the construction of the garden; but, in addition, the new style now required him to find suitably rustic expression for a host of architectural elements novel to garden design. These ranged from supporting walls and staircases to motifs specifically designed to emphasize major features such as monumental doorways, vistas and fountains – the last no longer comprising a simple stack of basins, as in the 15th century, but now truly monumental constructions, in which stone and marble formed a total composition with the water, sometimes as complete groups of statuary, often of Neptune and his followers.

Whether it was straight or curved, a wall could never be left plain; it had to be ornamented with niches containing statues or by a range of herms (human busts on pedestals, whose hybrid character went very well with the phantasmagoric setting of the garden; the ancient Greeks referred to them as *hermes* and they were often used as signposts at crossroads in the countryside). Needless to say, many kinds of bossage were used, principally for supporting elements; every landscape architect would have his own particularly ingenious examples and would also use several types of 'rustic' bonding in the walls.

The architect was also responsible for the construction in rock-work of the grottoes and nymphaeums which were to provide cool places of repose during the heat of the day or to serve as a setting for some mythological figure essential to the symbolic theme of the garden, commissioned perhaps by some humanist scholar who might also be the master of the house.

Along with architecture, and even more than the actual planting, water was fundamental to the Mannerist garden; this was the fluid element in the overall vision of the garden, which could be given any form desired. Jets could be made to rise vertically or at an angle; they could be single or arranged in groups. Water could take many other forms: bubbling streams (along the parapets of a staircase, for instance), translucent waterfalls, cascades of various forms, which were sometimes positioned in front of a portico to create a water theatre, canals, stairways (*catene d'acqua*) and hidden jets which could suddenly be switched on to drench the unsuspecting passer-by. Water could also be found trickling through rockeries or forming pools for duckweed and other aquatic plants,

The she-wolf of the Rometta. Villa d'Este, Tivoli.

or simply seeping down a wall. The water of the garden would finally come to rest in some pool or basin, to which the Italians gave the name of *peschiera* (fishpond). The force of the water was also used to drive automata or even to produce sounds in hydraulic organs.

The natural horticultural features so much loved by Renaissance gardeners were now banished from the planting scheme. The trees used in the shrubberies – anyway rather rare in the wild – had always been planted in a fairly strict and regulated manner and were chosen principally from species (yew, box and laurel) which could easily be trimmed to become virtually architectural features in their own right. Lines of cypress were popular, while the most common tree planted outside such groupings was the holm-oak (*leccio*).

It was recognized, however, that the master of the property might occasionally wish to commune with nature outside the garden; sometimes such a retreat was incorporated in the garden itself, but more often it took the form of a park (*barco*) a little distance away where the trees were allowed to grow as though in their natural habitat; this might even be part of the neighbouring forest. The garden, then, consisted essentially of vegetation, stone and water. Flowers were generally confined to secret gardens, enclosed by walls, and forming only a constituent part of the overall garden plan. However, pots or jars of varying sizes, containing flowers, were sometimes positioned near the casino or on the terraces.

THE ROMAN GARDENS

The two great centres of Mannerist garden design were Rome and Florence. Each city was surrounded by a ring of villas; wealthy Romans spent their summers at Tivoli (the Tibur of the ancient world) or at Frascati (Tusculum), thus following in the footsteps of their ancestors, partly because the latter would certainly have chosen the coolest places in the Roman countryside and partly to satisfy their own antiquarian tastes.

Both types of garden had individual characteristics: the Roman tended to be more grandiose and architectural, whereas the Tuscan was more restrained, adhering more closely to the Renaissance model, though they also incorporated the less orderly aspects of Mannerism in their design. But before examining the two forms in detail, it is worth looking at the most characteristic expression of the new humanism and also the most famous of Italian gardens, that of the Villa d'Este at Tivoli,

Old photograph of the overall view of the Villa d'Este, taken from the lowest level of the main axis.

which, even before it was finished, was exciting the admiration of all the courts of Europe.

As the youngest son of the all too notorious (though irreproachable as a wife) Lucrezia Borgia and Alphonse I of Este, Duke of Ferrara, Ippolito II was destined for a career in the church. By the age of 30 he had already been made cardinal. He represented Ferrara in France from 1536 to 1539, then returned to Italy as ambassador of François I to the pope, a post which he continued to fulfil for François' successor, Henri II. Among the traces of his stay in France are the magnificent portal which he commissioned from Serlio at Fontainebleau and a miniscule *giardino segreto* at the Cistercian monastery of Chaalis near Chantilly, where he was commendatory abbot; this was especially notable for its curious marble herms in the Mannerist style. In addition to the ecclesiastical benefices which he received from the church in Italy, the cardinal also had several more granted to him by the French king, finally making him a very rich man. He therefore had no problem in initiating his two great projects: his villa at Monte Cavallo in Rome, of which nothing remains (the site was built over again in the 17th century to create the Quirinal, the present-day residence of the Italian president), and his villa at Tivoli.

Ippolito had been appointed governor of Tivoli by Pope Julius II as a reward for his part in the pope's election. On 9 September 1550 he made a triumphal entry into Tivoli, in a carriage pulled by Moorish slaves and surrounded by 100 mounted guards. Doubtless he was attracted both by the beauty of the place and by the proximity of Hadrian's Villa, where he satisfied his penchant for archaeology by initiating excavations. The governor's residence, however, was only a humble convent, which he resolved to transform into a palace communicating with a grandiose garden, the like of which had never been seen before. Although his governor's mandate was suspended in 1555 after the disgrace of Paul IV, he was restored to favour under Pius IV in 1559. By the time he received Pope Gregory XIII with great pomp at Tivoli in September 1573, the villa was almost finished. Ippolito died shortly afterwards in Rome on 2 December 1573. Because of the terms of his will, the villa was later subject to varying fortunes. The will stipulated that it should always pass to a cardinal in the d'Este family or, if there were none, to remain within the gift of the dean of the Sacred College. The d'Este cardinals, when there were any, took reasonably good care of it, but under the deans it was neglected. This odd situation certainly brought the villa its ups and downs; some of the statues were

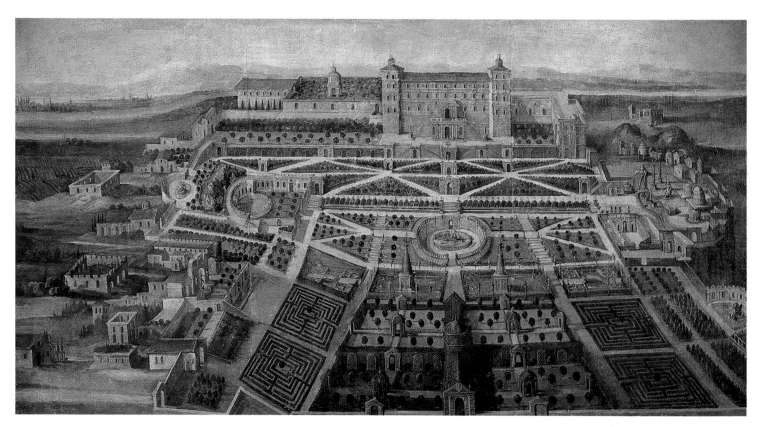

taken away to be displayed elsewhere or sold, while others replaced them. During the 17th century, Cardinal Rinaldo d'Este commissioned a number of changes to the villa in the Baroque style; the great fountain of the Bicchierone, for instance, was built by Bernini.

In 1802, Duke Ercole III d'Este, who was responsible for the upkeep of the villa, was overthrown by the French; it then passed to the Hapsburg family through his wife. In 1850, Cardinal Gustaf-Adolf von Hohenlohe wanted to make a cultural centre at the villa and rented it, but it was again abandoned after his death. It eventually passed to the Archduke Franz Ferdinand, who was assassinated at Sarajevo, and it was confiscated during World War I by the Italian state. The pre-war photographs by Alinari show its unkempt state before the restoration of the whole villa by the government. During World War II, it suffered no more than a few bombardments.

In spite of its chequered career, plenty of precious historical documentation on the villa still exists. There are two identical descriptions of it, dating from the 16th century, preserved in the Libraries of Paris and Vienna respectively; and a drawing by the French architect Dupérac, sent by Cardinal Ippolito to the Emperor Maximilian II in Vienna in February 1571, which is known through an engraving of 1573 dedicated to Catherine de Médicis, was included in an anthology by Lafreri entitled *Speculum Romanae Magnifi-*

centiae. Montaigne visited the villa in 1581 and expressed his admiration of it. The existence of such records have made it possible for the American scholar Arnold Coffin to recreate the primitive, though extremely coherent, symbolism of the house and its garden.

When Cardinal d'Este took possession of the governor's residence, then still part of the convent, two sections of garden already existed: a *barco* and a *barchetto*. The *barchetto* is still there; this is the horticultural feature, a secret enclosure serving both as kitchen and fruit garden, by the side of the palace. The *barco*, located away from the villa, was a natural park. It was enclosed by walls in 1564 to serve as an area for hunting, which drew protests from the local commune who claimed ownership.

The master planner commissioned by the cardinal was not particularly well known in the field of architecture, although he was famous in that of archaeology; this was the Neapolitan Pirro Ligorio (1510–83) who had lived in Rome since 1534. He was also the compiler of a formidable *Encyclopedia of Antiquity*, which remained unpublished and is now available in manuscript form in several European libraries. At the same time that he was commissioned to build the cardinal's villa, he was put in charge of the excavations at Hadrian's Villa.

The Villa d'Este is located on quite a steep slope. It can be visited in two ways: either by entering by the main gate (which is no longer

Panoramic view of the Villa d'Este, painted from the engraving by Dupérac. Private collection.

in use) and climbing up, or by descending, as the master of the house would have done. The latter route leads the visitor down a central staircase and across a series of pathways, all of which merit detailed exploration. The following description takes as its departure point the painting based on Dupérac's engraving, the original plan of garden, but of course it incorporates later modifications.

Pirro Ligorio first built a monumental double-flighted staircase against the wall of the old convent which gave access to the first terrace from the residential storeys of the villa. Opposite the steps a kind of belvedere jutted out into the garden from which the whole effect could be observed; this concealed a fountain dedicated to Leda. To the left was a dining room in a loggia that afforded views of the countryside; beyond, against the walls of the casino, was a real tennis court – the cardinal had brought the game back with him from France. The opposite side of the terrace gives on to the sacred garden mentioned above, which includes the Unicorn Fountain and, at the far end, a grotto dedicated to Thetis. The next transversal pathway, one level down from this terrace, is known as the Promenade of the Cardinal; it was here, in keeping with contemporary fashion derived from Classical precedent, that he liked to read, reflect or converse while walking. In the centre, beneath the belvedere terrace, there was a fountain to Pandora in a recess; it was replaced in the 17th century by the more elaborate Fountain of the Bicchierone, designed by Bernini, which was completed on 13 June 1661.

The next transversal pathway down is known as the Alley of the Hundred Jets. Several of the fountains spurt from 22 vessels, symbolizing the church, each separated from the next by three vases. Some of these were substituted in 1622 by eagles (emblem of the Este family) and *fleurs de lys*, while others were replaced by small obelisks in the 18th century. Beneath the fountains is a series of bas-reliefs recounting the *Metamorphoses* of Ovid.

This level of the garden is perhaps the most impressive feature of the villa. To the right it led to a curious group of structures called La Rometta, which consisted of small-scale copies of the principal buildings of Rome, dominated by a statue representing the city and another of the she-wolf. The whole ensemble was interspersed with fountains;

*A*lley of the Hundred Jets, Villa d'Este.

unfortunately, this miniature version of Rome was largely destroyed by a landslide, but we have a clear picture of it from engravings.

In the opposite direction the walk ends in a great water theatre, enclosed by walls. Recesses in the walls contain two fountains dedicated to Bacchus and one to Venus, while at the far end of the theatre is a pool surrounded by a portico which, with the pool, forms an oval. This portico is a nymphaeum and is decorated with ten statues of nymphs, from which spring powerful jets of water. It is dominated by the statue of the Sibyl of Tibur (Albunea), who looms over the entire feature above a great cascade; this tumbles into a basin in the pool, overflowing the sides. Known as the Oval Fountain, it is overlooked by a small wood, in the centre of which Pegasus, flying from Helicon, sends the water of the Hippocrene spring gushing from his hoof.

From the central point of the walk descends a circular staircase which encloses the Fountain of the Dragon. This many-headed dragon was the Lernean hydra, and the fountain was originally surmounted by an antique statue of Hercules; it was unfortunately replaced by one of Jupiter in the 17th century, completely destroying the garden's overall symbolism, since the Hercules had been the focal point of the whole plan. At the foot of the staircase is the alley leading to two secret gardens, each centred on a sort of triumphal arch, and enclosed by high walls. The first is still crowned by an owl between two *fleurs-de-lys*, but the birds which used to sing and chirp on the crest of the walls when activated by the water have long disappeared; along with the

hooting of the owl, it must have been quite noisy. Princess Kretzulesco-Quaranta may well be right, given the general theme of the garden, to see it as a symbol of Wisdom (the owl is the bird emblem of Minerva), bringing silence and harmony to conflicting philosophical and religious opinions. Concealed jets of water sprang from the paving of the garden. The fountain in the other secret garden is now known as the Fountain of Proserpine; the garden was originally dedicated to four emperors, represented by statues, who had built villas in the country near Tibur: Caesar, Augustus, Trajan and Hadrian.

The banisters of the three staircases which lead to the lower level of the garden are additionally used as water chutes. At this level the garden takes on a very different character.

The 17th-century water theatre, hiding the 16th-century Fountain of Nature, Villa d'Este.

Fountain of the Owl, from an engraving by G.F. Venturini, Villa d'Este, Tivoli.

TEATRO, E FONTANA DELLA CIVETTA CON DIVERSI GIVOCHI D'ACQVA

Gio-Francesco Venturini del et Sculp. 18

Fountain of the Dragon. Villa d'Este, Tivoli.

Dupérac's engraving shows two elongated pools at either end, in the centre of which is a *meta sudans* (a fountain at the top of which a trickle of water runs), copied from an ancient Roman monument. At the edge of the open country beyond is depicted a vast semi-circular fountain dedicated to Neptune, but this in fact was never built. After the two basins are two beds laid out as horticultural gardens, or gardens of simples planted with herbs. The survival of this utilitarian plot amidst a garden essentially laid out for display suggests that it was intended to be visited by descending from level to level rather than by starting from below, as Arnold Coffin has suggested; visitors to the house would hardly have been expected to enter through the vegetable garden, even if this had been concealed by galleries of wooden trellis. They would, rather, have approached the house by the crest of the hill, where all the outbuildings and services to take care of their carriages were located. To each side of this level of the garden, Dupérac's engraving shows two labyrinths, which were never planted, while the monumental fountains are positioned further to the side.

The garden presents a rather different appearance today; for instance, at the level where the *metae* should be located, there is an elaborate rustic-style structure crowned with the eagle of the Este which must date from the 16th century since it was being worked on in 1568. There are two recesses in this construction containing statues of Apollo and Orpheus, probably dating from the 17th century; they are framed by four herms, sirens with plaited hair above and two telamones below. The large central niche is now occupied by an aedicule placed there in 1611 to replace the many-breasted Diana of Ephesus, which was removed to a location behind the wall at the entrance to the garden, where it can still be found. This Diana is the work of a Flemish sculptor, Gillis van den Vliede, after an antique original in the Farnese collection. The symbolism is clear: Nature (Diana of Ephesus) was surrounded by the symbols of water (sirens) and of earth (telamones); she was to be positioned in front of the containing wall opposite the great Fountain of Neptune, which can be seen in Dupérac's engraving, but which was never built.

The statues of Orpheus and Apollo symbolize music. The Fountain of Nature was at the same time a water organ equipped with a hydraulic device to create sound, another imitation of a Classical model. It was built by French craftsmen who started work in 1568; the accounts of the house refer to a certain Lucha Clericho, no doubt Luc Leclerc, fountain maker, assisted by Claude Vénard.

The Fountain of Nature has certainly had its share of misfortune. It lost its principal statue in the 17th century, and then suffered the further indignity of being hidden by a curtain of water made up of powerful jets which eventually flowed in a cascade to feed the four ponds which stretched westward. The use of water in these ponds was especially subtle: plenty of movement in the first pond, less and less in the second and third, hardly a ripple in the fourth.

The original symbolism of this villa was, then, very rich and very clear, although it has since been somewhat obscured by the insensitivity of successive occupants and by the loss of numerous features and antique statuary now in museums. The imaginative range of this symbolism is even more evident if we take into account the lavish decoration of the casino, where a number of themes are illustrated.

Firstly, there are the pagan themes: Olympus in the garden and the casino; the grandeur of Rome (the Rometta); Nature in the casino as much as in the garden; abundant illustration of local history and mythology in the casino (the Tiburtine Sybil decorates one of the major features of the garden). Secondly, there are the religious themes, although these are only directly treated in the casino (the story of Noah, Moses, the cardinal virtues). In the garden itself, religion is exclusively evoked through allegory; the central idea, which is the struggle between virtue and vice, is therefore represented by the figures of Classical culture. This psychodrama reaches a climax in the centre of the garden in the theme of Hercules triumphing over the Lernean hydra, which embodies the forces of evil. Sin is signified again by Pandora (the exact counterpart of Eve in pagan mythology); the figure of Leda, now vanished, whose descendants caused the horrors of the Trojan War, symbolized the consequences of evil. Venus and Bacchus represent intemperance, while Diana embodies chastity. The Fountain of the Unicorn in the upper secret garden is another representation of purity. Venus, it seems, had fallen from the privileged position she held for the Florentine humanists in the 15th century, when she symbolized the origin of all things and the global sense of order. The Sibyl of Tibur is not only present to add a dimension of local history to the garden; she was also responsible for announcing the coming of Christ to Augustus. The standing child by her side could even be a representation of Christ and not Melicertes, as is usually supposed.

The central key to the symbolism of the

The garden of the Villa Farnese, Caprarola.

Villa d'Este was Hercules; an engraving by Venturini, in which the statue of that hero has already been replaced by that of Jupiter, shows another statue of Hercules along the same axis, but a little higher; this statue has now disappeared. Inside the casino is a cycle of paintings that tells the story of a metamorphosis of Hercules, the *Hercules Saxonus*. Hercule was a name much used in the d'Este family, but his repeated presence in a garden created by a prince of the church has a very special meaning. It was Boccaccio who first (*c.* 1372–83) emphasized the beneficent role of Hercules in Books 14 and 15 of his *Genealogia deorum gentilium*. This theme was further expanded in 1406 by Coluccio Salutati in his treatise *De laboribus Herculii*; and for the Dukes of Burgundy he was the model of the magnanimous prince. During the 16th century, Charles V and François I argued as to which of them should have him as 'patron'. Ronsard, in a poem which led him into direct dispute with the Huguenots, saw him as a prefiguration of Christ.

The cardinal himself was named Ippolito. And, on the first floor of the casino, a room remained undecorated, no doubt because it was to have been hung with tapestries retracing the history of Hippolytus, but these were never actually woven. However, the preparatory drawings by Pirro Ligorio are preserved today in the Pierpont Morgan Library in New York. It is perhaps in the cardinal's residence that we can find the explanation of the importance granted to the hero. The son of Theseus remained insensitive to the declared passion of his mother-in-law Phaedra, thus perhaps becoming a symbol of chastity, a virtue required in the ecclesiastical life and one which seems to have been observed by the ostentatious cardinal in keeping himself apart from the scandals of his time.

Apart from Versailles, no combination of house and garden is endowed with such rich and clearly displayed symbolism as the Villa d'Este which, in its wealth of mythological allusions, points to Pirro Ligorio as its originator. Although in the accounts for the villa he is never referred to as architect, he was used regularly by the cardinal as 'antiquary'. This term may very well have concealed his real work at the villa, which is hinted at by the fact that the statues destined for the garden were made to his designs. Indeed, a book by Fogliati of 1569, describing the activity at the

The loggia of the Palazzina at Caprarola.

villa, remarks: 'The inventor of everything there was the most famous architect of our time and my dearest friend, Pirro Ligorio, a man of great learning who also had considerable knowledge of antiquity.' The garden of the Villa d'Este was truly a creation of the humanist spirit, an Olympus where men could forget their earthly cares. In this case, the urge to relax in surroundings which, as in a Golden Age, evoked the life of the ancients, had a particular significance; both garden and house were built by a man of the church at a time when fundamental questions of dogma were under discussion at the Council of Trent and the representation of pagan gods had been forbidden. This ambiguity, very much of its time, is clearly evident in the whole ensemble. The true meaning of it draws on Christianity, but the beauty of its expression, as much of the ideas behind it as of the actual works of art, is derived from paganism. The transcendental unity which had been the

Villa Caprarola: the catena d'acqua *and the Fountain of the River in the upper garden.*

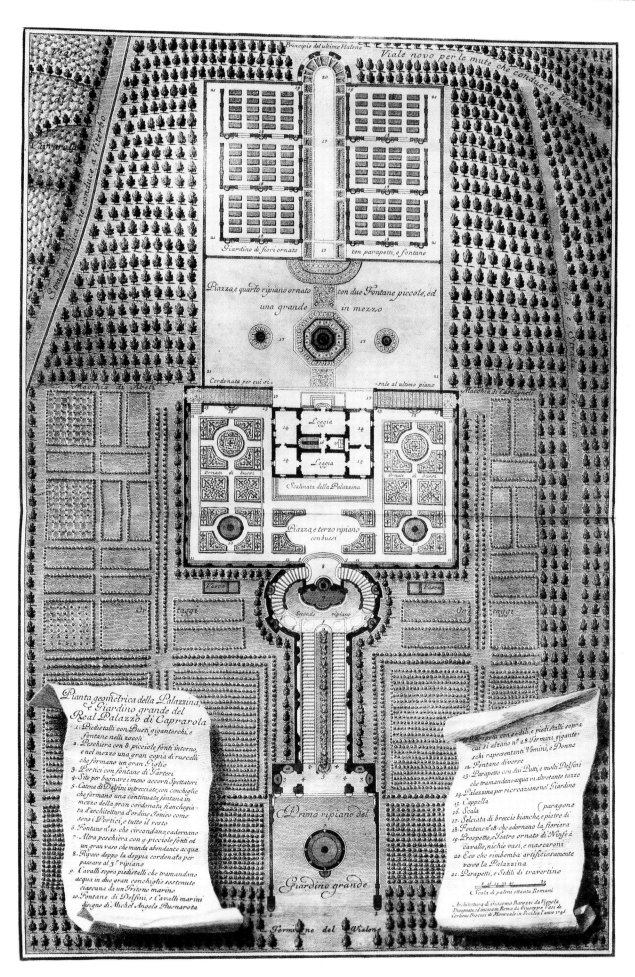

*C*aprarola: plan of
the Palazzina
and the gardens of
the Villa Farnese,
*after Illustrati Fatti
Farnesiani,* Rome,
*1748. Bibliothèque
Nationale, Paris.*

guiding principle of the Middle Ages had been broken.

The first Cardinal Farnese to bear the name of Alessandro, the future Pope Paul III, was a man obsessed with the feudal pride of his family, even at the beginning of the 16th century. When it fell to him to assemble the traditional possessions of the family and those he had acquired himself, he determined to create a symbolic 'capital' for the estate. For this purpose he chose a site at Caprarola, one of the highest places in Latium. There he decided to build a *rocca* or fortified castle. The commission was given to Antonio da Sangallo the Younger, who began the construction of a great pentagonal fortress flanked by bastions. But this building never got beyond its first foundations.

The design conformed very closely to the ideas of the 15th century and was already out of date when the second Cardinal Alessandro Farnese asked Vignola to build a palace on the existing foundations. The first stone was laid down on 28 April 1559, an event celebrated by a solemn mass.

The brothers Taddeo and Federico Zuccari were commissioned to carry out the interior decoration; their scaffolding went up as soon as that of the masons was taken down, and a team of painters and plasterers worked between 1560 and 1569 to complete an iconological programme contrived by two humanist scholars at the Cardinal's court, Annibale Caro and Flavio Orsini. When their work was done, not a square inch of wall remained which was not adorned with some image relating to the cardinal's family achievements, exemplified by the story of Hercules, to geography, astronomy, Holy Scripture or mythology, both in its own right and as an allegorical adjunct to all aspects of the cardinal's life – work, audiences, meals, meditation, prayer and sleep. The sheer quantity of things so represented must sometimes have become oppressive, provoking a need to escape from all those figures of gods, men and saints surrounded by grotesques and arabesques. The garden offered the ideal refuge; in fact, there were two rectangular gardens, laid out in traditional fashion at the same level as the *piano nobile*, one facing the suite of summer rooms to the north, and the other the winter rooms to the west. Each had a fountain in the centre and a grotto at the furthest extremity. One of these is known as the Grotto of the Tartars because of the strange statues of sylvans of both sexes which support the stalactite forms that hang from the ceiling. The other is known as the Grotto of the Shepherd since it served as the setting for the production

of *Pastor Fido*, a tragi-comedy by G.B. Guazini, published in 1590. These gardens now have a very simple air about them, planted with box trimmed in geometrical shapes. Like all secret gardens, they almost certainly contained flowers at one time. Yet these *orti* were still not enough; gardens were also settings for reflection and festivity – in other words, they had to represent an imaginary world other than that expressed in the decoration of the palace.

Vignola designed the great upper garden on several levels up the slope of a hill, linking them by a *catena d'acqua* which was fed by water from the Fountain of the Vase (Bicchiere) which in turn was fed by water from two river gods. On the penultimate level of this garden stands a *palazzina*, designed by Girolamo Rainaldi between 1584 and 1586; the area around it is flanked by a series of peculiar masculine and feminine herms carrying basket forms.

This garden gives a strong impression of being self-enclosed, perhaps because it lacks any obvious symbolism to direct or stimulate the imagination; although it contains a number of impressive hybrid statues, it still generates a sense of other-worldliness which can be somewhat oppressive. Where, for instance, are the gods we would normally expect to find here? In the house itself there are too many, yet here we miss them.

Vignola was the appointed architect of the Farnese and carried out other commissions for them, including the construction of the finest palace in Rome and the church of Gesù, which was built at their expense. The Farnese palace in Rome did not include a garden. When he became Pope under the name of Paul III, Alessandro commissioned Vignola to build a villa on the Palatine Hill, the most prestigious site of ancient Rome; the villa was finished under Alessandro's nephew, the

Panoramic view of the Villa Caprarola with its winter and summer gardens, c.1573. Painting from the gallery of villas in the Gambara casino of the Villa Lante at Bagnaia.

The Villa Lante at Bagnaia from an engraving by Jacobus Laurus, Rome, 1628. Bibliothèque Nationale, Paris.

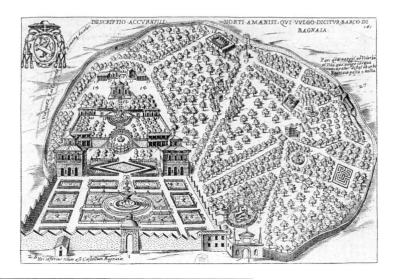

second Cardinal Alessandro, and Cardinal Ottavio, but the casino was never built. The *orti farnesiani* became famous, especially for their rare birds; two aviaries were built for these at the entrance to the villa, and their cubic bases still exist. The gardens were devastated in 1880 by excavations which brought to light the monumental portal, but it was a further 70 years before this was erected as the entrance gateway to the Palatine on the Via San Gregorio.

Vignola is also believed to be the architect of another villa at Bagnaia near Viterbo, an attribution which depends on similarities of style since no documentary evidence exists. This villa has always been known by the name of the dukes of Lante who lived there for three centuries before it was sold to Angelo Cantoni, a Roman businessman, who carried out a complete restoration. Even the two casinos were refurnished in the style of their date of construction. The villa now belongs to the Italian state.

The bishopric of Viterbo owned an area of land at Bagnaia which was reserved for hunt-ing; Ottaviano Riaro, who had been appointed a cardinal when aged only twelve, had this enclosed and also commissioned the building of a lodge for Pope Leo X, a hunting enthusiast. This was eventually inherited by Cardinal Gambara who in 1566 decided to build a villa by the lodge with a garden in the Italian style. The first casino was finished in 1573, the date inscribed on the cornice. The construction of the villa could easily have come to an end in 1580 after the visit to Bagnaia of Cardinal Borromeo, who told Gambara that he would have done better to spend his money in building a monastery. The Archbishop of Milan had been appointed by the dour Pope Pius V to be inspector of cardinals with the object of curtailing their lavish expenditure. This was very much the atmosphere engendered by the Council of Trent but, happily for the arts, little attention was paid to San Carlo Borromeo, whose strictures drew a very tart comment from Cardinal Farnese at Caprarola. On hearing Borromeo's remark, 'With all the money you are spending here, you could have brought relief to the people of the town,' Alessandro replied, 'I am doing better than bringing them relief, I am giving them work.' The sentiments seems rather more Calvinist than Catholic.

After Cardinal Gambara's death in 1587, the estate of Bagnaia, which belonged to the church, was bequeathed for life by Sixtus V to his nephew, Cardinal Alessandro Peretti, who assumed the name of Montalto. He completed the construction work and built the second casino. In 1656 a lease, renewed several times, was granted to Duke Ippolito Lante. He was responsible for alterations to the great parterre at the entrance to the garden; this was again changed in 1685 to conform with the French style.

However, the siting of the villa is entirely in the Italian manner, being arranged in terraces on the side of a hill. At the lowest level a monumental doorway opens on to a parterre done in French *broderie* style; in the centre of this is a basin divided into four sections, each of which contains the figure of a sailor on a galley emitting a jet of water. The centre of the basin is occupied by a fountain, the upper part of which depicts four Moors holding up the family emblem, the hills of the Monte Cimini. The water arches in the form of a crystal dome over the fountain. This bronze group has been attributed to Taddeo Landini, who was also responsible for the famous Fountain of the Tortoises in Rome.

The loggias of the two pavilions, formerly open, are on the same level as the parterre in the French style, but the pavilions themselves are actually set into the slope of the hill and are entered from behind at the first-floor level. The decoration of the loggia of the Gambara pavilion is especially memorable; between the herms are views of three of the great villas belonging to cardinals in the countryside around Rome: the Villa d'Este, Caprarola and the Villa Lante, together with a view of the town of Bagnaia. The idea of portraying villas and important houses in this manner originated in Italy and was then copied throughout Europe. In France, the practice reached its apogee in the tapestries of the royal residences woven by the Gobelins.

The upper garden is organized around the various forms of water which flow through the garden as cascades, fountains, rills or jets at several levels; at one point a rippling water chain leads to a great stone dining table through which the water runs in a narrow channel. The source of all this water is at the uppermost part of the garden in the form of a rustic cascade known as the Deluge. On either side of this are two pavilions complete with statues of the Muses, bearing the arms of Cardinal Gambara (a crayfish); these are set back from two balustraded areas surrounded by columns, some with Doric capitals and some without. The Fountain of the Deluge seems to symbolize nature in the raw, in contrast to the works around the fountain. Close by, yet unexpected, are two marvellous secret gardens which, in the time of Angelo Cantoni, would have been filled with the sweet scent of roses.

At the highest point of the garden is the great reservoir from which the water for the whole park is drawn; and beyond this is the old hunting lodge used by Leo X, now lacking its original labyrinth but still possessing an ice pit. It became the habit in the Middle Ages to drink liquid which had been cooled, and even Gothic castles were equipped with ice pits, although these have frequently been taken for oubliettes. The sorbet was invented in Italy in the 16th century and was then introduced in France by Catherine de Médicis. Ice was taken in the winter from frozen ponds or from the tops of neighbouring mountains. But since the winters were not always cold enough to

The Fountain of Pegasus at the Villa Lante.

A pergola of roses and vines painted on the vault of the semi-circular portico which connects the casino with the garden at the Villa Giulia, Rome.

guarantee this supply, quite a trade developed in transporting ice from Norway by boat.

Although the park surrounding the garden reminds us of the natural world beyond, it also contains one of the most grandiose features of the Villa Lante, the Fountain of Pegasus. Despite being constructed at the time of Cardinal Montalto, it had formed part of the original plan for the garden, as can be seen from the painted view of the villa in the Gambara casino. A great circular basin has been set in the hillside, contained on the deeper side by a curving wall from which project a series of herms spouting water, while the winged horse prances gracefully in the centre of the basin, surrounded by winged infant Cupids. As a symbol of poetry or of the supreme expression of the human genius, Pegasus constitutes a wonderful finale to the relatively simple symbolism of the Villa Lante – a symbolism which transports us from the world of Nature to the world of Man.

There is, in the Villa Lante and its garden, an indefinable balance between art and the forces of nature, from which now, as in the past (since there were few later modifications), we can draw a deep sense of harmony. In this, the villa must be reckoned to be the most perfect expression of the Mannerist style in planning. The Villa d'Este engages the intelligence by its subtle symbolism, but the Villa Lante extends a more friendly welcome; its garden is truly a place of delights, or *delizia*, as such pleasure villas had come to be known during the preceding century.

A number of villas were built within Rome itself. Inside the garden of the Vatican, Paul IV commissioned a secret garden, the Villa Pia, from Pirro Ligorio, which was eventually finished under Pius IV. This is much more a work of architecture and sculpture than a garden – a *diaeta* in the Vatican garden with an especially interesting symbolic structure. It is truly a place for refined pleasures which today houses the Papal Academy of Sciences.

The Villa Giulia (1550–4), built on the Via Flaminia at the gates of Rome, has lost almost all its natural features. The casino was built by Vignola; the subject matter of the paintings by Taddeo Zuccari and others is particularly fascinating. In one room is a frieze of views of the neighbourhoods of Rome. Some of them recall the *topia* of Graeco-Roman art, examples of which could have been seen by the artists in the excavations of the Golden House of Nero.

The façade of the casino gives on to the garden through a semi-circular loggia; on its vaulted ceiling are painted pergolas bearing vines, roses or jasmine, among which *putti* and birds disport themselves. The atmosphere of the garden is, then, immediately apparent on leaving the house.

During his pontificate, the pope did very little but concern himself with the construction of his villa; one of his main works was to divert a water course to provide for the residence, since water was in scarce supply to the west of Rome. Perhaps it was in celebration of this rare commodity that the nymphaeum of the villa was the subject of so much architectural and sculptural extravagance, an extraordinary combination of 'academic' and 'rustic' styles, characterized by amazingly voluptuous caryatids sculpted by Ammanati. The nymphaeum includes a number of 'cool rooms' in which to rest from the heat outside.

The alternation of architectural elements and gardens in the villa forms a sequence which is truly monumental in conception: first the casino with its exedra, then the first secret garden, then a loggia opening on to the great nymphaeum, which is virtually a water temple, and finally another secret garden with more columns at its far end. Little now exists of the architectural structure, but what remains is very fine. Indeed, the casino is today the admirable setting for Rome's Etruscan Museum.

The best preserved of the Roman villas is the one built by Cardinal Giovanni Ricci de Montepulciano in the Pincio and later acquired by Cardinal Ferdinand de' Medici. The latter created a garden of antiquities there which he transported to Florence when he became Grand Duke of Tuscany. Copies of the Niobides groups, the originals of which are now in the Uffizi, have recently been installed in the villa.

The theme of the villa is the quest for Paradise Lost, although the pilgrim may very well encounter Inferno along the perilous path!

In 1949 Mario Praz published an article in *Tempo* which introduced the 'monsters of Bomarzo' to a wider public, ensuring the lasting fame of the statues which were then still half buried in the earth and undergrowth. When Jean Cocteau and Salvador Dali came to see these extraordinary creations, they

The sacred wood of Bomarzo: the Mouth of Hell.

were filled with enthusiasm for the anonymous author of this *sacro bosco*, seeing in it a precursor of their own work. And even if the only affinity which the unreal world of this valley of the monsters has with the work of Dali is a state for the irrational, it certainly evokes the settings of Cocteau's film, *La Belle et la Bête*, which perhaps merely indicates that this cinematic masterpiece conforms to a very ancient poetic tradition.

After such curiosity on the part of writers and artists, it was the turn of the architects to work out the precise planning of the garden and the scholars to research the records; thanks to them, we now know much more about the mysteries of the monsters of Bomarzo.

This *sacro bosco* (the term used in a number of writings and letters) was the brainchild of a member of the Orsini family, the Duke Vicino, who inherited the estate of Bomarzo in 1532 and whose name can be found in an inscription in the house dating from 1583. The interval between the two dates clearly leaves us a considerable time span to examine, but a correspondence of 1554 between the duke and the humanist thinker Annibale Caro, in which the 'marvels' of the *sacro bosco*, then being constructed, are discussed, allows us to be much more precise about dating. In the past the sacred wood was approached through a rectangular plantation which bordered the house, then used as a summer residence. The peaceful atmosphere of this garden, which combined utility and pleasure, contrasted vividly with scenes along the valley of the brook known as La Concia. First, a giant apparently tearing the figure of a woman apart, then a colossal tortoise carrying on its back a figure with raised arms, a

bandy-legged Pegasus, several nymphs, lascivious sirens, bears (emblem of the Orsini), and finally a strangely sloping building with two storeys. Its symbolic function is very clear and is in any case explained in an inscription – the garden is full of inscriptions – noting that this is a place of repose but that constant vigilance is necessary in such a precarious refuge. Then comes a terrace where the most attractive monsters can be found – a Neptune with a floral beard, a very beautiful female figure, except that her back shelters a demoniac world of tritons and anthropomorphic figures, an elephant carrying a tower on its back and grasping a Roman soldier with its trunk, a dragon, and a *mascherone* in the form of a grotto, used for meals, which, according to the inscription, symbolized the mouth of hell. Cerberus, the dog with three heads, is close by at the foot of a staircase. We are then led to a terrace, where calm is at last restored, since it is in fact the plinth of a *tempietto* of the Tuscan order, consisting of a polygonal rotunda with a cupola at the end of a twelve-column pronaos.

The meaning of this extravagant symbolism is not to be found in Classical fable. This 'assault course' through many attendant dangers is of the type undergone by the knights of Arthurian romances who always found an ultimate haven of peace in the form of a chapel. We may, therefore, look for the origins of these fantastic creations in the initiation rites described in the romances which continued the traditions of the Christian mysteries. Although the *Jerusalem Delivered* by Torquato Tasso is too late (1572–3), a similar atmosphere informs the romances of Tasso's father, Bernardo, such as *Amadis* (1560). In this context, the *sacro bosco* can be

seen as the realization of the theme of the enchanted forest, where the hero must combat both the temptations and the terrors which are placed in his way. According to one of Vicino's contemporaries, Francesco Sansovino, who was also the historian of the Orsini family, the *tempietta* was a funerary monument built in memory of the beautiful Giulia Farnese, Vicino's model wife. The funerary emblems which decorate the podium of the temple do nothing to suggest that this interpretation is not accurate.

Indeed, the moral expressed by the drama in the garden seems to be well expressed by an inscription in the house: 'Conquer yourself – Live by your own precepts and you will be happy.' Another inscription expresses the moral thinking at the heart of stoicism and epicureanism, very much in the manner of the poet Horace: *Medium tenuere beati* – the morality of the happy medium.

The garden of Bomarzo only seems strikingly unusual in the context of 16th-century sculpture; the Mannerist painters of frescoes and decorators of villas were fascinated by this fabulous world, a taste inspired by Giulio Romano in his decoration of the Palazzo del Tè at Mantua, where he adopted a deliberately overblown style in his *trompe-l'oeil* painting of a struggle between the gods and the giants, a theme which Vicino had wanted to use in the decoration of his own villa and which Annibale Caro found totally in keeping with the extravagances in the garden.

THE TUSCAN GARDENS

As the 16th century progressed, civil peace came to the city of Florence; both external and internal threats to Florentine calm and prosperity died away and the power of the Medici family, now grand dukes, extended beyond the city and its immediate surroundings to the whole of Tuscany, which emerged as one of the great states of Italy. The family also developed a passion for building. The first three grand dukes had a whole circle of villas built around Florence. Francesco I (1541–87) and his brother Ferdinando I (1549–1609) were fortunate in being able to utilize the

The sacred wood of Bomarzo: the Tempietto.

talents of a brilliant architect, Bernardino Buontalenti (1536–1608), who also served them as Superintendent of Fine Arts. Practising virtually all the arts, he was a great military engineer and city planner. His interests also extended to the sciences, where he was responsible for a number of innovations and showed especial brilliance in the study of perspective, which proved significant in the decoration of the villas. In addition, he organized all the Medici celebrations, including games, triumphal processions and marriages, produced plays, and was so expert in the pyrotechnics of fireworks that he came to be known as 'Bernardino delle Girandole'.

Compared with the villas around Rome, those of Tuscany were generally smaller. They did, however, benefit from the fact that the artists who worked on them were of greater renown, such as the sculptors Ammanati, Bandinelli and Giambologna, whereas those responsible for the statuary of the Roman villas were second-class talents. All the Medici villas still exist today except, unfortunately, the most original of them, that of Pratolino, of which there are only a few remains. Not all of them are in their original state and a number have undergone substantial transformations over the centuries. For instance, the building of the great Baroque garden of the Boboli involved moving several statues which had been made for other villas. However, an outstanding record of their original state exists in the series of paintings commissioned from the Flemish artist Utens, which have already been mentioned in the context of the Renaissance garden.

The first villa to be commissioned by Cosimo I, from 1538, was that of Castello, situated to the west of Florence and looking over the valley of the Arno. The plans for the villa were drawn up by the architect and sculptor Tribolo (1500–38); it has been preserved, along with its decoration. Antique busts and statues are positioned everywhere in the garden in the Classical manner. The symbolism is very simple and may have been inspired by the humanist thinker Benadetto Varchi, a historian and friend of Cosimo, who lived in the nearby Villa Topaja and was therefore in a position to supervise the works. The formal garden, which is decorated with antique statuary, is the most human part of the whole. The Fountain of Hercules was originally balanced by that of Venus, now removed; however, we can still see in the former the struggle of Hercules against the giant Antaeus who could renew his strength by touching the ground, thus symbolizing the strength of the earth, a theme stated even more strongly higher up the garden. Deeper

into the garden, untutored nature is the theme of the grotto; the animal world is represented in stucco at the entrance, while the vegetable kingdom surmounts the upper part. The visitor to the natural part of the garden might well expect to find it free of all artificial elements, but is suddenly confronted by the bust of a bronze giant – January – rising from a stony outcrop, placed there by Ammanati in 1563. One curious feature which no longer exists was an oak in which had been built a wooden hut with a small marble table.

It was at the beginning of his rule, in 1576, that the Grand Duke gave instructions for work to start on the small villa of La Petraia, to be built around an old *rocca* which was also to be restored. The finest ornament in the garden was the bronze Fountain of Venus Anadyomene, which was brought from Castello in the 18th century and is now kept in a museum. With its *linea serpentinata*, this work by Giambologna is one of the most exquisite expressions of femininity.

Grand Duke Ferdinando commissioned the building of villas to serve as hunting lodges: Ambrogiana, La Magia and, finally, Artimino whose monumental casino is Buontalenti's masterpiece. This building is of especial interest, since the views of the Medicean villas, now in the Museum of Florence, were

The villa of Castello, owned by the Medici family, in 1599, part view from the painting by Giusto Utens. Museo Historico, Florence.

*T*he villa of Castello,
statue of January.

LA PRETAIA

The Villa Petraia, owned by the Medici, from a painting by Giusto Utens. Museo Topografico, Florence.

commissioned in 1599 from Utens as decoration for its main room.

The laying out of the gardens on the Boboli hill behind the Pitti Palace was begun in 1550, when the palace passed from the hands of the family who had built it in the previous century to Cosimo I and Eleonora of Toledo. It was their intention to turn the palace into a villa, taking advantage of the hilly site at the edge of the urban development which now spread across the plain below.

The garden was designed by Tribolo, who died only a few months later. He was succeeded by Ammanati, although no doubt Cosimo had his own ideas on the design and execution. Ammanati enlarged the old Pitti Palace, which now became the casino of the villa, by adding two wings and creating a courtyard below the palace. Buontalenti was only sixteen at the time and was yet to add his contribution to the design of the gardens.

The painting of the gardens by Utens shows us their layout at the end of the 16th century. A considerable number of parterres are ranged up the steep slope to the Belvedere built by Michelangelo, almost as though they were the divisions of a garden laid out on flat land. The Roman origins of the scheme are suggested in the overall design, notably the use of marble architecture and the combination of greenery and water. On the garden side of the palace, the hill has been dug out in the form of a U to create an amphitheatre or, rather, hippodrome, evoking memories of Pliny's villa in Tuscany. But the parterres themselves are arranged in a manner that makes no concessions to the curvature of the amphitheatre, which was only devised as a scenic feature of the garden in the following century.

As we enter the garden, the famous grotto is on the immediate left. The portico of the entry, built by Vasari, is crowned by an enormous Medici crest and framed by Bandinelli's statues of Apollo and Ceres, probably as contrasting symbols of intelligence and instinct. Certainly one of the most characteristic manifestations of Florentine Mannerism, the grotto was completed by Buontalenti between 1583–88 with the help of several sculptors, including Vincenzo de Rossi, Giambologna and the painter Bernardino Poccetti.

Four marble figures of slaves seem to support the main part of the grotto; Michelangelo had planned to use these statues on the tomb of Julius II, but had left them incomplete. Indeed their lack of finish make these athletic figures appear to represent some intermediary stage between a natural growth and the human figure. And it is the transition from the world of nature to the world of humankind which is the theme of the grotto. On the wall swarms a group of beings whose bodies seem immured in the rock as though entrapped in sticky mud – made, in fact, of stucco. The group includes all kinds of wild and domestic animals, a herdsman, fishermen and two river-gods. This teeming world is continued in the scenes painted by Poccetti on the vaulting, where an oculus, apparently supported by arches composed of rock-work and natural growths, reveals a sky full of birds. The grotto was formerly illuminated by light coming from above and then passing through an aquarium plentifully stocked with fish. On either side of the main grotto are two others which are more architectural in character. In one is the sculptural group of Paris and Helen by Vincenzo de Rossi; in the second is an exquisite sculpture of a very chaste-looking Venus in marble which appears to step out of the rock-work. The goddess is observed by two fauns, as she tries to protect herself as though from the cold. According to the author of a 16th-century guide to Florence (quoted by Detlef Heikamp in *L'Oeil* of 19 June 1964), the grotto illustrates the legend, recorded by Ovid, of Pyrrha and Deucalion, the only human

Fountain of the Anadyomene Venus at the Villa Petraia; the figure of Venus has since been removed to a museum.

*T*he grotto in the Boboli
   Gardens, Florence. The
first room appears supported
by the unfinished slave figures
of Michelangelo (the originals
have been replaced by new
casts).

*T*he group of
   Helen and Paris
by Vincenzo de
Rossi.

'*V*enus' by
   Giambologna
in the third niche of
the grotto in the
Boboli Gardens,
Florence.

*G*arden of the Villa
Pratolino: the
grotto of the
Apennine by
Giambologna.

couple to have survived the Deluge; the goddess Themis had ordered them to cast stones behind them which would eventually be transformed into human beings. This interpretation of the Deluge is worth noting, since it demonstrates how closely grottoes were linked to the theme of human origins. There was also a grotto of the Deluge at Pratolino.

The villa at Pratolino boasted a number of grottoes with automata which aroused curiosity throughout Europe and also had much influence on the development of garden design. Unfortunately this unique arrangement was destroyed in 1822 by Grand Duke Ferdinand III who could not be bothered with its upkeep. The garden had been a magnificent present given by the Grand Duke Francesco de' Medici to Bianca Capella, the Venetian with whom he fell in love and married after the death of his wife Joanna of Austria and with whom he remained until his death. The large house was extravagantly decorated and full of precious furniture, *objets d'art*, paintings and tapestries. The extraordinary garden was laid out by Francesco on land which he had bought in 1568 and was finished in 1586, when Francisco de Vieri published his short treatise on its 'marvels'. This guide, along with numerous engravings and the painting by Utens in the Museo Topografico in Florence, makes it possible for us to visualize with considerable accuracy the design of the garden. However, the representation by Utens only shows part of the whole and gives us no impression of what lay in front of the house. The garden was entered from the north, as can be seen from the complete plan drawn up by Sgrilli, dating from 1742. Almost immediately on entering, the visitor was faced with a labyrinth, symbolizing the uncertainties in human life. Shortly afterwards came a figure of Jupiter (now in the Boboli Gardens) positioned in a fountain, as if to affirm that the destiny of men was indeed in the hands of the gods. Then followed a *barco* through which ran three pathways coverging on a circle, and the *prato de l'Apennino*. Here, the Apennines, the backbone of Italy, were evoked by a gigantic statue in the 'rustic style' by Giambologna, which Montaigne saw in the process of construction during his travels in Italy during 1580–1. This is the only surviving feature of the garden. There are three grottoes within this man-made rock which forms a little island in a pool, never quite completed. This was the site of the reservoir which fed the whole hydraulic system of the garden. To the right, towards the villa itself, was a chapel (still in existence) and the fountains of Perseus, Aesculapius and the Bear.

The carriages would have had to make their way right round the villa to stop before a staircase made up of two circular flights. On the upper level, between the curves of these two flights, were the six famous grottoes: the Deluge, the Eruvi, the Galatean, the Sponge, the Tritons and the Samaritan, all themes which are related to water, here celebrated as a force of nature capable, in its practical application, of setting in motion all the hydraulic automata of the garden. At the lower level the grottoes of Pan, Fame (the fame of the Medici) and of the Frogs. Other grottoes in the garden included one dedicated to Cupid, where 'the water became subject to the passion of love', and one to Vulcan which was lined with coral and shells. The grotto known as the Sponge must have got its name from the fact that it was partly built from fossilized sponges, as was the small fountain in the third room of the grotto at the Boboli Gardens, where the sponges were combined with rock crystal.

There was an abundance of mechanical 'surprises' in the garden at Pratolino. In one part of the shrubbery was a figure of Pan playing his tunes, while at the end of the garden was a re-creation of Mount Parnassus, where the Muses operated water organs. In another fountain, a figure of Hercules brandishes a club from which a shower of water tumbled into a great shell containing the figure of a woman (Hercules caught between Vice and Virtue?). A number of themes were deliberately humorous, such as the pool of the washerwoman in which a young boy sprayed the laundress's work with a jet of urine.

The garden was full of antique statues and herms, which can be seen clearly in the painting by Utens; most of these were removed to the Boboli Gardens after the destruction of Pratolino in 1822. One curiosity which could not fail to astonish the visitor was a huge oak tree that also harboured a fountain. We can obtain a clear idea of the intention behind the creation of all these 'marvels' from the description given by Vieri: 'Here is an oak with two staircases . . . by which one reaches a platform composed of sixteen branches, where there is a magnificent fountain. This oak is a symbol of the rustic life led by the first men who lived off acorns. The dual staircase expresses the idea of the fidelity of one being to another under the eye of benevolent Cupid . . . the fountain is like the virtuous soul from which only acts of fidelity and love can spring, as they have done so frequently in the past centuries.'

As an indication of man's fascination with his origins, (usually accompanied by criticism of the present), the legend of the 'noble savage' began to gain currency during the

15th century. It was further elaborated during the 16th, fell out of favour in the 17th and reappeared in the 18th. For the artists and thinkers of the Mannerist period, the real meaning of things lay below the surface, and this true meaning could only be revealed by an understanding of symbols.

Perhaps the most novel feature of the garden at Pratolino was its layout. Instead of a series of rectangular areas monotonously succeeding one another, the garden seems almost disorganized in appearance. It was in fact made up of a large pine wood, interspersed with pathways, fountains and other features, almost as though it had been laid out, complete with ornaments, in virgin forest, which had the obvious advantage of providing the garden with adult trees. A wide central alley, lined with fountains, runs down the slope of the garden, dividing the whole area in two; on either side of it are ranged the subsidiary pathways – all straight, admittedly – which crisscross each other according to no apparent plan to create a completely asymmetrical scheme in relation to the great central avenue. To the east of the house, however, there was a secret garden for the cultivation of flowers and, beyond that, another, much larger enclosure divided into nine beds, which was the fruit garden (*pomario*). None of these features, however, conformed to a regular plan. In the western part of the garden was a system of pools through which water flowed to form Baroque cascades; the whole series followed at a long *linea serpentinata* through the garden. There was a similar system of pools to the east which was bordered by the plantation and laid out in the form of a curve. Everything in the garden seems to have been done to avoid the impression of symmetry: was it, indeed, Buontalenti, with his fertile genius, who was the true inventor of the English garden? Vieri draws distinctly moral conclusions from the whole mythology of the garden. Thus, the Apennine giant was one of the Titans expelled from Olympus for having tried to rival the power of Jupiter; this is taken to mean that, without the help of God, the world would be plunged into disaster. The grottoes are taken to be an allegory of the precious metals contained in the depths of the earth, evidence of the munificence of God. The labyrinth leading to a temple shows man how difficult is the way of truth, while Mount Parnassus is seen as a sign of encouragement to human beings to pursue that quest.

OTHER ITALIAN GARDENS

The greatest achievements in garden design

The lower part of the garden at Pratolino in 1599, from a painting by Giusto Utens. Museo Historico, Florence.

in Italy occurred in Rome and Florence. In the north of the country, at Ferrara and Mantua, for example, there was much less originality, partly because the gardens there did not have the advantage of being laid out on various levels which allowed the construction of terraces and the creation of designs affording panoramic views. The gardens in these areas tended to be constructed on flat ground and were more likely to be horticultural in character than pleasure gardens.

There are a number of examples of villas, as in Parma, where the house is still more or less in its original state, but where the garden has been reconstructed in the 18th and 19th centuries and opened to the public. In Parma the house has been transformed into a gendarmerie, but it is still decorated with 16th- and 17th-century frescoes, representing various mythological themes. These are mainly concerned with the celebration of love, a particularly suitable subject for a pleasure villa and one that continues to evoke a Golden Age where everyone embraces in a kind of universal pairing. Indeed, the representation of the Golden Age in this house is of central importance to the argument of this book.

The Palazzo del Tè at Mantua was one of the seminal works in the development of the Mannerist style, and one of the main architectural forces in that city was Giulio Romano, the pupil of Raphael, who went there in 1524. While building palaces for the Marchese of Gonzaga, Romano was also commissioned to design a villa, which was far more attractive than a simple country house, since it was sited on an island linked to the town by a bridge; this island was, in effect, an immense *barco*. The villa was completed very quickly and was ready, with its decoration, in 1530, when Charles V visited Mantua and promoted it from marquisate to duchy. The villa and its garden formed one of the most satisfying entities of the 16th century.

The approach to the villa was originally by way of the garden, although this has been closed by a large, arcaded exedra since the 18th century. The visitor then crossed a bridge over a pool, with fish, to enter a loggia; the pool extended the whole length of the villa, which was reflected in its waters. The atrium with its quadruple portico is truly majestic and grants access to the suite of rooms decorated with either painting or sculpture; one of these, depicting the famous story of Eros and Psyche, has already been discussed. The inscription in the room tells us exactly the intended purpose of the building: 'ONESTO OCIO POST LABORES AD REPARANDAM VIRTUTEM' (literally 'For wholesome leisure, to revive the spirits after work').

The garden backs on to the stables, which housed the famous stallions of the Duke of Gonzaga, some of which are represented in the paintings inside the house. A note of intimacy was struck in the garden by a small building called the *grotta*, which contained a secret garden, a basin with fountains, all surrounded by a rest space in the form of a grotto, decorated with frescoes of Aesop's fables.

It is curious that the new appreciation of the natural world did not inspire great developments in the art of the garden in Venice to compare with that city's extraordinary reclamation of land in the 16th century, and to the great advances in villa architecture, which achieved its perfect form in the hands of Palladio. A number of simply designed gardens did exist there, but these tended to be rather medieval in appearance, with enclosures, small rectangular beds, arbours and pergolas; we know the style from the work of a Flemish painter, Ludovico Toeput, who made these gardens almost his sole subject matter, which suggests his paintings were done for a specific clientèle. The lack of architectural elements or statuary explains why no trace of these gardens remains. Evidence of their lack of importance is confirmed by Vincenzo Scamozzi, the architect and heir to the mantle of Palladio, who cites the following as notable gardens in his *Idea dell'architettura universale* which was published in Venice in 1615: in Rome, the Villa Madama and the Villa Giulia; the Villa d'Este at Tivoli; Caprarola and Bagnaia in the Latium; Pratolino in Tuscany and the gardens of the Classical era. Scamozzi himself advocated the farm garden (*fattoria*) for the villa, with small, rectangular enclosures, whose charm would be enhanced by citrus fruits. The only element of perspective in the garden would be the *viale* of cypresses which led to the entrance.

Detail of the nymphaeum in the Villa Barbaro, Maser.

The Villa Emo, built by Palladio at Fanzolo, is the perfect example of the kind of agrarian residence mentioned above. The only Palladian villa with an elaborate garden is the Villa Barbaro at Maser. It looks on to a vast nymphaeum in the form of a rustic-style exedra, supported by telamones and with recessed niches containing statues of the gods. The style of the nymphaeum is totally out of keeping with the mood of Venice in the 16th century, when the city seemed suspended in the pursuit of the Classical ideal which it had inherited from Florence. Thus, while the rest of Italy, first on the example of Florence, then of Rome, embraced Mannerism, Venice remained apart. The style of the nymphaeum and the design of the house, both rather unexpected in the art of Palladio, suggest that the two owners of the house, the humanist Barbaro brothers, may have had something to do with their planning.

The serenity of the place is well expressed in the painted decoration of the villa, which was carried out by Veronese and remains the most complete to be found in any villa of the Veneto. It combines figures representing the nobility of the time with a very detailed rendering of the Olympian gods, thus creating a parallel between the two groups.

Perhaps we can see in Venetian society's scant regard for the garden a confirmation that this art develops most rapidly when there is a need to create an alternative to the world in which we live, where a person wearied by daily life may seek pleasure – and not in a social context where self-satisfaction is already very high.

OUTSIDE ITALY

In France, we almost have to leave the 16th century altogether to find a garden in the monumental Italian mode, with terraces ranged up a slope. In this case, direct Italian influence was seen in the person of the architect Etienne Dupérac, who had done the drawings of the Villa d' Este for Catherine de Médicis and Rodolfo II. In 1593, Henri IV commissioned him to take on the building of a new château at Saint-Germain-en-Laye on the edge of the promenade of the old château; this project had originally been commissioned by Henri II from Philibert Delorme, but only a beginning had been made. To incorporate the central part of the early plan, the château itself had to have four wings; the grandiose succession of terraces must have followed the lines of Dupérac's plan.

The garden and the château form a perfectly integrated ensemble; in this case, the garden is the dominant partner, while the château could easily be the casino of an Italian-style villa. The parterres were beautifully designed; at long last the French gardeners seem to have broken free of the monotonous rectangles which they had employed ever since the Middle Ages. The garden ascended the hill, like that of the Villa d'Este; on each of six levels were *broderie* parterres, fountains, monumental staircases and, especially, numerous grottoes. Indeed, there were even more than at the Villa d'Este and, since the architect had taken good care to vary the position of the staircases, their siting recalled another model: the Temple of Fortuna Primigenia at Praeneste (Palestrina).

At the summit of the garden there was a panoramic view of the plain through which the Seine winds its way to Paris. The Italianate style of the garden was consciously sought; Henri IV had asked his brother-in-law to send him the hydraulic engineers who had worked at Pratolino to install the automata. These were Tommaso and Alessandro Francini, whose family were to become naturalized French citizens under the name of 'Francine' and who remained in the service of the king until the end of the *ancien régime*. There were more grottoes than at Pratolino; in one; a young girl sat at the organ, while in another, Orpheus played the violin; elsewhere, Andromeda was freed by Perseus, overcoming the dragon and hurling it into the water, an obvious symbol (like that of Orpheus) of the peace-making role played by Henri IV. Another grotto was dedicated to Neptune. Aquatic surprises abounded throughout the garden, but the most extraordinary grotto was that of the Flambeaux, in which the visitor could witness a succession of metamorphoses: the sun gave way to a storm, then suddenly the royal palace appeared with a procession of the royal family, while the Dauphin descended from the clouds on a chariot borne by angels. Pratolino had been surpassed.

Apart from the grotto of Orpheus, of which the rock-work still exists in the only remaining pavilion of the château, the other grottoes are positioned normally under the terraces.

The grotto is associated with the bowels of the earth but, since French gardens were generally laid out on flat land, the creation of such caves in the Italian manner had to be done in one of two ways: either a place had to be found for it in the château itself or, if in the garden, a building had to be constructed to shelter it, as in the case of the famous grotto of Tethys at Versailles. However, such a siting necessarily subtracts from the character and symbolic value of a grotto that rises naturally from the ground. This is certainly true of the

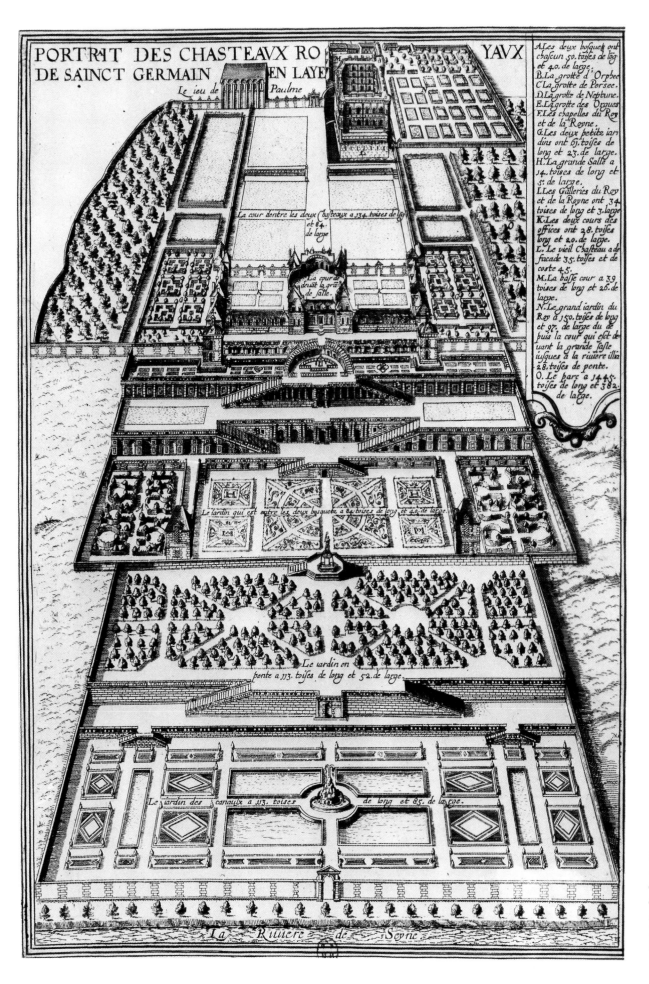

*T*he new château of
Saint-Germain-
en-Laye, from an
engraving by
Alessandro Francini,
1614. Bibliothèque
Nationale, Paris.

one that still exists at the Château de la Bastie d'Urfé, built by the father of Honoré d'Urfé, the poet of *L'Astrée*.

The famous grotto known as the Pines at Fontainebleau, built in 1543 after the designs of Primaticcio, who also decorated it with paintings, has survived the many transformations undergone by the château. Four heavily muscled, embossed Atlases stand on piles, their obvious strength evoking a sense of the Earth's natural forces.

The eventual fate of Saint-Germain-en-Laye seems to indicate that the French sensibility was much more at home with gardens laid out on level ground. The innovations of the château failed to elicit the praise of contemporary writers, although Louis XIV passed his childhood and youth there and the house was also used by the exiled Stuarts. Lack of upkeep, however, finally caused first the terraces and then the house to fall into ruin. While Versailles was being built, Saint-Germain continued to decay, a process which ended only in 1777, when the estate passed to the Comte d'Artois who decided to have house and garden demolished. The prince who had this folly built after his victory in a bitter war against his subjects had little time left to spend on the arts of peace. Although he resumed building operations at the Louvre and other sites in Paris, and at Fontainebleau, he still yearned to build something which was strictly personal, as Louis XIV would do later. But his achievement was never fully appreciated and, effectively, died with him.

Very few remains of the 16th-century gardens still exist: a circular temple on a double Ionic colonnade at the Bastie d'Urfé, and the

Grotto from the Hortus Palatinus by Salomon de Caus, Frankfurt, 1620. Bibliothèque Nationale, Paris.

two summerhouses of Brantôme. However, the first half of the 17th century did see one Frenchman of very broad culture become pre-eminent in extending the Mannerist style to garden design through the more explicit use of the symbolism of automata.

Salomon de Caus was born in Normandy in 1576 of a Huguenot family, which possibly explains his long absences from France. Between 1595 and 1598 he visited Italy; in 1601 we find him in Brussels, where he remained for about ten years and was appointed hydraulics engineer to the arch-dukes. In 1608 he moved to London where, in 1612, he published his *Perspective avec la raison des ombres et miroirs*, the first work on the subject to appear in England. In July 1614, Salomon emerges as engineer to the Elector Palatine in Heidelberg, sent there by the Prince of Wales to his sister Elizabeth, wife of the Elector. In 1615, still in Heidelberg, he published the *Raisons des forces mouvantes* which he dedicated to Elizabeth; during the same period he designed the Hortus Palatinus beside the castle in Heidelberg. The final six years of his life were passed in France as engineer to King Louis XIII; he died in 1626.

The application of pneumatics to cause motion was known to the scholars of ancient Alexandria and this knowledge had been revived and reapplied by Buontalenti at Pratolino. The work of Hero of Alexandria was already familiar in Italy from the 15th century through Latin and Arab translations, and an Italian translation by Alcotti was done in 1589. The book takes the form of a series of theorems – a form imitated by Salomon de Caus in his *Raisons*. Automata were not only used in gardens but also in the theatre. This was especially the case in England where masques – allegorical and mythological plays corresponding to the Italian *intermezzi* – were all the rage.

The achievements of Archimedes, Vitruvius and Hero of Alexandria were studied at length by Salomon before he applied their ideas in his own work. He was assisted by the fact that he had managed to interest the Queen of England, Anne of Denmark, and the Prince of Wales in his theorems. The gardens he designed for both of them incorporated automata. Furthermore, he redesigned the gardens of Somerset House in London for Anne and those at Richmond for the Prince of Wales. Unfortunately, we have to rely for our knowledge of these gardens on the descriptions of visiting foreigners, since no illustrations of them exist.

In some cases, the designs of Salomon seem like a direct response to one of Hero's theorems, so closely did the Frenchman follow the work of the Alexandrian. At Somerset House, the central feature of the series of automata was a Mount Parnassus, obviously inspired by the one at Pratolino. Even the plants on the rock were mountain species. Apollo was surrounded by the Muses as he played his violin – the lyre only appeared much later – while on the summit Pegasus took wing. All these automata performed their movements under a veil of water which sprang from multiple jets – one of the schemes described by Salomon in his *Raisons*. There was a *Tamesis* (Thames) in black marble, along with three other English rivers; and allusion must certainly have been made to Anne of Denmark. In a masque written in 1609 by Samuel Daniel, Anne is celebrated as Tethys, queen of the ocean and wife of Neptune (James I). From the 16th century the French court also staged allegorical spectacles with settings designed by Antoine Caron.

Henry, Prince of Wales, commissioned Salomon to carry out work for him at the Tudor palace of Richmond, which had originally been built to the commission of Henry VII. The garden included an imitation of the Apennine giant of Pratolino, perhaps designed by some Florentine who had worked at the house. However, the design of such a

*M*ount Parnassus, an engraving from the Hortus Palatinus *by Salomon de Caus, Frankfurt, 1620. Bibliothèque Nationale, Paris.*

giant was also included by Salomon in his *Raisons*; in the preface of this book, dedicated to Elizabeth, wife of the Elector Palatine, he mentions that he has included the designs of a number of features created for the Prince of Wales, the princess's brother. It is possible, therefore, that Salomon himself could have been the creator of the giant of Richmond.

Most of these gardens were added to houses which were already in existence. The Chelsea garden commissioned by Sir John Danvers, however, had the advantage of being planned at the same time as the house, thus forming a total design. For instance, there was a dining room situated in a tower, so that the guests could enjoy a panoramic view of the garden. Danvers also introduced the 'idyllic' or Arcadian style, which was to have great success later, by incorporating statues of shepherds and shepherdesses, symbolizing the innocence of the rustic life, in itself an allusion to the Golden Age. A similar intention informed his juxtaposing of a statuary group of Hercules and Antaeus with one of Cain and Abel.

It was during the reign of Charles I that English society began to develop a certain sophistication, and the taste for things Italian became widespread. The king himself acquired the art collection of the Gonzaga of Mantua in 1627 and eventually managed to assemble a truly unique collection of masterpieces; these were later lost to England to the gain of the French by the Puritan Revolution. In 1607, Inigo Jones returned from Italy bearing his personally annotated copy of the *Quattro libri dell'architettura* to initiate the central tradition of modern English architecture: Palladianism. Thomas Howard, Earl of Arundel, a passionate archaeologist who, long before Schliemann, dreamed of rediscovering Troy, had also bought drawings from the Gonzaga collection; he returned from a voyage in Italy with Inigo Jones in 1614 and began to assemble at Arundel House in London a circle of men of letters. One reason for their coming to his house was to admire the garden, which was a veritable museum of antiquities. Just as François I of France had done in the preceding century, Charles I of England sent a sculptor, Hubert Le Sueur, to Italy to bring back moulds and antique casts – a service for which he was paid in 1631. Many of these can now be found on the terrace of Windsor Castle. An inventory of the 'gods of the king' made in 1649 mentions 95 small figures, 175 busts and 20 marble pedestals in St James's Park.

In 1634 John Bate published his *Mysteryes of Nature and Art* which included one chapter devoted to every use which could be made of water. Francis Bacon's *Of Gardens* (1626) was

A panoramic view of the gardens at Wilton from the house, engraving by Isaac de Caus, The Garden of Wilton, c.1645.

Detail of the grotto at Woburn Abbey.

especially concerned with practical advice. A younger member of the de Caus family, Isaac, followed very much in Salomon's footsteps: the grotto which he created at Woburn Abbey for the extravagant Lucy Harmington in 1647 still exists as a prime example of the grottoes of the time, but without automata. Isaac also designed a Calypso grotto and a grotto to Mercury with Europa and Daphne. All these are closely related to the models of Pratolino. The garden at Wilton, commissioned from Isaac by the Earl of Pembroke, is known to us from the description left by the designer himself. The outside of the grotto has been preserved and a number of the statues in the park are still in place. The symbolic theme of the garden was the confrontation of love and chastity.

The mechanics of garden design had always been one of Salomon de Caus's chief preoccupations and in 1644 he published his *Nouvelle Invention de lever l'eau*. The design of English gardens was now to undergo a French influence in the opposite direction from that of Salomon de Caus towards much stricter forms of arrangement. This trend was certainly encouraged by the marriage of Charles I to Henrietta, daughter of Marie de Médicis. Inigo Jones was commissioned to refurbish Wimbledon House, which Charles had bought for Henrietta, while a Frenchman, André Mollet, the son of Claude Mollet, gardener of the Tuileries, was given the task of redesigning the garden. Mollet had worked in England, the Netherlands and Sweden, where in 1651

Fountain of Suzanna, garden of Wilton House, after Isaac de Caus, The Garden of Wilton, c.1645.

Interior of the grotto in the garden of Wilton House, engraving by Isaac de Caus, The Garden of Wilton, c.1645

The garden at Hellbrunn: the grotto of Orpheus. The detail shows Orpheus charming the animals.

he had published *Le Jardin de Plaisir* in Stockholm; the work appeared in three languages (French, German and English). He was paid in 1642 for his work at Wimbledon where he succeeded in creating a garden which was completely Classical in spirit.

There was surprisingly little of interest in the garden designed by Salomon de Caus at Heidelberg; both the garden and the house were later destroyed by the soldiers of Louis XIV. A truly Mannerist garden would have been a suitable complement to the palace which was a model of the style, with its numerous herms and caryatids.

In its ultimate form the Mannerist garden became a sort of living theatre, activated by water. Although all the English gardens in this style have now disappeared, there is still an example extant in Austria: the garden belonging to the villa of the Bishops of Salzburg at Hellbrunn, which is almost symbolic of its own location, since the name signifies 'clear fountain'. Both house and garden, which took only 15 months to build, were commissioned by Archbishop Markus Sitticus, Count of Hohenems, who had been brought up in Italy; they are probably the work of the architect Solari. By 1619 everything was finished, according to the illustrated description of Jean Steinhauser. 'Hellbrunn is a labyrinth of running water, a playground for water nymphs, a theatre of flowers, a capital of statues, a museum of the

Theatre in the garden of Hellbrunn, near Salzburg.

Graces,' wrote Dominique Gisberti, the court poet of the Prince-Elector Ferdinand Maria of Bavaria, in 1670.

The garden has not quite survived in its original form; around 1730–50 one of the bishops had some redesigning carried out according to contemporary taste; the hermitages were demolished and later the outside was further modified in the English style. However, the great hydraulic theatres are still there: the grottoes of Orpheus, Neptune, the Song Birds, the Fountain of Altemps and the five small grottoes where a variety of features can be seen in action: a grinder, a miller, a potter, Apollo flaying Marsyas and the inevitable Perseus delivering Andromeda. There are also the grotto of Midas and the Fountains of Mercury and Eurydice. Between 1747 and 1759 a mechanical theatre of semi-circular construction, bearing the arms of Archbishop André-Jacques, Count Dietrichstein (1747–53), was erected in the garden. At the centre of the theatre was a palace in the form of a tower and along the two sides were superimposed galleries. Here, in miniature, life at court was enacted as a reflection of life in the city outside. In this it might be compared to the Neapolitan puppet performances, notably the Christmas manger scenes (crèches). The clockmaker's art was also called in to supplement the hydraulics in the working of an organ.

The fashion for automata lasted into the 18th century. At Lunéville King Stanislas Leszczynski commissioned a mechanical theatre 250 metres long against the wall of the house. In mountainous surroundings, created out of stone from the Vosges, mills, workshops and huts, fashioned in stone, brick or wood, provided the setting where groups of wooden automata enacted all manner of daily activities. The king also had automata included his garden of La Malgrange. A shrubbery with songbirds can still be seen in the park of Schwetzingen. When Stanislas died in 1766 and Lorraine was returned to France, the various features of the parks at Lunéville and La Malgrange were offered for sale and, for the most part, were bought by German princes. The acquisition by the Elector Palatine Charles-Théodore of the effects of the garden of La Malgrange indicates just how strong the interest in garden automata remained, at least in Germany, at the end of the 18th century. At Schwetzingen, the birds and owls form an agreeable reminder of similar creatures first encountered at the Villa d'Este, but this time it is the night bird who is the victim of the smaller ones, being sprayed with water while suffering their scolding and provocations.

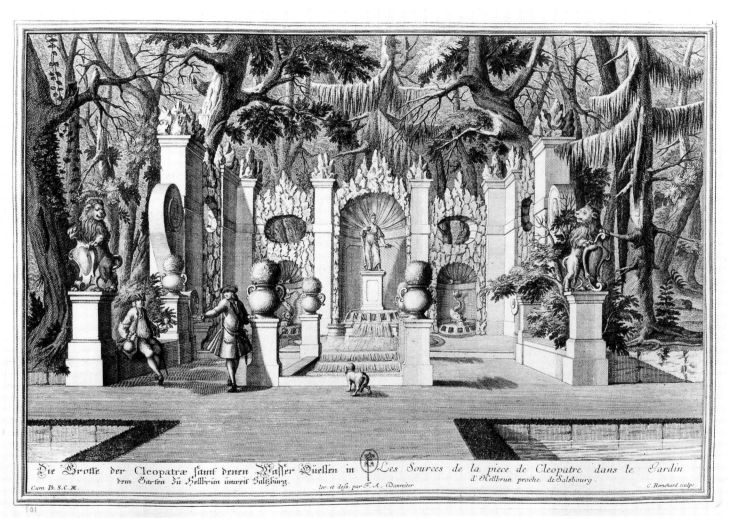

Die Grosse der Cleopatræ samt denen Wasser Quellen in Les Sources de la piece de Cleopatre dans le Gardin
dem Garten zu Hellbrün unweit Saltzburg. d'Hellbrun proche de Salsbourg.

Cum Pr.S.C.M. Inv. et dess. par F. A. Danreiter. C. Remshard sculps.

*T*he springs in the
grotto of Cleopatra
in the garden at
Hellbrunn,
engraving by Carl
Remshard from a
drawing by A.
Danreiter, 18th
century.
Bibliothèque
Nationale, Paris.

THE CLASSICAL GARDEN

In both their symbolic and artistic aspects, the Mannerist gardens developed empirically; they were never based on some pre-existing body of theory. Even the advice on their design given by Alberti was fairly elementary, and the *Hypnerotomachia* of Poliphilus was more an inspiration that a real guide. This was certainly not the case with the gardens designed in what is usually known as 'the French style'. Very much in keeping with the national character and especially with the spirit of the 17th century, these gardens were largely the product of theory. We have only to read the words of Boyceau de la Barauderie, superintendent of the royal gardens under Louis XIII and author of the treatise *Traité du jardinage selon les raisons de la nature et de l'art*, posthumously published in 1638, to realize the extent to which garden design was the subject of theoretical speculation. According to the author, the object of his book is 'to enter into the rationale of things, which is essential to all worthwhile work, and especially in this field'. 'Rationale' is clearly the key word here and the whole book is coloured by it; in gardening, for instance, the author distinguishes 'two types of rationale: that which is inherent in nature and from which depend the characteristics of vegetation, earth, climate, air and water . . . and that of art which enables us to estimate a task before it is done, so that when we do finally set to work we can repeat on a larger scale those things we have already planned in miniature.' No less than three members of the renowned Mollet family, which produced four generations of gardeners, were authors of theoretical treatises. From 1615, the second-generation Claude Mollet, pupil of the agronomist Olivier de Serres, worked on his *Théâtre des plantes de jardinage*, which only appeared in 1652, after his death. The year before, his son André had published *Le Jardin de Plaisir*, mentioned in the previous chapter, in Stockholm. Claude Mollet's work is less interesting to the historian of forms, since it is more concerned with the practical aspects of gardens than with their conception. He does, however, emerge as a remarkable botanist with a particular flair for combining different species of flowers so that the parterres could bloom throughout the year. He advocates laying out pathways wide enough to take account of the contracting effect of perspective; and he includes designs for labyrinths, deploring the fact that the common run of gardeners have no idea how to make them.

André Mollet's writing, however, does distinguish a number of principles which were to become central to the development of the French garden. The site had to be unrestricted and the house positioned in such a way that it could have a semi-circular or rectangular courtyard in front. On the other side of the house, the parterres would stretch away at right angles to the building so that the *broderies* would be clearly visible from the

Plan of a labyrinth from the Jardin de plaisir *by André Mollet, 1651. Bibliothèque Nationale, Paris.*

Versailles: the Bassin du Dragon.

windows of the château. His other concerns included the apparent diminution in size of the ornaments furthest away from the observers, and the principle that lawns should come after the parterres in the order of the garden. The majority of the alleys had to end in a focal point, such as a fountain or statue.

The greatest number of new ideas are to be found in the book by Boyceau. Although he admits that land which is 'hilly and uneven' can 'yield other pleasures and opportunities', he prefers it 'even and unified'; he also suggests that if such a site cannot be found, it is preferable to give up the whole idea of laying out a garden! Seen from above, the garden must present a unified spectacle: 'The unity of the different parts gives greater pleasure than the individual elements.' This suggests that the garden's main purpose is to provide a panoramic view rather than serve as a place of relaxation. Boyceau also advocates combining rounded and straight forms and using hedges of carefully clipped vegetation, the height of which should be one-third the width of the alleys. His plans for parterres are especially large-scale and varied; they were to include 'foliages, borders, moresques, arabesques, grotesques, guilloches, rosettes, glorioles, targes, escutcheons and devices'. The author's feeling for structure leads him to contrast the parterres to the higher planted areas, which might consist of trees arranged in clumps or in avenues, or of trellis-work forming arbours or other shapes.

Boyceau admires moving water in the garden, but he also recommends the inclusion of pools, the calm surfaces of which will provide a pleasant contrast. By varying their form they virtually become water parterres – a novel concept. His description of grottoes recalls those of the Château Neuf at Saint-Germain-en-Laye.

One interesting aspect of Boyceau's work is that, whereas in general it had become customary to envisage the various sections of garden as quite separate, he saw nothing wrong in combining the utilitarian with the pleasurable; so, ornamental parterres might have their place alongside kitchen gardens, orchards and herbal gardens, as was to be the case at Chantilly. And by making provision, too, for games areas, he clearly sees the garden as a universe of multiple possibilities.

Vaux-le-Vicomte is one of the great landmarks in the history of garden design, but possibly the impression it makes of being something of a miraculous achievement would be rather less strong had not all the previous famous gardens already disappeared. The Château de Rueil, for instance, begun by Richelieu in 1638, boasted the first of the great cascades which were to be among the most attractive features of French gardens. There were also three architectural grottoes and, to the north of the château, an arrangement of water features, consisting of a canal and pools of various shapes laid out in a manner that was to become a hallmark of the French garden tradition. The engineer responsible for the hydraulics of Rueil was the Italian Tommaso Francini.

In the garden of another château commissioned by the cardinal in Poitou, a great feature was made of water in the form of canals fed by a river, the Mable, which passed through the garden. Further ornamentation of this garden, belonging to a man of the cloth, was provided by a series of figures of pagan deities!

The finest garden in which moving water was a major feature, however, was that built at Liancourt by Roger du Plessis, Duc de la Roche-Guyon and Marquis de Liancourt. It included a fine arrangement of fountains, still pools, bowl-type fountains and high jets (including one which shot a hundred feet in the air), the whole effect completed by a canal running along the great parterre. Indeed, there was so much water in the garden that in one form or another, as at Chantilly later, it provided an ever-moving spectacle.

The dramatic events which caused the interior decoration of the Château de Vaux to be curtailed and which hastened the unfortunate end of the Surintendant Nicolas Fouquet, who had commissioned its building, also mark the importance which the garden was now to assume as a symbol of royal power. Fouquet had brought together a team of matchless ability: the architect Le Vau, the painter and decorator Le Brun and the landscape architect André Le Nôtre, who, between 1656 and 1661, jointly created the marvellous house and gardens on the plain of La Brie, to the east of Paris. Before the decoration was completed, Nicolas Fouquet wanted to show his creation to the king. The visit of Louis XIV on 15 August 1661 was marked by daylong festivities. Three weeks later, the Surintendant was arrested and, after his trial, imprisoned at the king's pleasure in the fortress of Pignerol.

The enigma of Louis XIV's vendetta against Fouquet has, if anything, deepened since the appearance of a book by Daniel Rousset in 1987; on the evidence of the Surintendant's account books, Rousset has proved that his fortune must have been considerable, since he was able to pay for the construction of Vaux with his own money. The court which the

*A*erial view of the château and park of Vaux-le-Vicomte.

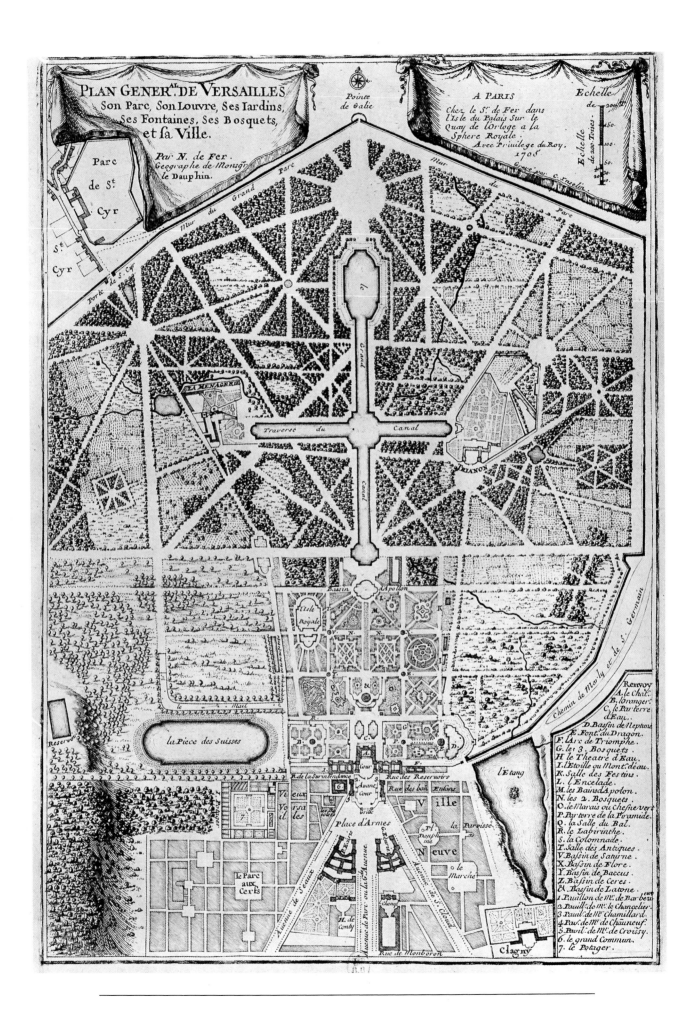

king imagined would condemn Fouquet to death in fact only punished him with a sentence of banishment, thus effectively acquitting him of at least the main charge, that of having breached the trust implicit in his office. But perhaps the real crime committed by Fouquet was one of *lèse-majesté*. At the time the king possessed only mediocre gardens, and a number of these were old-fashioned – at the Tuileries, Fontainebleau, Saint-Germain-en-Laye and at his father's château of Versailles. Perhaps he regarded Fouquet's construction of a house and garden of truly royal proportions as an act of insolence.

It is often tempting to compare Vaux with Versailles and always to the detriment of the latter. Vaux does indeed have certain advantages over its royal rival. It rises like a marvellous flower from the flat plain of La Brie, whereas Versailles is now surrounded by a town which hardly enhances the setting of the château itself. But there are fundamental differences between the two which make true comparisons difficult. Vaux-le-Vicomte was a pleasure château, whereas Versailles eventually became a state residence (1682). The abrupt end to work at Vaux meant that it retained the purity of the original concept, while Versailles, constantly modified according to the caprices of its creator and his successors, developed into something far more complex and heterogeneous – a drama of a hundred different acts or a poem dedicated to the changing fortunes of the nation. Moreover, the garden at Vaux also lays claim to be the most perfect expression of the French style.

The entry through the main courtyard prepares us for the grand spectacle to come. The homely brick of the outbuildings contrasts with the stone of the château itself but, at the same time, harmonizes with the turf of the four parterres and the foliage which appears at intervals between these buildings and the château. There is already a promise here of the effect to be made by the garden. By contrast, the entrance court at Versailles is a quadrilateral enclosed and paved, though somewhat less austere since the recent restoration of the colonnades linking the marble court to the water parterre. At Vaux-le-Vicomte, one of Le Vau's great successes was the siting of the various buildings. Even the outbuildings, set back from the château, show to advantage thanks to the parterres at the sides of the main house. And the house itself is truly inseparable from the garden; the long-neglected unity of these two elements is here perfectly realized. The house is actually surrounded by a moat, an archaic feature yet one that helps to reinforce the building's links

Plan of the château and park of Versailles from an engraving by Nicolas de Fer, 1705. Bibliothèque Nationale, Paris.

with its natural surroundings and its essentially rural character; and the house connects with the garden by way of an *allée* across a bridge. The eye is immediately engaged by the sense of space; at the end of a broad walk is a wall with arches, seeming to support the carpet of turf which slopes quite steeply upward to a colossal statue. On closer inspection, the wall and its arches turn out to be seven grottoes coated with shells and separated by herms, while a jet of water spurts from a mass of rock-work.

Two large *parterres de broderies* bring us to the transverse axis of the garden and a great round pool where the two axes intersect. A few steps lead down to a slighter lower level and the promenade continues between two parterres which are each centred on a basin in the shape of an oval quatrefoil. The alley is bordered by 14 floral fountains which were to have acted as 'water chandeliers' to form 'a crystal balustrade'. This alley is actually wider than the preceding one, but due to the effect of perspective they appear to be of equal width when observed from the château. It is worth remarking that Le Nôtre adhered to the principles of André Mollet in following the *parterres de broderie* with turf parterres.

We then come to the vast pool, truly surprising in its sheer size, and apparently fed by water from the seven grottoes which seem to be situated along one of its edges. This illusion, however, is swiftly dissipated by the discovery

that we are on the banks of a canal – in fact the river Anqueil – channelled over more than a kilometre and represented by the figure of a demi-god in a niche positioned at right angles to form a pendant to the figure depicting Tiber. The wall along the canal is adorned with 20 masks, all spurting water into basins. The designer's art has concealed this spectacular water theatre from the visitor until the last moment.

If we now look back towards the house, the reason for the vast size of the pool becomes apparent; its purpose is to reflect the château in its entirety. Thus, right at the other end of the garden, we can again admire the silhouette of the slate roof and dome against the sky, creating the landscape effect so characteristic of the Ile-de-France, where an infinite variety of roof forms is set against ever-changing skies. At Versailles, Le Vau departed in some measure from this native tradition in favour of Italianate terraces which tend to look better under clear, unvarying southern skies than under the shifting skyscapes of northern France.

Familiar with the optical laws defined by Descartes, Le Nôtre had obtained these surprise effects, along with the illusions and the reflection, by careful calculation of space, levels and angles. The art of the gardener had finally become a science.

The bank of the canal where the grottoes are located is reached by means of side bridges and from it rise a succession of steps, ramps

The grotto at Vaux-le-Vicomte with the Fountain of the Tiber.

and slopes which turn in such a way that the surrounding countryside can be observed from different angles. This ascent leads to the great fountain of La Gerbe, situated on the final horizontal plane of the garden. This is the starting point of the *vertugadin*, or raised turf (the term being derived from the osier frame or farthingale worn by women to spread their dresses). This stretch of the garden is bordered by foliage arranged like the flats of a theatre, but which used to form high walls akin to palisades. Finally, we reach the foot of the colossus, a modern copy in lead of the Farnese Hercules, which dominates the whole garden.

In other parts of the garden Le Nôtre laid out shaded promenades with the aid of raised parterres and shrubberies, their interest heightened by grottoes and other features, especially to the west, where the rising ground was arranged as a series of terraces.

Although the three artists responsible for Vaux undoubtedly collaborated very closely with one another, and Le Brun and Le Vau would certainly have offered advice on many points, Le Nôtre has to be recognized as the true creator of the garden. His father, Pierre, who had once worked for Claude Mollet, had been head gardener at the Tuileries. André, born in 1618, was thus from the best possible background to acquire a sound knowledge of gardening techniques. He also benefited from artistic training, having worked in the studio of the painter Simon Vouet, where he met Le Brun and where he also studied architecture. He was 34 when Nicolas Fouquet invited him to come to Vaux. He had already begun to remodel the gardens of the Tuileries, a task to which he was to devote much of his life. Because these gardens were too long for their width, Le Nôtre bordered them with two terraces to the north and south, while to the west he created the grandiose system of access staircases with double flights which exists to this day.

In the opinion of Saint-Simon, the site chosen by Louis XIV for the building of what was to be the greatest symbol of royal grandeur ever known was unsuitable for the purpose. Although the king hardly deserves such reproach, it is true, nevertheless, that the land was marshy, thus causing problems with drainage and with earth movement (it also explains why so many of the workmen employed on the site died of fever). This disadvantage in the siting of French-style gardens, arising from the type of terrain needed for their layout, was not uncommon. Completely flat land, such as the table of a plateau, was unsuitable, as was a steep slope necessitating arrangement in terraces. The ideal was a gentle slope running away from the château, itself built strategically on a ridge, and down the side of a valley towards the meandering and frequently marshy course of some river. An even greater drawback of such a site was the absence of running water or of a river with a current strong enough to provide sufficient force for effective cascades and fountains.

Yet, although the site presented its planners with certain problems, it lent itself admirably to the layout out of a French-style garden and to the display of all ornamental features.

Perhaps the dominant element in the character of Louis XIV was that of the artist. In every field he displayed a desperate need to create: in music, dance, theatre and in all the fine arts. He was also fully capable of providing firm personal direction to his various architectural commissions, as is shown by his work on the Colonnade du Louvre and even more by his correspondence with the absent Mansart during the construction of the Trianon. Indeed, so great was his involvement in his own building projects that a recently published book is entitled simply *Louis XIV architecte*[1].

[1]Jean Autun, *Louis XIV architecte*, Paris, 1981.

The Grand Trianon in the park of Versailles, by Jules Hardouin-Mansart.

The king was also an actor – appearing first in 1654 in the *Noces de Pélée et de Thétis*, in which he played six roles including that of Apollo – only giving up the stage in 1670. Saint-Simon noted, moreover, that Louis was a remarkably good dancer, a fact which ensured the success of the court ballet. Occasionally, his enthusiasm for dancing outran his energies; in two instances he danced so long that he came down with fever, and doctors feared for his health.

Louis regarded virtually every activity as an art, even that of war. On one occasion Vauban mounted a display devoted to methods of besieging fortresses, to which the king invited the court, including the ladies who were hardly appreciative of life on the battlefield.

Art – and not least the art of living (or, at least, living as a king) – preoccupied Louis, who once said: 'I can create twenty dukes and peers in a quarter of an hour, but it takes centuries to make a Mansart.' He had an undoubted gift for recognizing and encouraging various artists capable of giving expression to his dreams. He was surrounded by exceptional talents: Molière for comedy, Racine for tragedy, Lully for music, supported by that elegant poet Quinault for the libretti, Le Brun, master of all the figurative arts, Le Vau and then Mansart for architecture, and Le Nôtre for garden design. He also called upon an excellent team of sculptors, of whom only Coysevox and Girardon achieved individual fame, but who rivalled the achievements of antiquity in the gardens and who – even more than the painters – created French Classicism. Finally, Louis tempted the Keller brothers from Switzerland to make bronzes based on the ideas of his other artists.

Although the garden created by Le Nôtre at Vaux-le-Vicomte was perhaps the purest expression of the French style, it was not a truly regal garden. Now, in his project for Versailles, Louis was to provide his landscape

architect with all the means possible to fulfil that ambition. The king had already discharged his dynastic responsibility in contributing to the massive reconstruction of the Louvre. However, the works on the palace in Paris must have seemed to him interminable, and he obviously found the design of the other royal châteaux and gardens old-fashioned. Against this background it was hardly surprising that he should want to attempt something on a truly magnificent scale which would be entirely his own. After all, Richelieu had done it twice, at Rueil and in the Poitou at the place which bears his name, and more recently still Surintendant Fouquet had built Vaux-le-Vicomte, which may very well have acted as a provocation to the king.

Other motives may also have urged Louis XIV to abandon the Louvre in 1682 and to move his residence and the seat of government out of the city. As a child he had often been obliged to flee Paris during the insurrection of the Fronde and he must have become accustomed to a wandering life, as he moved from one château to the next according to the turn of events. His also inherited his ancestors' taste for nature and their instinct for the hunt. Unlike his grandfather Henri IV, he lacked the common touch, nor would he forget having seen the Palais-Royal invaded by the Paris mob when he was a child. Strong reasons, then, for his wishing to isolate himself with his court and to create a world of his own devising; in other words, he was driven by exactly that desire for an alternative life which lies at the root of the very idea of the garden. Initially, he sought this in a restless, continual change of scene but, tiring of the Louvre and the frequent journeys to the other royal châteaux, he eventually settled on Versailles, doubtless in memory of his father who had built a hunting lodge there. At first, Louis was happy to use this as his father had left it, but from 1661 he began to commission work

Versailles: the statue of La Seine by Le Hongre.

Panoramic view of the park of Marly from a painting by Martin des Batailles. Musée National du château de Versailles et de Trianon.

on the gardens, almost as though he wanted to create a great open-air setting for the presentation of spectacles to which his other gardens were so ill suited. The château itself went through several stages of development; first Louis built around the original house, then added further features until he had a façade, 670 m in length, giving on to the garden. Yet, having created this royal city, Louis inevitably felt the need occasionally to escape from it. The king's open-handed approach to court life attracted to Versailles 3,000 courtiers as well as countless hangers-on; the main qualification for appearing at court was the wearing of a sword and a plumed hat and, theoretically, every Frenchman had the right to see the royal person. The gardens were also open to the public. The king, then, still had the problem of how to escape the attentions of crowds who sometimes became so rowdy that they disrupted entertainments and even official receptions. To achieve some respite from the royal obligation of holding permanent audience, Louis built the Trianon de Porcelaine, later replaced by the Trianon de Marbre. His true place of refuge, however, was Marly, to which he would flee from the 'official' court to enjoy more intimate social contact and a less rigid court protocol.

It is hard to imagine Versailles being centred on anything other than the king's room, the inner sanctum, yet before 1701 the true heart of the palace lay elsewhere, in an apartment which no longer exists. According to Pierre Verlet, this apartment 'was like an annexe to the kingdom of Madame de Montespan'; this was the *appartement des bains*, begun in 1671 and still being furnished in 1680. It had several rooms and had been conceived essentially as a place for sensual pleasure; its decoration had an air of oriental luxury, with precious silks, the finest tapestries and rarest marbles. It was there, according to J.-P. Neraudau, that the 'sacred coupling' of the Sun King and his mistress took place. The apartment was located at the same level as the gardens which could be reached directly through a gallery since, in the 17th century, the central section of the palace communicated directly both with the gardens and the Court of Marble at ground-floor level.

From the *appartement des bains*, the royal lovers could see the grotto of Thetis, a small building completed in 1665 and demolished in 1685 during the construction of the north wing. Built in the rococo style with aquatic features, it contained a mythological group symbolizing the setting of the sun. This group was subsequently moved several times before 1781 when, after a plan of 1778 by Hubert Robert, two years later than the general reforestation of the park, it was installed as part of a theatrical display in the English romantic style in a huge nymphaeum known as 'Apollo's Bath', which looked as though it had been formed from natural rock. There, his daily course run, Phoebus Apollo could take his rest, attended by nymphs, with respite too for the horses of the sun.

The gallery which formerly led from the *appartement des bains* gave on to a terrace marked to the north and south by vases representing Peace and War, corresponding to the rooms bearing the same names which were located at the end of the Galerie des Glaces.

The decorative elements on the façade of the château overlooking the water parterre form part of the cosmological symbolism of the garden. At attic level on the three projections from the façade the months of the year are represented as twelve statues of the Zodiac arranged around the figures of Diana and Apollo. But in this fictional world, where everything must appear as in Classical antiquity, the year starts according to the Roman calendar, with the month of March. There is another detail which shows the subtlety of this symbolic language. On the windows of the ground floor, the masks of male and female faces age as the year gets older.

The water parterre underwent three transformations before assuming its final form. In 1674, a year in which several large-scale projects were carried out, a reading of Ovid had inspired Le Brun to create a number of features based on particularly complicated mythological themes; these included a Mount Parnassus and had some of the ambiguous quality of Mannerist allegory. It was almost certainly Louis himself who brought a Classical simplicity to the project in the form of two immense stretches of water, their borders lined with 24 bronze statues which symbolize the kingdom by its network of rivers (eight of the statues represent respectively the Loire, the Loiret, the Rhône, the Saône, the Garonne, the Dordogne, the Seine and the Marne), water by the nymphs, and the vitality of the kingdom by those groups of children,

*O**rnamental heads on the keystones of the ground-floor windows in the central part of the château of Versailles. The heads form part of a symbolic system expressing the passage of time and show different effects of ageing according to their place in the year, the months of which are also represented along the outside of the attic floor.*

*L**e repos des chevaux du Soleil, one of the three groups from the old grotto of Thetis and Peleus by Girardon, de Marsy and Guérin.*

here playing in pairs, which Louis XIV caused to be repeated in all his buildings and gardens. Children, in fact, occupied a relatively unimportant place in family life – at least in the great families. The significance of these statues of infants at Versailles is that they represent a return of the *putto* of Classical antiquity, symbol of vital energy and a figure of allegorical consequence in the gardens of Pompeii and Herculaneum. So although the children look quite natural, they are in fact symbolic of a France flourishing under the rule of Louis XIV. This group of bronzes, which were executed by a number of different sculptors at Versailles, is one of the major works of Classicism. However, the remarkable unity of the group should not surprise us for, like all the statues of the park, they were designed by Le Brun.

Taking up the themes of the statues along the upper storey of the château, those of the two fountains in which the parterre terminates have as their theme the passing of time: Daybreak, Noon and Evening are represented, as well as Air and Water. The depiction of animals in combat on the façade may very well be derived from one of Ovid's texts describing the gates of the palace of the sun. This is all that remains of the mythological symbolism envisaged by Le Brun, along with, on the terrace, the statues of Apollo, Bacchus, Mercury and Silenus, all expressing the fundamental union of opposites.

If we follow the advice given in *La Manière de montrer les jardins de Versailles*, written by Louis XIV and revised by him as he transformed the gardens, we now proceed towards the edge of the water parterre following the longitudinal axis of the garden. There we may stop to contemplate the perspective view of

Versailles: Départ du char de Soleil, *group by Girardon.*

the canal, 3,200 m in length, which stretches from the château to the west gate.

The central Allée Royale or lawn, which leads from the Bassin de Latone to the Bassin d'Apollon, formerly had a more markedly architectural appearance, since the trees were then trimmed to form a hedge, and the visitor would take his promenade between walls of greenery. One of the lesser known but still extraordinary feats of Louis XIV was the reforestation of the park. This was achieved by using adult trees which were brought to Versailles in their hundreds; those that did not survive replanting were immediately replaced. In 1688, for example, 25,000 trees arrived from Artois.

Le Nôtre's handling of grand effects can now be admired. Given that the garden of Louis XIII ended at the Bassin des Cygnes (which retained this name for a long time before providing the setting for Apollo and his chariot), Le Nôtre virtually remodelled the whole slope of the garden. This enabled him to reshape the approaches to the château, using the water parterre and the marvellous amphitheatre of Latona. The Allée Royale was then left to descend gently towards another amphitheatre, that of the Bassin d'Apollon, at which point the garden becomes horizontal again.

The Bassin de Latone is positioned within the horseshoe shape of a magnificent staircase. The marble statue of Latona is turned towards us, her appeal for help expressed in her raised hand, while her children, Apollo and Diana, whom she is trying to protect from the fury of Juno, press themselves against her. In the basin itself are the lead figures of the peasants of Lycia, who had refused shelter to Latona and had then been turned by her into frogs; these are shown at different stages of metamorphosis. The amphitheatre of Latona, bordered by statues and herms and by urns of stone, lead or bronze, is the heart of the garden of Versailles. One might have expected to find here a work of somewhat greater authority and majesty than this expression of anguish and reference to dreadful events – so rare at Versailles. Doubtless the dramatic subject of the group was intended to symbolize the punishment which awaited all those who rebelled against the king's power. And there were other reminders in the garden of the troubles of the Fronde.

The meaning of the fountain in the Bosquet de l'Encelade needs little explanation. It takes its name from the huge bronze figure representing the giant Enceladus from which a jet of water rises 23 m; the figure itself seems crushed beneath a mass of rocks which have fallen from the slopes of Mount Olympus

Versailles: the vista of the Allée Royale from the Bassin de Latone.

*V*ersailles:
*L'Orangerie and
the staircase of the
Hundred Steps, from
a painting attributed
to Martin des Batailles.
Musée National du
château de
Versailles et de
Trianon.*

which the giant had attempted to climb.

While the carts bearing the trees were arriving at Versailles, other forms of land and water transport were being used to bring antique statues from Rome. The fact that so many projects were completed in such a short time indicates the king's urgency to finish the palace and gardens and the enterprise of his minister Colbert. The statues which now arrived to join those that Colbert had already ordered in France were either original antiques or copies of Classical masterpieces made by the pupils of the French Academy in Rome. The king initially purchased so many of these that the pope had to set a limit to the number which could be exported. In the Bassin d'Apollon the god holds the reins of the horses and seems to be urging the chariot of the sun to leap from the surface of the water. Logically, the chariot should be directed towards the west, but the rhetoric of Versailles dictated that even a god had to face the human individual of whom he was the mythological expression: the Sun King.

The flatness of the site in no way detracts from the majesty of the amphitheatre which surrounds the Bassin d'Apollon; bordered by herms, antique statues and antique reproductions, it is almost as impressive as the Bassin de Latone. It opens out on to the grand canal, one of the first works carried out at Versailles, dug between 1667 and 1668. Some 120 m wide and 1,560 m long, it is cut by a transverse canal, 1,013 m in length, which formerly ended to the south at a menagerie, now demolished, but formerly one of the finest buildings of Versailles, and to the north at the Grand Trianon. The great canal was often the scene of nocturnal festivity and a whole flotilla of boats was moored on it, including the royal galley and numerous gondolas, manned by Venetian gondoliers who were lodged in the buildings which even today bear the name of 'Little Venice'.

An entire monograph could be devoted to the innumerable urns at Versailles. They come in a variety of materials – stone, marble, bronze or lead; some even recount specific narratives. Many of them stand on the Parterre du Nord and the Parterre du Midi which flank the water parterre and extend along the corresponding wings of the château. This was also the best position for floral display, since the flowers could be seen from the windows of the house. Under Louis XIV, they were kept in pots and changed during the night, so that each morning the king could gaze on a new design in *broderie*. The most attractive feature of the Parterre du Midi is that it overlooks the Orangery. Built by Mansart between 1684

The Bosquet de la Colonnade, by Mansart.

Versailles: Bosquet de la Salle de Bal (detail of the water staircase).

and 1686 to replace the one by Le Vau, this splendid building boasts the finest barrel vaulting in France. Although the Parterre de l'Orangerie has its own selection of ornaments, it is at its best in summer, when orange trees, lemon trees and, nowadays, date palms are removed from the main building and placed outside in a geometrical arrangement.

To gain access to the Orangery, Mansart built a staircase known as the 'hundred steps', although in fact there are 103; the same way south also led to the immense stretch of water known as the Pièce d'Eau des Suisses, so called because it was dug out by the king's guards to drain a particularly unhealthy piece of marshland. To climb the staircase, where each step seems to have been made for a giant, is one of the great experiences of the park; until the very last steps only the sky, one of the essential elements in the art of the garden, is visible, so that the staircase becomes a veritable Jacob's Ladder.

The larger Parterre du Nord is more richly decorated and has a greater number of statues. At the end of the central *allée* is the graceful Fontaine de la Pyramide; below is a water table decorated by Girardon with a bas-relief of a *Bain des nymphes*, a subject which was later to inspire Renoir.

The Allée des Marmousets, or the Allée d'Eau, is bordered by four urns in Languedoc marble, again showing children at play together in a celebration of health and the joys of living, a theme to be found everywhere in Versailles. Sloping more sharply, the *allée* leads to the most powerful fountain in the whole park, which shoots upwards from the Bassin du Dragon. This is a circular expanse of water, 40 m in diameter, in which the monster struggles against the gentler creatures – swans and dolphins. The presence of the dolphins may be another reference to the infant king's experiences during the Fronde, while the swans could well refer to Louis's love of birdlife. The jet of water from the basin can rise to 27 m, although a device attached to the fountain limits it to 11 m, the maximum height only being used during the visits of ambassadors and royalty. The necessity for such a device reminds us of the problems encountered by Louis in bringing water to

Versailles, despite the massive (and not always successful) works which were undertaken to this end.

Behind the Bassin du Dragon is located the biggest water theatre ever built. The work of Le Nôtre, it was constructed between 1678 and 1682 and enlarged in 1738; the Bassin de Neptune was adorned with an entire mythological group on the themes of the oceans and water. The water in the theatre could be displayed in 99 different ways to form an extraordinary monument in crystal.

Everything we have seen up to this point, principally the parterres which follow one another along the east-west axis, has been part of the official and visible aspect of the park. But Versailles also has its secrets, the 'rooms' or 'closets' hidden in the *bosquets*. These varied from the ballroom designed by Le Nôtre to La Colonnade, an elegant circle of arches in pink, white, blue, turquoise and violet marble, each one framing a jet of water shooting up from a fountain basin. The design was taken by Mansart from an illustration in the *Hypnerotomachia Poliphili* and includes, as part of the decoration, clusters of infant musicians who form a joyful garland apparently suspended in the air.

Four octagonal fountains, positioned at the intersections of *allées*, are decorated with lead figures symbolizing the Four Seasons, thus underlining the message found on the façade of the château and which permeates the whole garden – how the universe is governed by the passing of time and how birth and death alternate.

From time to time the king undoubtedly tired of the pomp and circumstance of his château and garden, and his first 'retreat' was built on land which he owned near the hamlet of Trianon, some distance into the park. This was the Trianon de Porcelaine, so called because the building was covered with ceramic tiles of various origins, although there was a preponderance from the Netherlands. The house was commissioned by Louis from Le Vau in 1670 for Mme de Montespan as a love nest, which induced Mme de Maintenon to yearn for its destruction. This was virtually a secret garden, a *hortus conclusus*, within the great park; the intimate and secretive nature

Versailles: entrance to the old labyrinth, painting by Jean Cotelle. Musée National du château de Versailles et de Trianon.

of the place was emphasized by the exaggeratedly luxurious decoration of the three parts of the building. There were even special perfume closets.

A second house was commissioned from Mansart, supported by Robert de Cotte, to be built on the site at the northern end of the transverse section of the grand canal. This was to be larger than the first house and was called the Trianon de Marbre, because of the extensive use of Languedoc marble and marbled green for the columns and the entablature friezes, while the Ionic capitals were in Carrara, all displayed to the greatest advantage by the marvellous honey colour of Troissy stone. Impatient to see the building completed, the king took a close interest in its construction; and it was finished so quickly that he was able to sleep there with Mme de Maintenon on 22 January 1689. The decorative details carved on the window piers are of a beauty and elegance which speak highly of the talent of the craftsmen who worked at Versailles. The variety is extraordinary, including battle trophies, musical instruments, garden tools, fruit and flowers.

The building consists of a single storey grouped in several sections; the dry ditches of the entry courtyard signify that this is a country house. Far from being enclosed, the garden of the Grand Trianon opens on to the great garden beyond by the grand canal and, more subtly, by the entry court. This gives the house a much greater feeling of openness than is evident at the château, reinforcing its role as a place devoted to pleasure, where the king could at last be free of the obligation to be constantly available. The mythological sym-

bolism here was limited to the lead figures of children on the edges of the basins, made from Languedoc marble; in the parterres flowers were the dominant element, which gave the alternative name of the Palais de Flore to the Trianon. The Trianon was conceived as a château in its own right; beyond the parterres lay the wooded part of the park which stretched as far as the hahas which marked its boundary. The expression 'haha' is derived from the exclamation of surprise uttered by the unsuspecting walker who, believing that he is following a path straight across the fields, suddenly finds this sunken obstacle underfoot. The purpose of this feature was to allow an unbroken view to the country beyond, impossible in a park enclosed by walls. The security of the château could thus be ensured even where the wall was broken and even a formal garden could then relate directly to the countryside through the openings among the trees of the park.

On the southern slope of the garden of the Trianon, Louis XIV had orange trees planted out in the soil; these were protected, as at the Trianon de Porcelaine, by wooden constructions.

One of the advantages enjoyed by the gardens of Versailles over those modelled on them – as in the case of Tuscan compared to Roman gardens in the 16th century – was the quality of its works of art. As a magnificent museum of sculpture, the park has no rival; indeed, some of the great masterpieces have had to be stored and replaced by copies. Versailles certainly represents a peak in the art of French sculpture – an art which was one of the finest achievements of Classicism.

Versailles also included within its bounds an old medieval or Renaissance-style orchard, the fruit and vegetable garden managed by M. de la Quintinie. So in this respect the king and his court needed to look no further for their supplies.

The palace of Versailles is one of the two masterpieces of garden design (the other is the Villa d'Este) to exhibit an overall pattern of structural symbolism wholly associated with its owner. The symbolic metamorphoses and allegories to be found on the walls of the château and in the garden are at once simple and complex. They celebrate the cult of the Sun King, repeatedly emphasizing this royal emblem, yet their symbolism, unlike that applicable to his predecessors, no longer derives from Hercules, but from Apollo.

There is also a certain hermetic significance in a number of the allegories at Versailles. For instance, one figure behind Latona is scooping up water in a deep receptacle, while another is tearing up books. According to J.-P. Neraudau, the alchemist must purify base metal to obtain gold; he can then tear up his books once he has found the way to transform metals. At the heart of Versailles, then, is this expression of the spectacular triumph of the alchemist's quest. Elsewhere, Neraudau writes: 'It is here that the prophecy of Campanella seems to have been realized; Versailles is the Heliopolis dreamt of by the ancients; it is the City of the Sun, Heliaca. And if it is the triumph of gold (the gold of the sun) that we witness here, may we not also see the successful transmutation of metals through the agency of the king, himself the philosopher's stone?'

Versailles is an excellent illustration of the central argument of this book, that the garden is born from a sense of frustration. In France, the whole concept of royalty was permeated with this feeling. The nation had seen the most popular of her kings, Henri IV, assassinated. The monarchy of his son, Louis XIII, had been a retiring one, during which the queen mother turned against her son and the queen betrayed state secrets to a foreign power. The order and power of the state were only preserved by an opportunist minister equal to the enormous task before him, Cardinal Richelieu. Both for the bourgeoisie and the great families, the minority of the long-awaited Dauphin, the future Louis XIV, was a period of unprecedented struggle for power. Only with great difficulty was civil order maintained, thanks to a skilful adventurer whose reward was to be reviled on all sides. Once Louis XIII was dead, the royal ideal came to reside in the child who was to become Louis XIV, a ruler of genius who raised the monarchy to such heights that it was possible once again to talk of 'divine right'. And it was from this revival of royalty that Versailles derived its grandeur. The shadow cast by Louis XIV maintained the idea of divine right into the following century, but there it was vested in monarchs who were no longer obliged to display it in public, but preferred to withdraw into their private lives. The decline of the monarchy, then, was hardly a surprise, but it turned Versailles into an immense theatre, forever abandoned by its actors.

Yet Louis was responsible for what was perhaps an even greater architectural and landscaping triumph than Versailles: Marly. Versailles underwent so many modifications in the making of its complex design that total unity there proved elusive. Marly, on the other hand, was a unified, concrete expression by Mansart of the ideal of monarchy, the like of which had not been seen since the time of the Romans, the Babylonians, the Medes and the Persians. In any case, Louis was far more deserving of his royal title than Darius or Xerxes, whose immense armies had retreated when faced with a few resolute adversaries. In everything he undertook he was worthy of his title. But it was in the garden of Versailles – that universe of marble, bronze, gold, greenery, sky and water – that he achieved the highest expression of his royal ideals and one that every minor princeling in Europe yearned to imitate. Every garden is a reflection of human nostalgia for the promised land and, in the case of Versailles and its grandeur, this was evident in the wish of Louis XIV and Le Nôtre to restore the lost notion of the royal ideal to the collective consciousness. Yet the question of unity was never satisfactorily

The park of Saint-Cloud: the Great Cascade in the 18th century, from a painting in the Museum of Montreal.

resolved, even by the many modifications which were carried out from 1661, when the garden was begun, to the end of the reign; these entailed either rearrangements of the interior decoration or the creation of new *bosquets* at the expense of the forest. The various attempts – all unsuccessful – made to link the palace to the park in a harmonious whole included the positioning of the mirrors in the Galerie des Glaces, which in the event gave only an imperfect reflection of the view directly over the terrace, and the introduction of the passage through the ground floor of the central pavilion.

The garden at Marly (1679) was planned in relation to the position occupied by the Pavillon de Soleil (the façade incorporated an image of the sun) which was based on the design of Palladio's Villa Rotonda in Vicenza and is the only example of the influence of that architect in France. Stretching away from the house on either side of an arrangement of basins and parterres were twelve pavilions destined for the use of the king's guests. These were linked by pergolas of jasmine or honeysuckle and each bore one of the signs of the Zodiac and the name of one of the great gods. The pavilions were divided into two series of six on either side of the garden, one for the lords and one for the ladies.

The decoration of Marly was especially rich (at one point there were even frescoes on the outside walls) and really more Baroque than Classical in spirit. The central motif of the garden was a great cascade in the form of a water staircase, located in front of the château; this water proceeded to feed, via a number of different levels, several basins and fountains, until it reached, at the end of the garden, a triangular stretch of water known as 'the Trough' which had been completed in 1698.

The Sun King's successor had very little feeling for this retreat, and disfigured the garden by turning the watercourse into a lawn. Marly was also robbed of its statues which were sent to other houses, including Versailles. Two equestrian groups, *La Renommée* and *Mercure*, ordered in 1699 from Coysevox and which provided a finishing touch to the garden near the Trough, were removed in 1719 to decorate the terrace at the Tuileries. Their pedestals remained vacant until Louis XV ordered replacements in 1739 from Guillaume Coustou; these were the splendid *Deux Chevaux échappés retenus par des palefreniers nus* (of which one was a black). During the Revolution, which saw the destruction of Marly, the two groups were taken to adorn the entrance to the Champs

Elysées in 1795, in which position they remained famous as the *Chevaux de Marly*.

The destruction of Marly is a cause for permanent regret, fuelled all the more by the many documents still in existence relating to the château, most of which are in Stockholm.

In 1704, near Mainz, the Prince Palatine Lothar-Franz von Schönborn commissioned a replica of Marly, though reduced to six pavilions, from Maximilien von Welsch and his head gardener Dietmann. He called the house La Favorite and it also came to be known as the Petit Marly. It was destroyed in 1793 by French troops.

Other châteaux and gardens were subsequently commissioned under the influence of Versailles, to be built for members of the royal family or ministers by Le Nôtre: Saint-Cloud for the king's brother, Sceaux for Colbert, and Louvois for the minister of the same name, who was also responsible for the remodelling of Meudon, where Le Nôtre had to base his design on existing buildings and landscaping.

In 1665, the Duc d'Orléans, brother of the king, asked Le Nôtre to improve a garden already laid out on the hilly land of the château built by the Condé at Saint-Cloud. The centrepiece of the duke's garden was the Grandes Cascades; ranged over nine levels on the side of the hill, they overlooked the Seine and constituted one element of Italian design which Versailles could not rival.

Colbert, who had purchased the barony of Sceaux in 1670, naturally asked Le Nôtre to design the garden. The flat terrain lent itself easily to a classic combination of parterres and *bosquets*. The cascades were even more elaborate than those of Saint-Cloud. Of this park, designed to reflect the prestige of the minister, nothing now remains except the grand canal and seemingly endless lawns, at the end of which is the graceful building known as the Pavillon de l'Aurore. The name signifies Colbert's intention that his park should everywhere be open to the sun. The cupola, painted by Le Brun, shows Aurora led by Cupid along the path of the Zodiac, while the Seasons, too, can be seen participating in the universal joy which precedes the sunrise. The Orangery, which is fortunately still standing, was built by Mansart to a model which has lasted to the present (see, for example, the Jardin de Bagatelle in Paris), with high curved bays and walls with sharp projections at intervals. Our only view of the original cascade, said to have been more impressive than the one at Saint-Cloud, is in engravings.

The garden of the château at Chantilly was considered the most beautiful in France after that of Versailles. Any important figure or

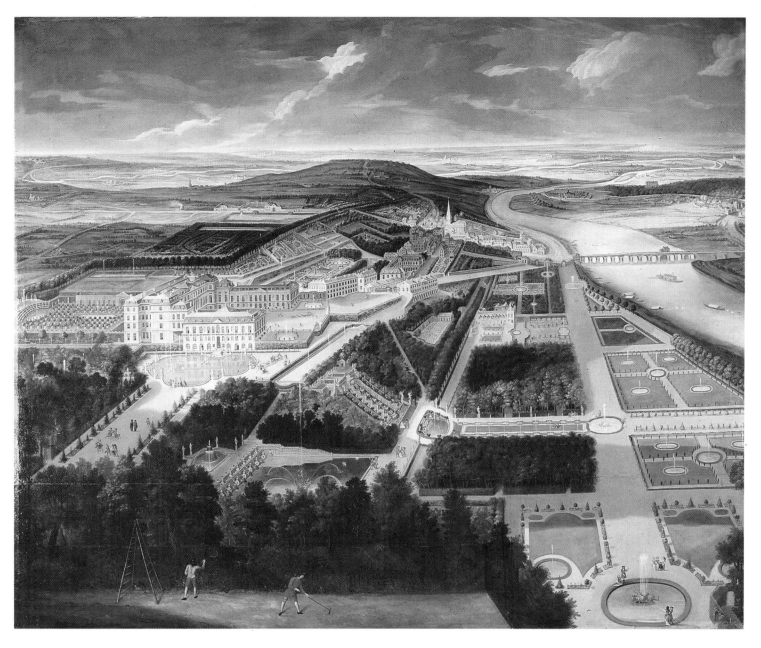

*V*iew of the park of Saint-Cloud, from a painting by Etienne Allegrain. Musée National du château de Versailles et de Trianon.

*T*he cascade in the park of Sceaux at the end of the 18th century, watercolour by Meunier. Musée des Arts Décoratifs, Paris.

PARC du CHATEAU de CHANTILLY — Les Trois Allées

*P*ark of the château of Chantilly: the hedges at the separation of the three allées, from a photograph taken at the beginning of the 20th century.

foreign monarch visiting the country was bound to be taken to see it. The Grand Condé, second prince of the blood, was the most culpable of the leaders of the Fronde and, when a clause of the Peace of the Pyrenees (1659) had restored his titles and privileges, the king advised him to 'rest' at Chantilly. However, it was not until eleven years had elapsed that the king actually went to visit him there, in 1671; this occasion was marked by great festivities and the serving of 1,500 meals a day. But a shadow was cast over the celebrations by the suicide of the prince's *mâitre d'hôtel*, the renowned Vatel, whom Condé had taken from Fouquet.

Condé's wish to preserve the buildings put up by the Connétable de Montmorency – a small château retained in its original form and a larger one brought up to date by Mansart – led Le Nôtre to adopt a highly individual plan for the gardens. Assisted by his nephew Desgots and the architect Gitard, he laid them out fanwise around the central point of the château. The gardens of Chantilly derived much of their beauty from the abundance of its waterworks which were so famous that Bossuet recalled, in the funeral orations for Condé, the victor of Rocroi, that 'they stopped neither day nor night'. These marvels were the work of a Dutch hydraulics engineer, M. de Manse, who diverted a spring and a river (La Nonette) and managed to produce all manner of varied effects despite the relatively low pressure of the water.

The esplanade is reached by a magnificent formal staircase which leads to the long terrace supported on a series of arches; here are a number of grottoes similar to those at Vaux-le-Vicomte. This vantage point provides a view over a vast stretch of water, on either side of which are arranged a dozen bright fountains divided by grassy areas. This watery expanse is set at right angles to the immense canal, 80 m wide and 2 km in length, which runs along the east-west axis of the garden.

Seen from the present château, built by the Duc d'Aumale at the end of the 19th century, the view of this stretch of water is superb, since this vantage point allows the observer to look down on it and across it at the same time, thus encompassing the greatest possible surface. When a few white clouds against the blue sky are reflected in the water, the effect is quite stunning, reminiscent perhaps of the gardens of Kashmir.

In a wooded area to the north-west of the garden was developed the Parc de Sylvie; its features included rooms or closets of greenery, various forms of games and a labyrinth. On the west, close to the château but separated from it by a wider stretch of the moat, are

beautiful *broderie* parterres framed by the wings of Mansart's Orangery. Still further to the west is a curious succession of gardens which are a mixture of floral parterres, orchards, vegetable beds, fountains and two cascades, one large and one small. The larger one was a water theatre as big and impressive as that at Saint-Cloud.

Constant additions were made to Chantilly by the Bourbons during the 18th century; it was also one of Le Nôtre's own favourites among all his designs. In his *Tableau de Paris*, Sébastien Mercier described it as 'the most beautiful marriage ever made between Art and Nature. Rarely have they been in such agreement.' Many would agree that these gardens are among the most beautiful ever designed.

Laden with honours, André Le Nôtre died in September 1700 at the age of 87 in his house in the Tuileries, which he had filled with paintings, *objets d'art* and silver. He had ceased to accept any further commissions in 1693, in preparation for death. He had been on very close terms with the king, who often allowed his artists such familiarity, while keeping the distance prescribed by etiquette from the notables of the realm, his dukes and ministers. Indeed, it was in the company of men whose genius and talent he respected and who gave concrete form to his dreams that the king's true humanity emerged. Le Nôtre left behind him a considerable body of work, of which we have only been able to study three examples in detail. But before the century had come to an end his achievement was already beginning to have an influence abroad.

In 1679 Le Nôtre had travelled to Italy to carry out an examination of the equestrian statue which Louis had commissioned from Bernini. He had little time for the Italian gardens, although he may have been consulted

View of the grand canal and the water parterre of the château of Chantilly, from a 17th-century painting in the Musée Condé at Chantilly.

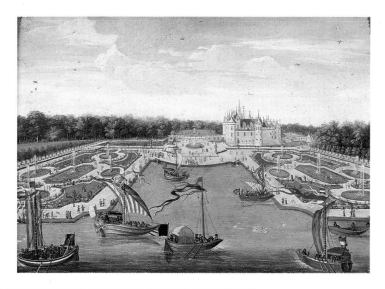

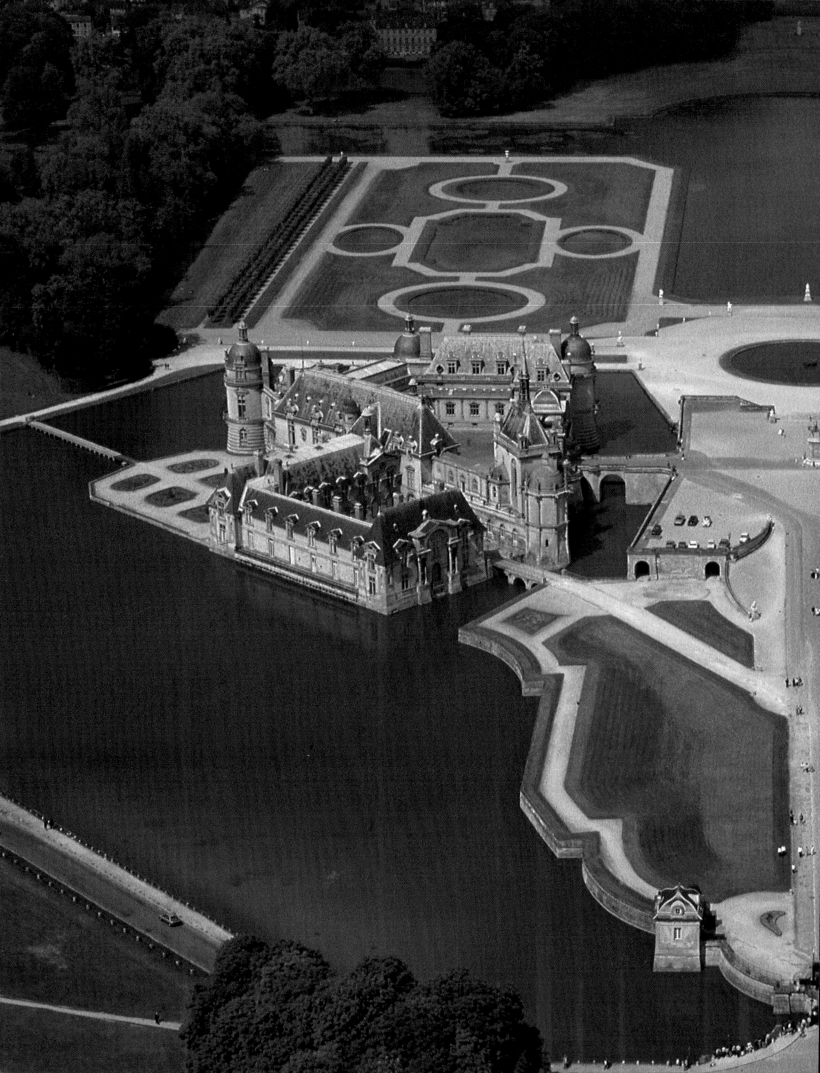

fashion eventually reached the Midi where Le Nôtre drew up plans for a garden with follies at Castries near Montpellier. In 1730 a superb water garden was started in Nîmes, planned around an ancient temple, La Source, and the remains of the Roman baths. The whole site was dominated by a wooded hill crowned with an antique tower, thus evoking the continuity of the ancient and the modern. The town of Montpellier, not to be left behind, commissioned the Promenade de Peyrou to accommodate a statue of Louis XIV in 1718 and a water château: a fine staircase led up to a hexagonal temple in pure Classical style to which water was brought, in true antique fashion, by an aqueduct.

In the last decades of the century many writers advanced theories on the art of the garden. In one of the most paradoxical of such statements, Dézallier d'Argenville (author of *Théorie et Pratique du jardinage*, published in 1709 and subsequently revised up to 1747) claimed that Le Nôtre had 'handed over Art to Nature'; he found that the gardens of Saint-Cloud, Chantilly and Sceaux were very 'natural' in style. The French style of garden design undoubtedly underwent some simplification during the 18th century; Dézallier, for instance, was especially critical of high hedges formed from clipped trees, over-decorated fountains, loggias, columns and trelliswork, in fact of anything which smacked of artifice. Extravagant parterres of *broderie* were considered unacceptable in favour of simple English-style lawns. These might be concave in shape, an effect known as *en boulingrin*, a word derived from the English 'bowling green'. The parterre could also be centred on a floral dome form known as a *corbeille*, which became especially popular in the 19th century.

The division of Germany into principalities tended to favour the development of the French-style garden there. Princes and princelings, influenced by the French palaces and their settings, proceeded to demolish their old houses and hunting lodges to conform to the new style. Many French artists were invited to Germany, an emigration facilitated by the revocation of the Edict of Nantes (1695), which caused many Calvinists to leave the country. A great number of these Huguenots found a warm welcome on the other side of the Rhine.

Under the Elector Ernest-Augustus, the Hanoverian court was profoundly influenced by French culture; Molière, Corneille and Lully all worked for him. When he decided to redesign the gardens of his summer residence (Herrenhausen), he turned to a French gardener from the court of Celle, Henri Perronet,

on the planning of the royal garden in Turin. It is hard to tell whether he ever visited England, although it is certain that Charles II, restored to the throne, asked Louis XIV in 1662 to allow Le Nôtre to come and work for him. Louis agreed to the request but whether the architect complied or not remains a mystery. There are many indications that he obliged with plans and advice, but none that he actually went there. However, he did send his nephew Claude Desgots, who had worked at Chantilly, recommending him to the Duke of Portland in a letter written on 21 June 1698, two years before his death.

Until the final third of the 18th century, every new garden in France was planned according to the new style. At Ménars and at Champs, the gardens (now restored) created for La Pompadour, the favourite of Louis XV, were in the spirit of Le Nôtre's creations. In this, the nobles imitated the king who was continually introducing modifications to his gardens at Versailles. The process of imitation then spread to the lesser gentry and the

*P*anoramic view
of the park of La
Favorite, designed for
the Prince Elector of
Mainz by
Maximilien von
Welsch. Engraving
by J.A. Corvinus
from a drawing by
Salomon Kleiner,
1726. Marburg
Klassischer
Staadtarchiv.

who came to Hanover in 1672. Another Frenchman, Michel Charbonnier, brought from Osnabruck, succeeded Perronet in 1682 and gave the garden its present form: French *broderies*, marked out in a check pattern and ending in a semi-circle, then a large wooded section divided into *bosquets* by paths leading out from a central round pool. Between 1689 and 1693 he built a garden theatre in the Italian manner.

One of the most distant imitations of the French-style garden was at the castle of Schlobitten, built by the Burgrave von Dohna at the end of the 17th century, which bears certain resemblances to Vaux-le-Vicomte.

The Calvinist landgravate of Hesse-Kassel was a refuge for Walloon or French nonconformists well before the revocation of the Edict of Nantes. Its wealth was so great during the long reign of Karl (1677–1730) that a special neighbourhood was built for the Huguenot refugees. The architect for this project was Paul de Ry, himself a Huguenot, and the head of a whole dynasty of architects responsible for many buildings in the landgravate.

The layout of the garden of Karlsaue, created between 1694 and 1729 by a number of gardeners, including two Frenchmen, Elias Bourguignon and J. de Marne, is in the French style, while the bathing pavilion, known as the Marble Bath, was also the work of a French architect, Pierre Etienne Monnot, who had come from Rome. Executed between 1721 and 1728, this is one of the finest sculptural groups in Germany.

In 1715, Lothar-Franz von Schönborn commissioned a garden to be laid out at the foot of the old castle of Gaibach, almost certainly the work of Maximilien von Welsch, it was in the French style and included a fine orangery. Von Welsch was also the designer of the imitation of Marly commissioned by the same prince at La Favorite, mentioned above. The Palais de Soleil was replaced by an orangery and the six pavilions were positioned in two oblique lines.

We have no certain proof that the garden at the castle of Gross-Sedlitz near Dresden, where J.-S. Bach liked to walk when he visited the Saxon capital, was the work of the Frenchman Zacharie Longuelune. But since this artist, whose work was much admired by Auguste le Fort, was so involved with the office of public buildings in Dresden, there is every likelihood that this was the case. The design of the garden was exceptionally original in its very narrow central section, flanked by two U-shaped parterres; the various levels of the garden were enlivened by numerous statues.

*P*lan of the garden
of Karlsaue, pen
and wash drawing on
canvas.

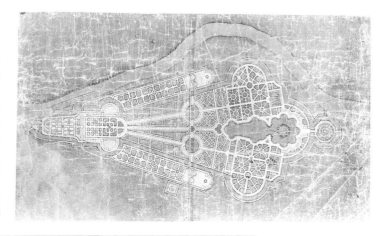

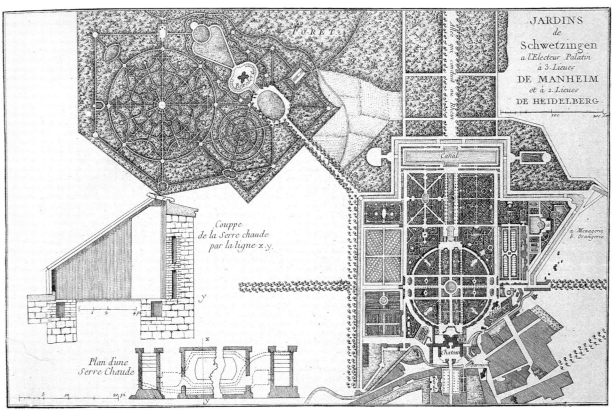

P lan of the garden and castle of Schwetzingen by Le Rouge, Le Jardin anglo-chinois à la mode, 1776–89. Bibliothèque Nationale, Paris.

No building in Germany reflected Versailles more faithfully than the castle of Lietzenburg, which became known as Charlottenburg in 1705 on the death of Charlotte, the philosopher queen for whom it had been built. The commission to enlarge the existing pavilion was given to Eosander von Göthe who had visited Versailles in 1700. The long façade with its terraces evokes the side of Versailles which looks over the park; another similarity is that the castle had to be built in several stages and was only finished by Frederick II. An engraving of 1717 after a drawing by Eosander von Göthe shows a grandiose vision of the gardens, beginning with parterres on either side of a courtyard, which was never actually completed.

Behind the castle and to the left of the main axis of the garden were planned other parterres, since the garden could not be developed on the right because of the Spree. When the garden was finally completed it was promptly spoiled by Frederick-William II, who modified it according to the English style.

Max-Emmanuel III, ruler in Munich from 1679 to 1723, brought numerous French artisans to the city to form the nucleus of a craft guild, just as Louis XIV had done at the Gobelins. The most important of these was Dominique Girard, who was master of the fountains and inspector of the court gardens. He was also the designer of the gardens of Nymphenburg, which the Elector described in a letter to the Countess of Arco in 1715 as worthy 'of being placed in the middle of France'. Although they have been much transformed, they do contain a jewel in the Pavilion of Amalienburg, the work of the Belgian Cuvilliés, who also worked in Paris; the interior is a masterpiece of German Rococo. The park which adjoined the castle of Schleisseim, also designed by Dominique Girard but built by the Italian Zucalli, was very Classical in style; it included an *allée* with 34 water jets and a cascade. This garden was also extensively modified, but there still remains the grand *allée* which leads from the castle to that of Lustheim.

On several occasions, Dominique Girard was authorized by the Elector to spend time in Vienna (1717, 1719, 1722), where he worked for Prince Eugène of Savoy on the garden which linked the lower and upper Belvederes.

The finest Classical garden in Germany is that of Schwetzingen, the work of the Frenchman Nicolas de Pigage, architect of the Elector Palatine Charles-Théodore. His original plan for the house was quite magnificent and entailed extending the low wings of the old electoral hunting lodge in quarter circles to form one complete circle. In this he laid out the parterres, groves and fountains of the first part of the garden; the parallel *allées* of the circle were marked out in two groups of three to form a Greek cross, at the centre of which was the great Fountain of Arion; the whole composition was finished off by another fountain in the form of two stags. The main axis of the garden then ran through a *tapis vert* bordered by two paths and framed by four parterres to a transverse canal, beyond which were two statues representing the Rhine and the Danube. The view to the west stretches to the Rhine.

T he garden of Schwetzingen: one of the two fountains with figures of stags, by P.A. von Vertschaffelt, 1767.

*P*eterhof: the
*Fountain of
Samson and the
water theatre.*

The prestige of the gardens of Louis XIV had reached the ears of Peter the Great long before he visited Versailles in 1716. The designs and plans of the Sun King's residences had certainly been sent to him, as is evidenced by the names of Monplaisir, Marli, Monbijou and L'Ermitage which he gave to his pleasure villas on the coast of the Gulf of Finland, close to the landing stage he used for sailing to the port of Kronstadt. After his visit to France in 1716 he brought back with him J.B.A. Leblond, who became his superintendent of buildings. He had already commissioned the building of a house at Peterhof in 1715, from which a canal was to be dug to the sea. The palace was built by Leblond but was enlarged and entirely refurbished for the Tsarina Elizabeth by Rastrelli. The garden was constantly modified and new features added right up to the time of Tsar Nicholas I. The Peterhof gardens were destroyed by the Nazis during World War Two but have now been reconstructed to constitute once again one of the most remarkable arrangements of fountains in the whole of Europe.

The residence and its garden are positioned on the edge of a plateau with a commanding view over the Gulf of Finland. Above the house is the upper garden consisting of a conventional arrangement of parterres; the centrepiece of the arrangement is a Fountain of Neptune embellished with numerous bronze figures,which has a rather curious history. It was originally executed for the town of Nuremburg in 1660 by Richter and Schneider; but because it was impossible to supply sufficient water it was never assembled, and the sections were kept in a municipal repository until 1799, when they were acquired by Tsar Paul I.

A narrow terrace gives on to the lower garden where the central axis leads towards the sea through a remarkable display of fountains. Water spurts from the five arches of a grotto framed by two cascades with seven levels. These are lined with statues which emit further jets of water, eventually falling into one central cascade above a round pool, where all the other water collects. In the centre of the pool is the Fountain of Samson surrounded by a water spray; the huge gilded statue depicts the biblical hero pulling apart the jaws of a lion. The figure of Samson was chosen in preference to that of Hercules to commemorate the battle of Poltava, which signalled the end of Swedish power and which occurred on St Samson's day. The pool is a true water spectacular, with jets shooting in all directions, its high point the 20 m spout issuing from the figure of Samson itself. The water from the pool feeds directly into the

*P*eterhof: the
*Fountain of
Samson and the
canal.*

300 m canal which leads to a landing stage. This canal is lined with 22 fountains of the 'candle' type, the jets of which formerly rose 6 m into the air; more water spurts from the muzzles of lions who project from the edges of the canal. The problem with this display of water features is that it can only be seen properly from the first floor of the house; even the terrace affords only the sight of an immense wall of water. Paul I then had two side staircases built to permit a better view of this marvellous spectacle; their rails were decorated with copies of the most famous remains of ancient Rome. Towards the Gulf the lower garden opens out to include the pleasure pavilions of Monplaisir, near the shore, Marli, L'Ermitage and L'Orangerie. Fountains are located everywhere, in ever more ingenious arrangements, including the Pyramid Foun-

tain, its spray surrounding the figures of Adam and Eve, and the great cascade known as the Mountain of the Dragon. The Mountain of Gold at Marli is so called because the steps are covered in copper as well as being lined with statues. The jets from the Fountain of the Bell set a number of glass balls tinkling. There are also Roman fountains, French fountains and the Lion Fountain, from which the water flows via the stylobate of an Ionic peristyle.

Orianenbaum, built to the designs of Menchnikov and also located on the Gulf of Finland, had a typically French garden. This house was given the German name for orange-tree by the favourite of Peter the Great. In a country which was subjected to the rigours of winter for eight months of the year, nothing was considered to be more sophisticated and refined than to cultivate the

fruit of the Hesperides, yet another expression, perhaps, of the desire in northern Europe to model itself on the gardens of the Mediterranean.

In Sweden, the influence of Le Nôtre was introduced by the architect Nicodème Tessin (1654–1718). He visited Versailles and the royal châteaux in the company of Le Nôtre, whom he also consulted about the gardens of Drottningholm during their construction. The bronzes in these gardens had been originally commissioned from Adriaen de Vries by Wallenstein for his own palace and were part of the booty from Prague obtained in October 1648 by Königsmarck after the Treaty of Westphalia and sent by him to Queen Christina of Sweden, already a keen collector.

The park of the castle of Schönbrunn is directly descended from Le Nôtre: it was designed by L.F. de Nesle, otherwise known as Gervais, a pupil of Desgots (the nephew of Le Nôtre). He was from Lorraine and had remained in the service of the future emperor Francis, the husband of Maria Theresa, first in Tuscany and then in Austria. The various elements of the garden are arranged around a central axis in the French style, although the problems of the site would have been better solved by a garden in the Italian style (by then completely out of fashion), since the ground slopes steeply upward some distance from the castle. The parterres are arranged around a vast fountain (by J.C.W. Bayer) dedicated to Neptune ; the central statue of the sea god dominates symmetrically arranged groups of figures. The place of honour in this garden was bound to be taken by water, since the estate derives its name from that of a spring.

The castle of Schönbrunn: the triumphal arch by Hohenberg and the Fountain of Neptune, by J.C.W. Bayer.

The gaping expanse of the horizon was masked by Hohenburg with a kind of open-arched triumphal monument, surmounted by the imperial eagle and known as the Gloriette; its image appears mirrored in a pool of water.

It needed the shock of the French Revolution to put an end to the era of the Classical garden which had, by then, spread its influence throughout Europe. In 1763, Prince Miklos Esterhazy of Hungary began to extend his castle of Süttor (now known as Fentöd), which he then named Esterhaza. He added a magnificent garden in the French style; during its construction he visited Versailles twice, in 1764 and 1767. His life at the castle must have been one of considerable ostentation, what with his court and, as master of music, Joseph Haydn who was responsible for arranging the castle festivities as well as writing operas. The guests of Prince Miklos were so dazzled by what they saw that Cardinal de Rohan, the French ambassador in Vienna, remarked that he had rediscovered Versailles at Esterhaza. Years later, Goethe was to recall with some emotion the festivities he had witnessed there.

The house itself is arranged around a courtyard; the first, semi-circular part is limited to one storey and houses the stables. Two wings, now demolished, were built at right angles to the main body of the house, one to serve as an orangery and the other as a gallery for the famous collection of paintings begun by Miklos's father.

By the façade of the house which overlooked the park was a water staircase framed by two curving flights of steps leading to a terrace. From there, the visitor saw three *allées* branching out and extending into the far distance. The central one led to a pheasantry in the form of a harmoniously designed exedra; beyond it was Monbijou, the hunting box. The *allée* on the left led to a hexagonal enclosure, the reserve of wild boar. It needed a full hour and a half on horseback to cover the whole park.

Amid the many basins, statues and fountains, the visitor might also have come across an opera house, a puppet theatre, a Chinese pavilion, a hermitage, complete with a live hermit, and temples of Venus, Diana, Fortune and the Sun. None of these marvels, however, survived the reign of Miklos. He died in 1790 and Antal, his son, abandoned Esterhaza for Kismarton, now Eisenstadt, in Austria. There he had the castle reconstructed and added a garden in the English style. The furniture, statues, urns and many of the other ornaments of Esterhaza found their way to Kismarton, while the deserted garden of the old house reverted to nature. This process was completed by revolutions and wars but, happily, the estate was never broken up and it eventually became a school for horticulture and a centre for botanical research. What remained of the original decor of the house began to be restored in 1957. The remaking of the park forms part of an overall plan for the restoration of the historic gardens of Hungary under a landscape architect in the Service of Historical Monuments.

The existence of contemporary plans and a detailed description from 1784, the time of its greatest splendour, should enable the restorers to rediscover some of the garden's original magnificence. At the height of its luxury it was as beautiful as Schwetzingen as well as being on a grander scale.

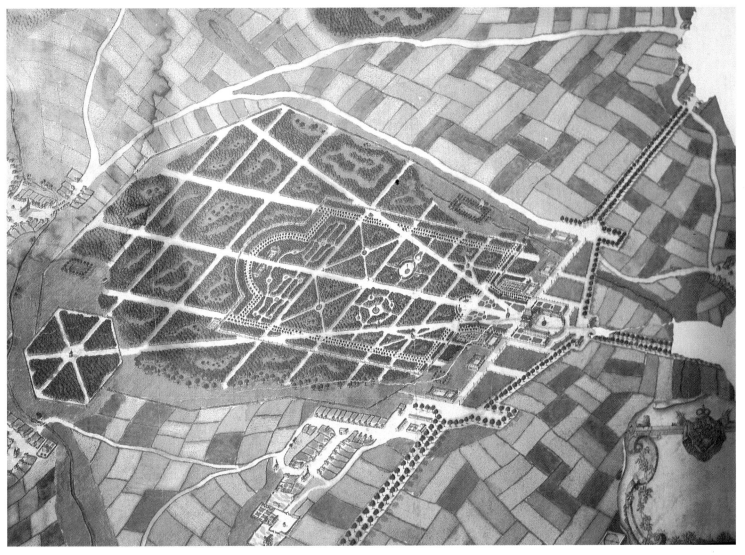

*P*anoramic plan of the castle of Esterhaza, 18th-century watercolour. Hungarian Historical Monuments Service, Budapest.

THE BAROQUE GARDEN

It is sometimes tempting to believe that there are only three important types of garden in the West in modern times: the Mannerist (Italian), the Classical (French) and the Landscape (English). But another important form does exist, the Baroque, though in garden design the style is hard to categorize. It embraces many different types of features, does not lend itself easily to interpretation and is truly international. In the Italian garden it was the natural outcome of the Mannerist style, as it was in the other arts.

We can, however, note some of the distinguishing characteristics of the Baroque garden: the grandiose scale of its design, the taste for shock effects, expressed in a multiplicity of other overblown and monstrous forms, and an exaggerated love for rocaille and for ornamental expressions of power and strength.

The gardens of Italy are one of the country's relatively unknown treasures. Although many are open to the public for several hours a week during the summer months, very few of them are much visited. In conjunction they form a remarkable part of the national heritage, carefully maintained by their owners who are often descendants of the families who created them and have either received them by direct inheritance or have repurchased them for the family. Foreigners, too, especially Americans, have been busy acquiring villas in Italy and restoring them. In the gardens of such houses it is not unusual to see carefully clipped hedges 10 m in height, magnificent topiary and all the original features functioning perfectly.

The Villa Aldobrandini at Frascati, the Tusculum of the Romans, is a very good example of the transition from the Mannerist to the Baroque garden. The siting of the villa at Frascati is of particular historical interest, for it was there that the ancient Romans came to escape the pressures of the city; during the second half of the 16th century, their successors, the high society of Renaissance Rome, also began to retread the steps of their ancestors in search of country air. In the 16th and 17th centuries the hill of Frascati became covered with villas. During the Second World War, these suffered from heavy bombing because of the presence of the Allied Headquarters in the area; however, the Villa Aldobrandini was one of the least affected and has now been restored to its original splendour by Prince Clemente Aldobrandini with the help of the architect Clemente Busiri-Vici.

Cardinal Pietro Aldobrandini (d.1617), the nephew of Pope Clement VIII, had been responsible for the inclusion of Ferrara in the Papal States. As a gift, he received from the church the Villa Belvedere, where he was to build a new and truly magnificent villa during the first two decades of the 17th century. The first stage dates from 1601 and was carried out by Giacomo della Porta, who simply enlarged the old house. A much more extensive programme of building was begun in 1602 under Carlo Maderno, assisted by his uncle, Giovanni Fontana, in the hydraulic work. The house itself is a very good example of that period of austerity which succeeded the extravagances of Mannerism at the end of the 16th century. The garden is in the Italian

The Villa Aldobrandini at Frascati: the Grotto of Polyphemus, sculpture by Ippolito Busti, 1605; Polyphemus, by Jacques Sarrazin, 1621.

The Villa Garzoni at Collodi: end of the main vista, with the sculptural group of Fame and the statues of Florence and Lucca.

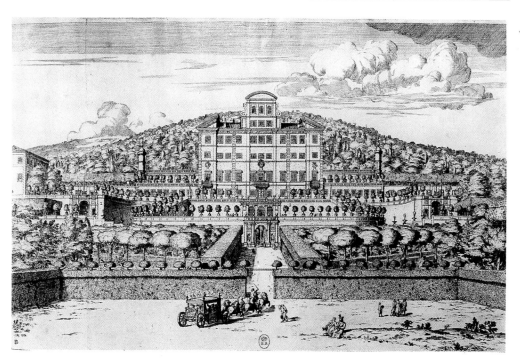

The Villa Aldobrandini at Frascati: view of the upper garden with the central part of the nymphaeum. Grotto with the statue of Atlas by Jacques Sarrazin, 1621.

style, sloping but, unlike that of the Villa d'Este, opening out as it rises up the hill. The high walls of the house form a screen in front of the garden. The curved drives leading to the house, which rise through two levels, run on either side of a kind of hippodrome, a reminder of the villas of the Romans. The house has only two levels at the rear from which to contemplate the garden, and the effect of surprise is total. Directly before the observer is a façade, 108 m wide, in the centre of which is a nymphaeum in exedra form. The Baroque spirit of this feature is evident in the juxtaposition of a refined Classical style (Ionic order in marble of three colours) and the rustic manner, expressed in the herms of satyrs or sirens, occasionally with their bifid tails twisted together. This magnificent opening feature to the garden also boasts five grottoes. The most important one, the central, is the work of the French architect Sarrazin and contains a colossal figure of Atlas holding up a graduated celestial globe, emblem of the Aldobrandini. The Atlas was formerly accompanied by a figure of Hercules who, as we know, once relieved the giant of his burden. The representation of the Hesperides has also disappeared, but the head of the fallen giant Enceladus can still be seen at the edge of the fountain. On either side are grottoes full of rock-work; in one is the figure of Polyphemus playing the pipes and in the other is a Centaur playing the horn, both works by Ippolito Busti.

Behind the façade are a chamber to Apollo, several cool rooms and a chapel dedicated to Saint Sebastian. The ceiling of the Apollo room is decorated with a ravishing pergola of

The Villa Aldobrandini at Frascati, from the side of the main entrance, engraving by D. Barrière Maxiliensis, 1647. Bibliothèque Nationale, Paris.

The Villa Albani (or Torlonia) in Rome: the kaffeehaus and parterre, by Carlo Marchioni.

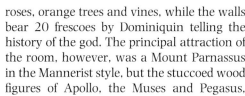

roses, orange trees and vines, while the walls bear 20 frescoes by Dominiquin telling the history of the god. The principal attraction of the room, however, was a Mount Parnassus in the Mannerist style, but the stuccoed wood figures of Apollo, the Muses and Pegasus, which decorated it, have not survived.

The water for the garden was formerly brought a considerable distance by aqueduct to arrive as a torrent in the open air via a water theatre with a cascade flanked by two huge spiral pillars, before continuing its course towards the great nymphaeum by means of another high cascade in the rustic style. This aqueduct no longer exists and the current now seems to flow naturally out of the hill amidst rocks and vegetation, before following a canal to the water staircase between two columns covered with mosaic work; the whole watercourse is lined with tall hedges of clipped box. A spiral gutter on each column leads some of the water up to the tops of the columns from which it spurts in a pair of jets. A number of other fountains formerly in the garden have since disappeared.

Atlas, Hercules and a *mascherone* similar to the one of Bomarzo symbolize brute force, a suitable theme for a mountain villa. The impression is of mother earth herself opening to allow her life-giving fluid, water, to gush out. In contrast to this physical world is the realm of the spirit, expressed in the Apollo room. It has also been suggested that the figure of Atlas bearing the canopy of heaven was identified with Clement VIII as upholder of the church, while the figure of Hercules (now vanished) represented his nephew.

Even a cursory acquaintanceship with G.B. Falda's *I Giardini di Roma* shows us to what extent Rome was a garden city. The greatest gardens, laid out during the 17th century, were those of the Quirinal, the Villa Borghese, the Villa Ludovisi and the Villa Pamphili-Doria. Most of these gardens have been destroyed by the creation of modern Rome. The largest of them, that of the Villa Ludovisi, had all its traces erased when the Via Veneto neighbourhood was built on the site of the garden. One building remains of the villa, the Ludovisi casino, containing an allegorical painting of Aurora by Le Guerchin which can be interpreted as a symbolic rendering of time. The garden of the Villa Borghese was originally laid out in the 16th century and enlarged in the 17th, with work continuing right up to the 19th, and has many of its architectural features still intact; but even this has been crossed by several busy roads, completely destroying its attraction. Although it has been similarly cut into three parts, the Villa Pamphili-Doria on the Janiculum suf-

The Boboli Gardens, behind the Pitti Palace in Florence. In the foreground is the fountain by Ammanati and Tribolo. Behind is the amphitheatre laid out in the 17th century and modified in the 18th.

fered less and, indeed, enjoyed some final moments of grandeur under a wealthy Belgian patron, Ambassador van der Elst, before being purchased by the Italian state, when the garden was divided into smaller sections. This garden was laid out on level ground in the French style; the fine house, known as *Di Bel Respiro*, was built between 1644 and 1652 on the central axis of the garden with a vast *barco* to one side.

Dating from the end of the 16th century and also from the 17th, the collection of buildings which makes up the Villa of the Quirinal has remained intact. The garden, which has been substantially modified several times, is laid out to a rather monotonous geometrical plan – an English-style garden dating from the time of Gregory XVI (1831–46). During the pontificate of Benedict XIV (1740–8), a small eating place of the kind currently known in Rome as a *kaffeehaus* was constructed at the bottom of the main garden by Fuga.

We should note here a *trompe l'oeil* decoration painted by Francesco Nubale (*c.*1770) in the anteroom to the chapel of the Villa Chigi, representing a cave-hermitage in the middle of rocks inhabited by Franciscan friars. Meditation rooms of this kind can also be found in the Palazzo Chigi alle Quattro Fontane; in the Altieri and Colonna palaces; outside Rome, in the Villa Cetinale near Siena; and in the Villa Garzoni at Collodi near Pistoia. We have already encountered the hermitage as a garden feature at Gaillon; later, we shall see what form it takes in the hands of a margrave of Bayreuth.

We end this brief survey of Roman villas of the 17th and 18th centuries with a look at one which was a protest against the Baroque: the Villa Albani, better known by its association with the Prince Torlonia who bought it in 1804. The villa was built by Cardinal Alessandro Albani (1692–1779). A nephew of Clement XI, Albani was, along with Winckelmann who lived in his villa, the most respected authority in contemporary archaeology. The villa, designed by Carlo Marchioni, was finished in 1757 as part of a harmonious arrangement which also included a *kaffeehaus* in exedra form opposite the main house. The villa was planned as a setting for the cardinal's archaeological collections, which also spread to the garden. It was here, too, that Raphael Mengs painted his fresco of *Parnassus* to demonstrate Winckelmann's theories on allegory. The German archaeologist also advised the cardinal to have four antique temples built in the garden, of which one was to be a ruin. The garden was laid out in the French style between two buildings; following a strict geometrical plan, there are four

The Boboli Gardens in Florence: the Viottolone (main avenue) joining the two parts of the garden, lined with antique and modern statues.

The Boboli Gardens: detail of the Isolotto.

broderie parterres between the villa and the *kaffeehaus*, which still retain the same design shown in engravings of the first years of the garden.

The Tuscan gardens of the time tended to be more restrained in extent, as they had been during the preceding period. The countryside around Florence was covered with villas and their fine gardens, of which that of Gamberaia at Settignano is the best known.

However, Florence was eventually to see its ruling family build a garden which fully complemented the Pitti Palace in size. The palace itself had now been elevated to the status of principal residence and substantially extended during the 17th century. Along the main vista of the garden behind the palace, the hippodrome, which had been constructed in a natural hollow, as we can see from the painting by Utens, was now stripped of its plants. Instead, its sides were lined with stone tiers, behind which an arrangement of tabernacles and statues was added during the 17th century to create the effect of a real amphitheatre. The new work was carried out by the brothers Alfonso and Giulio Parigi, who continued to lay out the garden up the hill in the direction of Rome.

A mass of sea-horses, sirens and tritons cling to the rocks in the rocaille Fountain of Neptune. This fountain is positioned on the main axis of the garden from the amphi-

The Villa Garzoni, Collodi: the Italian garden.

The Villa Garzoni, Collodi: the French-style garden below the Italian garden.

theatre, while the furthest point of the vista is dominated by the statue of 'Abundance'. A wide *allée* (*viottolone*), lined with antique and modern statues, leads down to the south-west part of the garden and the *isolotto*. This is an oval basin measuring 70 x 40 m; its centre is occupied by an island on which is a statue of the Ocean by Giambologna, surrounded by the Nile, the Ganges and the Euphrates (symbolizing the three stages of life). A figure of Venus is situated on another small island in front of the *isolotto*.

Lacking any coherent overall plan, the Boboli Gardens underwent constant modifications, but the hill, which is their major drawback, has never been reshaped. Indeed, without the famous grotto, the gardens would hardly deserve their reputation.

The most beautiful garden in Tuscany adjoins one of the 60 villas which dot the countryside around Lucca – that built by Romano Garzoni at Collodi at the beginning of the 17th cen-

tury. The estate is some distance from the house, erected at the beginning of the century on the site of an old castle belonging to the family, and the garden divides neatly into two parts: a semi-circular lower garden with fountains and parterres and an upper garden in the Italian style. The architect of the garden has used the slope brilliantly, breaking it up into several different levels. The Classical garden below serves as a sort of prelude to the harmonious spectacle of the Italian garden with its three sets of matching pairs of staircases, leading to a theatrical group of statuary framed by tall hedges of clipped box. Trumpet in mouth, the statue of Fame looks down on those of Florence and Lucca and a pile of rocks over which flows the stream feeding the rest of the garden. At the level below the statues, a faun and his mate are seated in stone scrolls attached to pillars and turn towards the observer as if in invitation to admire the glories of two cities, rivals for so long, but now joined in common cause.

The Villa Borromeo (Isola Bella) on Lake Maggiore: the sculptural centrepiece of the upper garden.

Veduta a mezzo di dell'Isola-Bella sul Lago Maggiore di Sua Ecc^{za} il Signor Conte Carlo Borromeo Arese

Veue (du Coté du midi) de l'Isle belle sur le Lac Majeur de son Ecc^{ce} mons. le Comte Charles Borromeo Ares

Marcus Antonius Dal Re, delineavit et Sculp.

The garden also boasts an open-air theatre at the end of a transverse *allée* which leads to the house. This type of theatre began to make its appearance during the 17th century and by the 18th dramatic production had become a favourite diversion of aristocratic society, in which the master of the house and guests would sometimes take part. In the garden theatre at the Villa Marlia (formerly Orsetti), three terracotta statues grace the stage: Colombine, Harlequin and Pulcinella.

If the Baroque garden was often an exercise in scene setting, then this aspect of its development found its ultimate expression in the garden of the Villa Borromeo at Isola Bella on Lake Maggiore. It took some 50 years of colossal enterprise to transform a barren rock of mica-schist into an island of Cythera. First, it was necessary to create a stable island capable of supporting the villa and its garden, with all the additional soil that was required. This Herculean task was given to Angelo Crivelli in 1620 by Carlo Borromeo II and his son

Vitaliano VI, then later to Pietro Antonio Barca who was responsible for the works until 1671. Ten terraces, reaching a height of 32 m, were built above the lake. The residence, unfinished, is located towards the centre of the island; beyond it is a small fishing village. Facing the house is a huge and theatrical architectural assembly, consisting of buttresses, obelisks, rocaille, grottoes, herms and statues, including numerous winged figures, which forms the backdrop to a series of terraces. This construction is crowned by a unicorn which faces the house and, like Pegasus, seems about to take wing. The unicorn is in fact the emblem of the Borromeo family but, oddly, this fabulous creature and symbol of chastity is here mounted by a winged genie. As Princess Emmanuela Kretzulesko-Quaranta has pointed out, it is all reminiscent of the *Hypnerotomachia* and the quest for true love as understood by the Neoplatonists. Very probably the figures of the genie and the unicorn are an allusion to the love of Carlo III

The Villa Borromeo (Isola Bella) on Lake Maggiore: panoramic view engraved by Marcus Antonius Dal Re. Bibliothèque Nationale, Paris.

The Palace of Caserta; the rustic cascade and sculptural groups in marble, inspired by episodes in the myth of Diana.

for his wife Isabella, who was very beautiful and who gave her name to the island in the punning form of Isola Bella. As well as the unicorn, other symbols of purity in the garden include white birds, doves and peacocks.

The garden of the palace at Caserta was designed by Luigi Vanvitelli for Charles IV of Naples, under whom that state regained its autonomy. Despite the numerous features of the garden over its 3–km length, these often seem lost in its apparently boundless space. The many marble statues which play out the drama of *Venus dissuading Adonis from going to the hunt* and the tragedy of *Diana causing Actaeon to be devoured by his dogs* appear somehow lifeless. Neoclassical sculpture tended to see the human form in isolation, an attitude which made it difficult to evoke a sense of action, let alone the movement of figures in a group. The quality of movement in the sculptural groups at La Granja is much more expressive and more suited to its natural environment. The stiffness of the statues of Caserta is further accentuated by the contrast they form to the gigantic cascade which hurtles down the rocks above them, conveying the water from the mountain to the basins. There is certainly an imbalance between the various elements of the garden and the exaggerated form of some of these only indicates the essential decadence of the artistic impulse. The gardens of Caserta emphasize the futility of trying to prolong a particular style when all life has long since left it.

We have already seen how little the 16th-century Venetians cared for the art of the garden; the villas of Palladio tended simply to be built in the unembellished countryside. During the 17th and 18th centuries, however, far more attention was paid to the immediate environment of the house. In the case of the 18th-century Villa Levada at Piombino Dese, for instance, the arrangement of the various farm and residential buildings in a very simple garden (canals, lawns and avenues) is particularly harmonious. The villa and garden accord so well with the surrounding countryside that the passage from the one to the other seems utterly natural and totally satisfying to the spirit.

In an angle of one of the buildings is a charming orchestra of monkeys arranged on consoles. The monkey seems to have held a particular fascination for the Italian sculptors, although it does sometimes make an appearance in French interior decoration. Undoubtedly, however, statuary became increasingly common in the Venetian gardens of the 17th century. Its subject-matter was very varied: innumerable gods, seasons, and the inevitable nymphs, although these were often included without any precise regard for their symbolic significance. Other types of statue were inspired by the theatre, such as the Italian *commedia* and the plays of Goldoni: subservient peasants doffing their hats, servants at the entrance to the villa doing likewise, dwarfs, Turks, Chinamen, negroes, mous-

tached soldiers garbed in a more or less oriental style, pandours and Hungarian hussars. There were Brandenburgers, riflemen and pipe-smoking Germans – a picturesque crowd of theatrical characters mingling with the gods, whose symbolic significance no longer appeared to be understood.

All these developments made the garden a much friendlier place. The enclosed garden which surrounds the Villa Emo Capodilista at Montecchia di Selvazzano is full of groups of young peasant lads paying gallant attention to the peasant girls by bringing them flowers and the fruits of the hunt – rabbits and roe-deer. We are now truly in the 18th century, the era of Rousseau, when only in the simple souls of the countryfolk can true love be found. The interior decoration of this villa is notable for its extravagance, being entirely in trompe-l'oeil. Each morning the master of the house would awaken to the garden painted on the walls of his bedroom, windows open, blinds lowered and the eternal sun outside. Yet the ambiguities here go beyond mere artifice to take in an urge to escape – almost to flee – the home.

During the 16th and 17th centuries, the owners of Venetian villas were able to call on a number of remarkable painters well versed in the rendering of secular subjects; these included Veronese, Zelotti and Tiepolo. The themes of their work were usually drawn from Classical antiquity, but were often imbued with a moralizing quality which attested to the strength of the Christian ideal, even when it had to be dressed up in pagan clothes.

The new developments in the Venetian villas were certainly conducive to a pleasant life, but they hardly expressed a strong crea-

tive impulse. In this regard, however, two villas do stand out from the rest: the Villa Barbarigo at Valsanzibio in the 17th century, and the royal villa of Stra in the 18th.

Begun in 1689, the villa at Valsanzibio is laid out in the French style; the choice of its relatively flat location must have been deliberate since it is at the foot of the Euganean Hills and the architect could therefore easily have opted for the Italian style.

The main axis of the garden and house is marked by an immense avenue which stretches up to the house and continues at the back through a circular arrangement of figures of gods which serves as the courtyard on the garden side. The vista is then extended by a long *allée* bordered by hedges of perfectly clipped box, 6 m in height. The *bosquets* on either side of the main axis take various forms; some have been clipped to form dark tunnels; one conceals a labyrinth, while another is a rabbit island which also contains an aviary. Yet another, reached by steep rock steps, contains a colossal statue of Time, which resembles a figure of Atlas bending under the weight of the Earth, here represented by a cubic polyhedron. The formal part of the garden, however, is arranged very differently. It is laid out along an axis at right angles to the main vista and opens with a monumental group known as 'The Bath of Diana' to complement the group at the entry to the garden which shows Diana with lance in hand, hunting the stag and accompanied by Endymion and Actaeon; the arms of the Barbarigo family are also included in the group. Behind, the lovely fountain of children spurting water around a swan is positioned in front of the monumental fountain to Aeolus and the Winds, a rare subject to find represented in

The Villa Barbarigo, Valsanzibio: vista showing the entrance to the garden (The Bath of Diana) and, in the foreground, the back of the Fountain of Aeolus.

The Villa Barbarigo, Valsanzibio: the Fountain of the Putti.

this way. The crossing of the two axes of the garden is marked by four statues. Then comes a 'natural' basin, full of duckweed; its upper edge is made of rocks on which the figures of two river gods have been carved. The garden continues up the hill as a *barco*, after yet another *allée* with a basin. The whole design celebrates the power of nature; even in the *bosquets*, blocks of solid rock are scattered about, producing a more natural effect than that achieved by the use of rocaille. The nearby mountain, which is reflected in the water of basins, lends a quite exceptional grandeur to this garden, which is undoubtedly one of the most beautiful in Italy. An inscription on the circular feature in front of the house proclaims it as a work due not to Art but to Nature.

The banks of the canalized river Brenta made a delightful setting for a country dwelling; it was near Venice and accessible by water. Inevitably, many villas were built there, although the majority of these are now in dire need of restoration. However, it is here, at Stra, that we find the grandest Venetian villa, commissioned by Doge Alvise Pisani in 1735. Sometimes described as 'imperial and royal', it belonged in succession to the viceroyalty of Italy under Napoleon (who spent one night there), the Austrian royal family and finally the Italian royal family. The villa has, unfortunately, been very badly maintained; its furniture has been removed to other residences and much of the statuary has disappeared.

The façade of the villa presents a mixture of Baroque and Neoclassicism; the pediment is supported by Corinthian columns and at the first floor level are giant herms in lion skins, carrying the club of Hercules to whom they are intended to be a homage.

The ceiling of the grand drawing room by Tiepolo is dedicated to the glory of the Pisani family, which they owe to an intercession by the Virgin Mary.

The parterres of the park are turfed, but the architect Maria Preti created an incomparable effect of water reflection. The back of the house, which is entirely Neoclassical, faces another building, in the form of a temple, in the same style. But the axis of the vista between the two buildings is occupied by a canal which is so positioned that it can reflect either façade.

Hercules is much honoured in this garden. Figures of him occur five or six times along the edges of the canal and there is also a group showing the carrying off of Deianira. Although the statues in the park demonstrate pagan themes, the theological and cardinal virtues are set out on the terrace of the stables – which seems a rather curious location for them. Such allusions to religion occur frequently in the iconography of these villas; it is surprising to see Christian morality invoked so fervently by the Venetians of the period when they practised it so little.

The walls of the park have one rather unusual feature; at intervals they are interrupted by openings crowned with a pediment but closed off by a grille. The reason for these openings becomes apparent within the park. Not far from the labyrinth, made famous in d'Annunzio's *The Flame of Life*, is an octagonal building with arches and concave sides. If one stands in the exact centre, the view through each arch lines up with a corresponding opening in the wall, so revealing the countryside outside the park. This seems an ingenious way of obtaining the same effect achieved by the use of the haha in French gardens. The juxtaposition of the octagon and the labyrinth suggests a deliberate relationship between the two features. The latter carries the risk of imprisonment, whereas the former holds out the hope of freedom by allowing the eye to embrace the view far beyond the confines of the park.

Another strange feature of this park is a monumental doorway with an ironwork spiral staircase attached, let into the boundary wall of the park, thus giving an observer an oblique view of the surroundings.

The labyrinth, one of the rare examples with a belvedere tower in the centre, is of the type so heavily imbued with symbolic meanings that it came to be a major decorative feature in gardens from the Middle Ages onwards.

During the 17th and 18th centuries the labyrinth was popularized in a number of engravings and treatises. The symbolism is generally fairly explicit: after the dangers of the maze itself comes the recompense. In the case of garden labyrinths, the prize for finding the way was often food. The *Tenet error amantem* of Ovid is illustrated in an engraving by Hieronymous Sperling (1695–1777). Cupid is shown in the centre of a maze of clipped box, holding his bow and a flaming torch; a blindfold *amour* has just appeared and will leave later fully draped. One odd feature of this engraving is in the lower part which shows two doves drinking from the same spring, an allusion to the deceptive pleasures of love, seemingly derived from the early Christian symbol of doves drinking from a bowl.

There are a number of instances in 17th-century French engraving where the labyrinth is shown as a setting in which men and women give themselves to all kinds of pleasures, including copulation; in one example,

*T*he garden of the
Villa of Stra: the
canal with the stables
behind; in the
foreground, a statue
of Hercules.

The park of La Granja; The great play of water around the Fountain of Diana.

La Granja, Segovia: the central vista with the water staircase.

the naked couple, though very small, is quite clearly visible in a corner of the labyrinth's centre. At the entrance to the labyrinth a fool plays a lute (an instrument condemned by the clergy as a means of enfeebling the soul and predisposing it to thoughts of love) while a group of young scholars are turned away from this place of perdition by their guardian angels who guide them towards a palace where the values of the mechanical and liberal arts are expressed by allegories. A dog bites the heel of one child who is about to succumb to temptation. This engraving does indeed have a very earnest moral message to deliver.

The labyrinth remained a highly regarded feature in gardens until the end of the 18th century. An account of the reception given in 1784 in the labyrinth of Chantilly for the visit of the Tsarevitch details all the preparations, the finery, the surprises, the delicacies, the disguises and the musical diversions that accompanied the games; there were even children disguised as Cupids to lead the participants astray. The labyrinth could thus be seen as a love trap, as Sperling's engraving shows.

There is a certain ambiguity in the taste for such games with their elements of self-abandon to the torments as well as the delights of love. It is this tension which is so brilliantly translated into scintillating music by Mozart in the garden scene which closes the fifth act of the *Marriage of Figaro*: a scene which could well be glossed as a game in a labyrinth!

After a visit to Philip V of Spain, the Duke of Saint-Simon reproached his host with having positioned his summer retreat of La Granja the wrong way round, with the vista facing the mountains instead of opening towards the plain of Segovia, as a French garden would have done. The grumpy duke did not understand that La Granja was not to be compared to Versailles but rather to Marly, likewise intended as a retreat; the king had no wish for a view of the outside world, but sought rather a feeling of enclosure. The choice of such a mountainous site for a French-style garden has often been criticized; but where else, north of Madrid, could the king go to escape the heat of the city in summer? As at Marly, the vista from the first floor of the house is terminated by a water staircase, here made of marble, which is crowned by a pavilion at the edge of the forest.

It was in 1721 that Philip V, grandson of Louis XIV, hired a team of French artists and architects to build a residence at La Granja. The original La Granja, meaning 'farm', had been a place of retreat for the Hieronymites of the monastery of Parral at Segovia during the hot season. Philip V bought the estate from them and commissioned his superintendent of buildings, Théodore Ardemans, to build the house. The landscape architect was Etienne Boutelou and the sculptors were René Frémin and Jean Thierry, soon to be followed by four more. Under Frémin's direction, this group was responsible for the 26 fountains which are the glory of La Granja.

As at Valsanzibio, the setting of forest and foothills lends the house and garden a certain grandeur. The site is certainly restricted, but within it is a combination of sculpture and water so marvellous that nothing in a European garden can be compared to it. Extraordinarily, the artists managed to inform the whole work with the true spirit of the Baroque, although this had long passed from fashion in France, and to link it directly with the achievements of Bernini in the preceding century. The most impressive arrangement of fountains is that known as the 'Horse Race', which consists of three basins dedicated respectively to Neptune, Apollo and Andromeda, designed by Frémin and forming a glorious aquatic cavalcade. In the Fountain of Fame, with its Mount Parnassus, the winged horse seems to be somersaulting over the Muses on the rocks as it takes flight. The jet of water which rises 35 m from Parnassus is visible in Segovia. In the Fountain of Diana the goddess is seen bathing, accompanied by 20 nymphs. There is also a basin dedicated to Latona, a reference to Versailles. Additional fountains are positioned at the eight-branched crossways of the *bosquets*. In the centre of one such crossway is a *Carrying Off of Pandora*, surrounded by eight other fountains,

The park of La Granja: the Fountain of Neptune's Chariot.

dedicated respectively to Saturn, Minerva, Hercules, Ceres, Neptune, Mars, Cybele and Victory. The whole ensemble achieves an effect of unprecedented splendour.

The garden should really be seen when all the water features are working. Nowhere else are the effects of water so abundant, bountiful, varied and unexpected. In the Horse Race, one figure emits a great fan-shaped spray of water, giving the name to that part of the fountain. The Fountain of Diana is so deeply submerged in the water which plays all around and in every direction that it seems almost afloat in the basin, while the various jets spurting from the figures of frogs dispersed around the basin of the Fountain of Latona create a veritable deluge. In the Fountain of Aeolus the fury of the winds is echoed in the tumultuous sound of the spray; the bronze figures of horses, gods and goddesses, demigods, cupids and children all appear to be swimming furiously in the water, floundering, twisting and turning, occasionally clutching a rock or a shell, or reaching out for a dolphin or some other beast.

If the prince ever tired of so much noise and activity, he could climb up to the great reservoir which, at an altitude of 1,249 m fed all the water features of the garden, there to sail the royal galley (still in existence) and admire the reflection of the mountains in the water.

The beautiful urns which alternate with the statues along the *allées* or line the *boulingrins* (lawns) bring a slight note of sobriety to all the excitement, although they are in the rococo style seemingly derived from the rather breathless designs of Meisonnier.

La Granja is one of the greatest achievements of the Baroque and the same spirit was not to be repeated at Aranjuez, but, then, that garden was not Philip's personal creation. The site had been occupied since the 16th century, with further buildings and gardens being added later.

A popular form of ornament in the gardens of Portugal are the ceramic tiles known as *azulejos*, because of the dominance of blue in them; they may be used for pure decoration or to create images, both sacred and profane. The garden of La Quinta in Lisbon, built by Antonio Colaço Torrès between 1745 and 1775, includes an arrangement of arbours and pergolas supported on pillars made of *azulejos*, with benches made of the same material. The garden of the great cloister of the convent of St Clare in Naples, built between 1739 and 1742, is also famous for its decoration in a similar style, using the local *piastrelle*.

The finest example of this form of ornament in *azulejos* is to be found at the palace of the

Marquis de la Fronteira at Benfica near Lisbon. The garden itself is arranged in squares of clipped box in the Renaissance style; along one of its sides runs a pool of water which mirrors a terrace flanked by two square towers reached by straight staircases. In each of the arcatures below the terrace is an equestrian figure in *azulejos* of one of the generals of the War of Independence. Along the terrace itself is a series of niches holding the busts of the kings of Portugal except, of course, those of the two Spanish usurpers. João Mascarenhas, the second count of Torre, appointed Marquis de la Fronteira by D. Pedro in 1670, had been one of the heroes of that war. A garden of Venus overlooks the park from the first floor of the palace and also serves as the entrance court to the chapel; nearby is a terrace with twelve allegorical figures of the Arts. The whole garden, which has the many levels of meaning to be expected from its learned creator, easily absorbs the images in *azulejos* into a satisfying whole.

After his travels in Italy, the Landgrave Karl of Hesse-Kassel (1654–1731) brought back with him an Italian architect, Giovanni Fran-

The Octagon at Wilhelmshöhe, engraving by W.C. Mäyr, from a drawing by Funck. Bibliothèque Nationale, Paris.

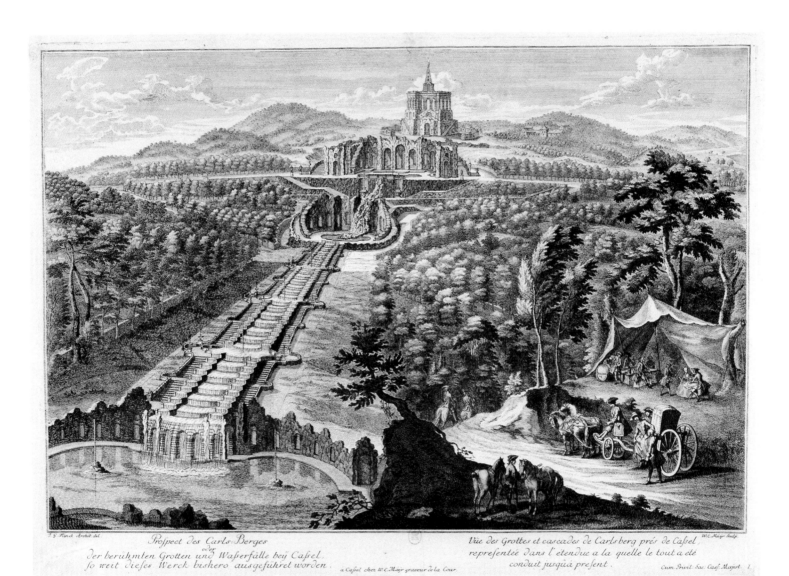

Profpect des Carls-Berges
oder
der berühmten Grotten und Wafferfälle bey Caffel.
fo weit diefes Werck bishero ausgeführet worden.

a Caffel chez W.C.Mäyr graveur de la Cour.

Vüe des Grottes et cascades de Carlsberg prés de Caffel.
reprefenteé dans l'étendue a la quelle le tout a eté
conduit jusquà prefent.

Cum Privil: Sac: Caef: Majest. I.

The main vista at Karlsberg, engraving by W.C. Mäyr, from a drawing by Funck. Bibliothèque Nationale, Paris.

cesco Guarniero (*c.*1665–1745), whom he then commissioned to build a garden for his hunting lodge at Wilhelmshöhe. Guarniero prepared a plan in 1701, which showed an immense cascade of water flowing over the rocks from a huge reservoir, known as the Octagon, set on a hill and built from rustic materials. On top of the reservoir was a pyramid surmounted by a gigantic statue of Hercules, so that the whole construction was 71 m high. The project was finally completed in 1718. The water flowed out from a grotto in the Octagon on either side of a representation of the head of Enceladus, the giant killed by Athene and the very embodiment of evil. The hunting lodge was later replaced by a large Neoclassical house in 1787–94, the work of the Frenchman Louis de Ry, which offered a better view of the aquatic spectacle. The glory of Hercules, symbol of strength and justice, would never again be celebrated in quite such a grand manner.

We have already seen how Roman princes commissioned *trompe-l'oeil* paintings for the walls of their quiet rooms, the antechambers where they composed themselves before entering chapel. One margrave of Bayreuth, however, took this decoration a stage further, from *trompe l'oeil* into the world of reality. Georg-Wilhelm, a former soldier, decided to construct a hermitage near the New Castle. This was built in large blocks of uncut stone and included separate cells furnished only with chairs, wooden tables and camp-beds. The margrave then obliged his wife and cour-

The new castle at Bayreuth: the hermitage of the Margravine Wilhelmina.

tiers, dressed as hermits, to spend a certain amount of time there devoted to ascetic pursuits. The building was finally ready for these performances in 1718.

In this, the margrave was a leader of fashion, since hermitages were to become very much *à la mode* and many of them were built in English-style gardens. Professional hermits would be engaged for the season (while the house was inhabited), required to grow a long beard and to live in the necessary state of squalor.

The cult of the garden was really a response to the need to satisfy certain deep desires. So the garden had to be a kind of theatre, with countless roles and changes of scene. Suffer-

Bayreuth: the hermitage of the Margrave Georg-Wilhelm (detail).

ing in his human state, man pretended to be a god; fed up with being a god, he play-acted a hermit; soon tiring of this, he would become a peasant or even a servant. The cycle would thus be complete and the flight from self reached its final stages as a whole civilization started to crumble.

It may very well have been a sense of contrast which led the Margravine Wilhelmina to build an elegant, semi-circular pavilion with a central rotunda, possibly inspired by La Colonnade at Versailles, and to call it a hermitage. In the rotunda a jet of water holds a double crown in balance. The sister of Frederick II was also extravagant and fashion-conscious. She commissioned her French architect, Joseph Saint-Pierre, to build a theme park in 1745–7, known as 'Sans Pareil'. The chosen theme was *Les Aventures de Télémaque* by Fénelon, a work which contributed as much as *La Nouvelle Héloïse* to spreading the humanitarian ideas behind the French Revolution. The garden consisted mainly of a winding pathway under trees, set at intervals with rocaille grottoes dedicated to Aeolus, Sybilla, Calypso, Diana, Vulcan, Mentor and Pan. Only two constructions still remain from this literary garden.

There is generally an air of serenity about the figurative ornaments in a garden, which may be derived from their debt to antique models and their symbolic significance. Although the Baroque brought much greater animation to such figures, as at La Granja, they still retain a nobility in action, born from their mythological origins. Towards the end of the 18th century, however, Austrian and German painting (Maulbertsch) and sculpture (Ignaz Günther) began to portray the human figure in frenzied and convulsive movement, with faces often contorted and tortured. This 'rococo' effect was also evident in garden statuary, as in the garden of the castle of Vertshöchheim, planned from 1763 onwards by the Bishop of Würzburg, Philipp von Greifenklau. This garden is one of the most important in Germany and, iconographically, one of the most complete.

There are certainly some very charming elements in the garden: the putti, who dance in pairs and look as though they are about to stumble, and the mischievous airs of the dancers and ballerinas. But why are the Seasons so exaggerated in their gestures, and why is Venus made to look so saucy as she indulges in amorous conversation with Mercury who offers her a bouquet? Pallas-Athene, too, seems to have totally forgotten the virtue of wisdom which she is supposed to embody, as

The park of the castle of Vertshöchheim: Mount Parnassus, by Ferdinand Tietz.

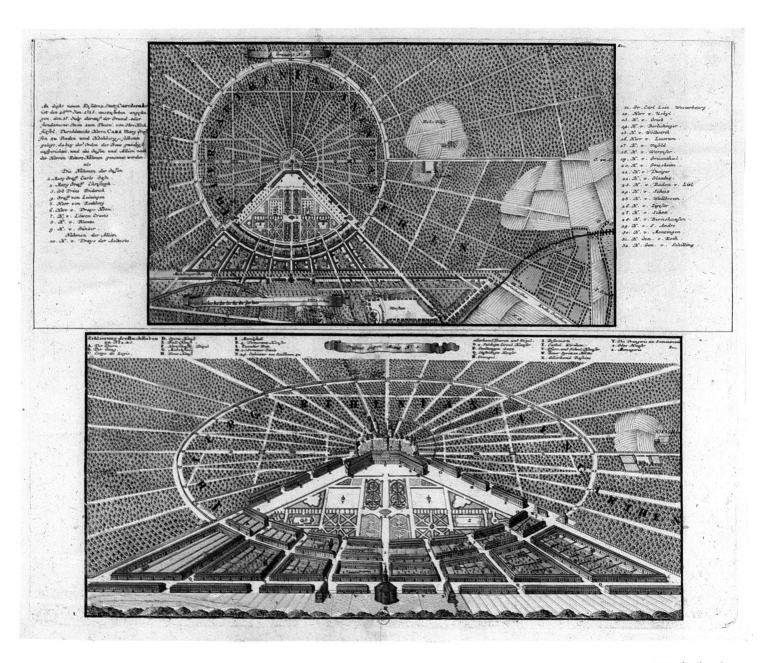

*K*arlsrühe: plan and perspective of the castle, the forest and the town, tinted German engraving of 1715. Bibliothèque Nationale, Paris, Cabinet des Estampes.

she gives her reply to Hercules. Even less comprehensible is the figure of Europe (the Holy Empire) courting America, Africa and Asia. The sphinx, that mythical beast, which often expressed noble qualities in the parks of the 17th century, is here depicted as a vulgar, untidy, sneering woman in contemporary dress.

The centrepiece of the garden is a Mount Parnassus in a vast basin, sculpted by Ferdinand Tietz in 1765–6. The Muses appear oddly dressed and so restless that they seem to be about to throw themselves into the water. The figure of Diana by the same sculptor, however, is quite magnificent; the hair of the goddess streams in the wind as she blows her horn, while the figures of the stag and dog at her feet complete a polymorphous group.

This is really more of a theatre than a garden, which is why the figures, grouped in pairs, appear to be talking to each other. The sense of continual interchange lends this exquisite garden its air of frivolity. The serious purpose of the garden, as understood by the Olympians and the philosophers, seems to have been forgotten, here to be replaced simply by an ideal of amusement, an invitation to the dancers, trumpeters and bagpipers to herald the end of the garden as an art form.

The radial plan of Karlsrühe, drawn up in 1775 under the direction of the Margrave Karl Wilhelm of Baden-Durlach, included within its 32 arms the town, the French garden, the wings of the castle and, beyond, 23 avenues through the forest. From a tower situated at the central point of the layout, behind the castle, the prince could contemplate the whole of his domain and consider himself a reflection in miniature of the Sun King, as he gazed towards the radiant horizon. The original plan for the estate was probably derived partly from the concept of the Ideal City and partly from Heliaca, Campanella's City of the Sun.

The forested park of the castle of Fredensborg in Denmark was also planned radially. The castle, as its name indicates, was built in 1720 to celebrate the peace between Denmark and Sweden, which may indicate some symbolic intention in the plan.

THE SACRED GARDEN

During the period of the Baroque, a new type of garden made its appearance in the West: the sacred garden. Some, but not all, were gardens belonging to monasteries, many of which, principally in Germany and central Europe, were exceptionally beautiful. The most remarkable is the French-style garden belonging to the Austrian abbey of Melk. It has a sumptuous eating pavilion (*lusthaus*), built in 1747 by Franz Munggenast, and decorated in 1763 by Johann Bergl with motifs of animals, flowers and people from East and West grouped around a representation of the Light of the World shown on his journey to the four parts of the known world, an allusion to the universal reign of Christian truth.

These gardens tended to disappear as the political influence of the French Revolution spread; this was even true of those belonging to monasteries converted to other uses.

The most elaborate of such gardens which I have seen is the one belonging to the head of the order of Benedictines in Portugal, at the abbey of Tibães in the Minho-Douro. Although now in great need of restoration, it still has many attractions. During the recon-

The sanctuary of the Bom Jesus at Braga: general view.

struction of the monastery, the then abbot decided to re-use some of the Romanesque and Gothic remains, including columns and architraves, from the demolished buildings to build vine pergolas. A magnificent *catena d' acqua* runs down the slope of the hill, with fountains at ten of its levels and flanked by two staircases, an arrangement imitated from the Italian villas.

Again in Portugal, the Bishop of Castelo Branco, Don João de Mendoça, commissioned a historic and sacred garden to be built around his palace. The garden was finished in 1725. Between the basins and the parterres stand statues of the Twelve Apostles, the theological and cardinal Virtues, the four seasons, the twelve signs of the Zodiac, the four corners of the earth and various saints. One great staircase is lined with statues of the kings of Portugal as well as the Twelve Apostles: Don João de Mendoça was also a historian.

The true sacred gardens of the period, however, were not so much those of the monasteries as the landscape parks which provided a setting for the Way of the Cross, the alternative to a real pilgrimage to Jerusalem. The idea of this substitute pilgrimage had first emerged in the Middle Ages, but it was to enjoy its greatest success during the Baroque period in the form of the Sacro Monte. The constructions in such gardens consisted of chapels dedicated to the different stations of the cross. Groups of sculptures illustrated episodes from the Passion and were built along a twisting track which wound up a hill. Beginning with representations of Golgotha, the sculpture would then take on a more universal character, some of it dedicated to the Virgin Mary. The finest of all such gardens is that of Varallo, to the north of Milan, which occupies a magnificent site decorated with floral parterres. There are about fifteen of such Sacri Monti between Lombardy and Piedmont; the best known are those of Varese and Varallo, but the most poetic is that of Orta. As the pilgrim passes from chapel to chapel through a magnificent beech wood, he sees below him the lake of the same name. The way in this garden is that of Saint Francis of Assisi, the stigmatist, who relived the Passion of Christ. The first stone to be laid of these chapels was blessed in 1591.

The finest expression of the Sacro Monte, however, occurred in Portugal. The best time

The sanctuary of the Bom Jesus at Braga: the upper terrace with the statue of Saint Longinus.

to see the Bom Jesus near Braga is in February and March when the red camellias are in bloom; it is as though the whole mountain were running with the blood of Christ. The iconology of the garden, however, is very subtle. In the first part of the garden, a staircase leads through a wood from chapel to chapel and from fountain to fountain, each one of which is dedicated to a planet. After all, at this stage Golgotha is the centre of the universe. Then follows the climb up the magnificent Staircase of the Five Senses, which have a double meaning: that of the humanity of Christ and that of the sins of the flesh. Then follow the church of the pilgrimage and several chapels, including those of the Passion and those dedicated to the evangelists, until the highest part of the garden, with trees, flowers and fountains, is reached.

The greatest sculptor in Bohemia, Mathias Bernard Braun, once received the amazing commission from Count Sporck to carve a number of figures from the rock of a wooded hill belonging to the Hospice of Kukus (Kuks). The park came to be known as Bethleem Wald. The sculptures are still in a fairly good state of preservation and include a Saint Francis of Assisi receiving the stigmata, a Birth of Jesus with the adoration of the shepherds, the Christ child and the Samaritan at the well, the arrival and the adoration of the wise men, and dramatic figures of the hermit saints Onufre and Garinus; the latter sought shelter in a tomb between 1725 and 1730.

It is curious how certain ideas tend to circulate at the same time in different places. Far from Kukus, at Cetinale in Tuscany, a cardinal had a very similar idea. In the oak wood on the edge of his *delizia*, built in 1680 by

Carlo Fontana, Cardinal Flavio Chigi, nephew of Pope Alexander VII, built a meditation room to expiate the sin of having killed a rival in love. The approach to the villa, guarded by a colossal figure of Hercules, is now direct, but formerly the drive, which leads all the way from Siena, divided into two some distance from the house. The parting of the ways was marked by an inscription, still in existence, which gave the visitor the choice between the way to the left and the way to the right, the first leading to pleasure and the second to penitence. The path to the left did indeed lead to the *delizia* and its garden decorated with emperors and gods. The path to the right led by a portico to the place of penitence by way of a steep track through the woods, lined with statues of saints and hermits. The rocks on the ground are occasionally carved with the forms of lizards, toads, reptiles and dragons, reminding the visitor of the temptations to be conquered along this way of initiation. The pilgrim finally arrived at a portal surmounted by a screen protecting a large fresco of a hermit at prayer (Saint Paul?) to whom a crow is bringing bread. Beyond the portal lies a chapel.

In some ways, the Sacro Monte is a return to the archetype of the garden as a sanctuary in its simplest possible form.

The Villa of Cetinale: the Latin inscription offering the visitor the choice of two ways, one leading to the asceticism of the Thebaïde and the other to the amusement of the pleasure garden.

THE LANDSCAPE GARDEN

The Botanical Gardens at Kew: the Pagoda, 1761–2, by William Chambers.

The different forms of the garden which we have looked at so far – Renaissance, Mannerist, Classical – succeeded each other through continuous evolution. At any given time, there was no strong opposition to the prevailing style which might have promoted new and revolutionary forms of expression in the art. This is not, however, the case with the landscape style, which certainly *was* a revolution in garden design, and which happened to coincide with the revolution occurring in the political field. Towards the end of the 17th century and the beginning of the 18th, England was gradually easing itself into democracy. The attempts by Charles II and James II to restore absolute monarchy were thwarted by Parliament which had acquired the habit of wielding governmental power during the period of the Long Parliament. Eventually, the vagaries of the English royal succession brought to the throne a foreign dynasty, that of Hanover, whose first two representatives helped to reinforce the status of an elected prime minister dependent for this power on being the leader of the majority party in Parliament. Opposed by the more conservative Tories, the dominant party for a third of a century was that of the Whigs, who associated themselves with the ideals of liberty, free discussion and a generally open approach to political and social matters.

One significant outcome of the political situation was the massive decline in influence of the court (George I could only speak German and Latin and was frequently in Hanover). The important landowners were therefore more disposed to live on their own estates and to take an interest in the building of their houses, in nature and agriculture and the art of the garden. This was the period when gardening first became a serious and competitive business. As the owners tried to outdo one another, the gardens of the day were continually modified to keep up with contemporary taste. In 1681, George London, the king's gardener, left his royal post to set up an independent business with Henry Wise, with whom Charles Bridgeman was also associated. In 1751, Lancelot Brown, a pupil of William Kent, gave up the post of master gardener at Stowe to set up business in Hammersmith. His skills as a landscape gardener were recognized to be so remarkable and thorough that he became known as 'Capability' Brown. Valleys, hills and even whole villages would be razed to make way for his grander schemes.

A reaction against such drastic treatment of natural features marked the work of Humphrey Repton (1752–1818), who felt that the designer should respect the qualities of the site. The effects sought by Brown were essentially intended to rouse deep emotions, whereas Repton felt that a garden should open much more naturally, not giving the observer the impression that it consisted of a series of dramatic set-pieces prepared by the gardener.

The gardens of the Restoration period, however, were still very much in the classic mould of contemporary European gardens, designed with a central vista and symmetrical arrangements of other elements on either side. The *Jardin de Plaisir* (1657) by André

The park at Stowe: the Palladian bridge, 1742.

Mollet was still the most frequently consulted work, and both André and Gabriel Mollet were invited to London by Charles II. And although Le Nôtre may only have been consulted by the court, his nephew Desgots certainly visited England. Interest in the formal garden, which survived in England for a much longer period than is often realized, probably inspired John James to translate the work of Dézallier d'Argenville under the title *The Theory and Practice of Gardening*, four years after it had appeared in French. This treatise contained a mass of technical information.

Most English gardens of the period have either disappeared or have been substantially modified, though fortunately many of them were reproduced in the *Britannia Illustrata* of 1707 as engravings by Johannes Kip, after the paintings of the Dutch artist Leonard Knyff, and again in 1724 in the *Nouveau Théâtre de la Grande-Bretagne* by the same artists. Some of the gardens, such as Lord Conway's design for Ragley in Warwickshire, were laid out to such a rigorously symmetrical plan that a drawing of only half the garden could illustrate the whole design. Others were modelled on the French style but with certain 'English' features, frequently a combination of axial and radial layouts. The finest examples of this are the semi-circular garden at Hampton Court, from which the main *allées* spread out radially, or that of Longleat, designed by George London and Henry Wise about 1680 for the Wiltshire estate of Lord Weymouth. There, the main axis of the geometrical part of the garden leads to a magnificent wood which is crossed by ten avenues. Cassiobury in Hertfordshire is one of the oldest examples of a radially planned garden; planned by Moses Cook about 1669, it may have been influenced by John Evelyn, an ardent advocate of the garden *in sylva*. He certainly made an impact on London and Wise when they laid out their wooded gardens at Melbourne Hall in Derbyshire about 1704; this latter is one of the very rare examples of a formal garden which has remained more or less intact.

Charles Bridgeman was the last of the great English gardeners to design within the French tradition. The plan of Eastbury (Dorset), for example, which he designed about 1720, was very much in the style, except for instances of a freer approach in the arrangement of certain features on either side of the main axis. The garden is opened up to the surrounding countryside by the use of hahas, inspired by the French practice. This first step towards the development of the landscape garden had already been taken by Mansart at the Grand Trianon in Versailles, as we have seen above; the beginnings of the native English style can be envisaged as a modifying process of French garden conventions. The *broderie* parterre, for instance, came to be considered a very 'unnatural' feature and the movement towards simplification resulted in its substitution by the 'English' parterre, consisting of a lawn with a floral border, from which it would be separated by a narrow gravel or sand path, or of a 'bowling green', the slightly concave lawn employed for that game. Some aspects of the art of topiary were also considered excessive, especially when it went beyond the bounds of the very simple geometrical shaping of a few plants to become the figurative sculpture which was so fashionable during the reign of William III. The increased speculation on the true nature of a garden can perhaps be seen as a renewal of the age-old quest for paradise lost. Although Milton's poem of that title had already appeared in 1667, it was not fully appreciated until much later, when an article by Joseph Addison in *The Spectator* drew attention to the stature of the work. The description of the Garden of Eden in Book IV must surely have been based on Milton's memories of the English countryside prior to his going blind. This augmented feeling for nature added a further dimension to the exploration of human origins already expressed in the Classical symbolism of the Italian and French gardens; it was closer to English religious belief and laid emphasis on nature in its original state. The Garden of Eden joined the Golden Age as a central inspiration in the art of the garden, and Biblical simplicity allied to a concept of the natural world derived from Classical antiquity came to have a crucial effect on the shaping of the English sensibility. In his *Upon the Gardens of Epicurus* (1685), William Temple provided a nostalgic evocation of walks in the gardens and orchards during the age of the philosophers.

Alexander Pope, who began his translation of the *Odyssey* in 1715, sang the praises of the gardens of Alcinous. At Stowe, William Kent set out to evoke the Elysian Fields, searching for his images of Arcadia in the paintings of Poussin, Claude Lorrain, Gaspard Dughet, L'Orizzonte and Van Lint. Classical antiquity, which had so deeply inspired the Mannerist and Classical gardens, now made an equal impact on the designers of gardens which were almost their opposite in style, as if the antique vision of the world were sufficiently all-embracing to provide a model for every situation, even the most divergent.

The park of Blenheim Palace was begun *c.* 1705 and finished around 1720 to the designs of Henry Wise; it would have provided a wonderful example of the early evolution of

*T*he park at Stowe: the triumphal arch and commemorative monuments, after Le Rouge.

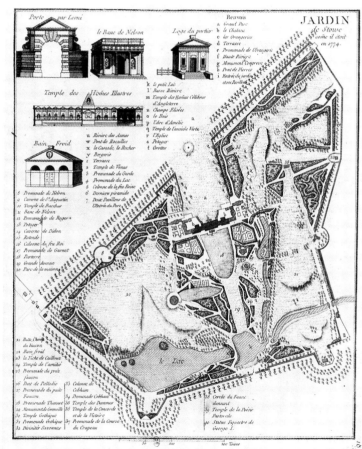

*P*lan of the park at Stowe, after Le Rouge.

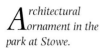

*A*rchitectural ornament in the park at Stowe.

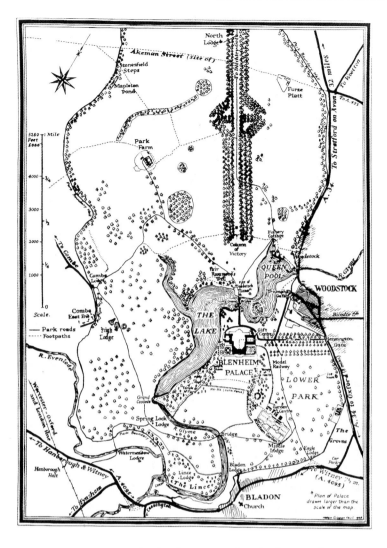

the landscape garden, had it not been constantly modified and elaborated during the 18th century by Capability Brown and William Chambers and, during the following century, by the French landscape designer, Achille Duchêne, employed by the ninth Duke of Marlborough who acceded to the title in 1892. Duchêne's additions to the original plan are undoubtedly disconcerting at first sight, consisting of French-style *broderie* and water parterres and an arrangement of Italianate features centred on a fountain in the style of Bernini.

A long inscription on the palace's main portal, built by Nicholas Hawksmoor who was working for Sir John Vanbrugh, describes it as a gift from Queen Anne and Parliament to the Duke of Marlborough. The gift was made in recognition of the duke's victory over the French at Blenheim in August 1704. The sovereign's generosity may be partially explained by Anne's favouritism of Sarah, the Duchess of Marlborough, and the problems of finishing Blenheim were certainly the result of the latter's fluctuations in the queen's favours.

The site on which Blenheim was built is legendary: the old estate of the manor of Woodstock, where Henry II had imprisoned the fair Rosamund. A plan was drawn up in 1770 to make a special feature of the spring by including it in a great Neo-Gothic arrangement, including baths, but this was never carried out.

The great size and mass of the house gives an overwhelming impression of strength, while the regal decorations on the terraces, the many representations of trophies, flares and heraldic beasts and emblems make Blenheim, in effect, a triumphal monument, unique in Europe.

The house was built in a bend of the river Glyme. Initially, a parterre in the French style was laid down in front of the south façade, but nothing now remains of this. The only feature surviving from this first stage of work in the garden is the colossal bridge across the river. Like the house, this was designed by Vanbrugh as a triumphal monument, although this aspect of its appearance was never fully realized and, without the open gallery which was to have formed its upper level, it resembles some kind of fortification embedded in the countryside. From the moment the first foundations of the bridge were laid in 1708, it was the subject of argument between the duchess and her architect. Sarah bemoaned the cost of the construction which, she claimed, would have enabled her to add a further 22 bedrooms to the main house. The majestic presence of the bridge was further reduced by the intervention of Capability Brown, who modified the course of the river to form a lake, thus raising the level of the water to cover even more of the stonework.

The ornamental bridge was to become an essential element in the English landscape garden, and the bridge at Blenheim marked the beginning of a series of such features, later to be followed by bridges to Palladian designs. Like these later versions, the bridge at Blenheim had no utilitarian purpose, not even that of facilitating access to the house. It was set in order to be seen from the Column of Victory which, after the duke's death, replaced the projected obelisk to Rosamund Clifford. The gigantic column in Roman Doric style measures about 50 m in height and is crowned by a huge lead statue of the Duke of Marlborough holding up an emblem of victory. The base of the statue is surrounded by figures of eagles. In addition to its impressive size, this column recalls the emblem and trophy gardens of the Tudors. The arrangement of trees behind the column, planted by the ninth Duke of Marlborough, reproduced the line of battle at Blenheim.

*T*he park at
Blenheim: the
bridge by Vanbrugh.

Apart from this column and a few other decorative elements, there is no other allusion in the form of mythological statuary to the achievements of the duke, neither in the garden nor the house; even Hercules is absent. We can only imagine the profusion of symbolic ornament which would have decorated the garden of such a hero in France or Italy 50 years earlier.

This relatively simple garden was completely transformed by Capability Brown when he modified the bend of the river to create a lake with curving banks, ending in a cascade, after which the river continues on its original course. Other water features play an important part in the garden. On the banks of the lake, an Ionic temple to Diana was built by William Chambers.

The garden of Blenheim also boasts a kitchen garden and a remarkable floral one, whose vivid colours form a pleasant contrast to the pink brick of the retaining walls. The sale of plants, vegetables and shrubs is now one of the most important sources of revenue of the estate.

There is an apparent contradiction in the fact that the rise of the landscape garden coincided with the growth of the architectural movement known as Palladianism. At the beginning of the 17th century, Inigo Jones had fallen under the influence of Palladio, which shows clearly in a number of works by the English architect that have been preserved. This first Palladian period, however, was brought to an end by the architectural formalism propagated by Wren in the second half of the century, which wavered between the Classical and the Baroque. After a further excursion into the Baroque in the work of Vanbrugh and Hawksmoor, the architectural values of the master of Vicenza returned to fashion, achieving worldwide currency in the second quarter of the 18th century. The inspiration behind this movement was not a professional architect, but one of the dominant personalities of the Whig aristocracy, Lord Burlington (1695–1753). A great patron of the arts, he was a source of encouragement to some of the prominent figures of the time: Berkeley in philosophy, Pope, Swift and Thomson in literature, Handel in music, and many other architects, painters and sculptors. He completed the Grand Tour in 1714–15, travelling through France and northern Italy to Rome. The deep impression made upon him by seeing the works of Palladio was reinforced by the appearance of the *Quattro libri dell' Architettura* in the English translation by Leoni in 1715, and by a second visit to Italy in 1719. It was then that he decided to build his country house at Chiswick in the style of a Palladian villa.

While in Rome, in 1719, Lord Burlington had met another Englishman, a coach painter named William Kent (1683–1748), who was completing his artist's training under Bernardo Luti. They agreed to meet afterwards in Paris and to journey to London together. By the end of the year they were both back in London and Kent was installed in Burlington House, where he was to live until the death of

the earl. Under the latter's guidance, Kent was transformed into an architect and, in 1727, he was commissioned to design the garden at Chiswick, which was finished in 1730.

It is difficult to distinguish between the work of Kent and his patron in the garden of Chiswick; Burlington had already been active in the old park before the new works were begun. The radial arrangement in front of the north-west façade of the villa seems to predate the house, since it does not occupy the same axis. The temples must have been built by Burlington between 1717 and 1724. Kent's main contribution to the garden was probably the area on the other side of the river which winds serpent-like through the park. There also exist designs by Kent for the rustic cascade and the exedra with statues of Caesar, Pompey and Cicero from Hadrian's Villa at Tivoli. But the most distinctive of Kent's contributions to the garden were the tracks and paths winding through the spaces between the straight *allées* which extend from the house and through the wooded section on the other side of the river. The laying out of paths in curves and counter-curves was attributed to the type of Chinese garden known as *sharawagi* by Sir William Temple in his essay *Upon the Gardens of Epicurus*. The author did not show any particular enthusiasm for this feature and it was a long time before it became current. It appears in a design by Stephen Switzer of 1718 and in another by Batty Langley in the *New Principles of Gardening* of 1728,

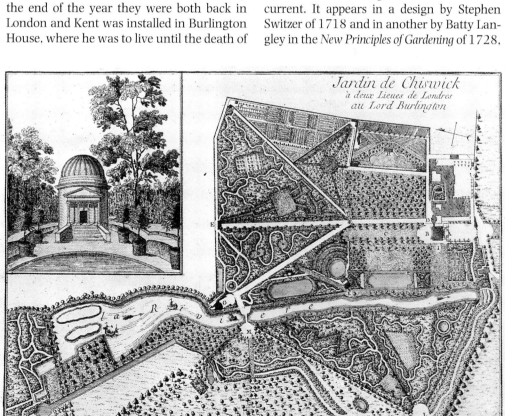

*P*lan of Chiswick House and its garden; upper left, the Pantheon, after Le Rouge. Bibliothèque Nationale, Paris.

where the system of winding paths is again enclosed by a network of straight *allées*. The enclosing elements were soon to disappear completely. There may be some justification of Pierre Grimal's theory that the English inclined to this form of layout because of the long tradition of labyrinths in their gardens.

Kent had hardly enjoyed a free hand in his designs for Chiswick, and his contribution to the art of the garden can be much better assessed from his work in transforming the garden at Stowe, which had originally been planned by Bridgeman as a complement to the house of Sir Richard Temple (later Lord Cobham). In 1730, Kent was commissioned to remodel that part of the estate which had been laid out in the oriental style to create 'the Elysian Fields'. The result marked an end to the austerity visible in the style of Blenheim. Straight lines had disappeared and there were now a large number of architectural features; the landscape garden had taken on as 'busy' an aspect as any preceding style. Ornament succeeded ornament down this 'happy valley': an Egyptian pyramid, an Italian belvedere, a Saxon temple, a Chinese house, a temple of Ancient Virtue, a Corinthian arch, temples of Venus, Concord, Victory[1], and Friendship, as well as a shepherd's hut, a cemetery and, on an island, the tomb of the dramatist William Congreve. The Temple of Victory was inspired by the Maison Carrée at Nîmes. The grotto where Dido gives herself up to Aeneas is covered with Italian-style rocaille, while close by is a Chinese house on piles. The Temple of Modern Virtue was deliberately left as a ruin to counterbalance that to antique Virtue which was, naturally, complete in every aspect.

One of the most interesting constructions in the garden is the Palladian bridge (1742), built as a free interpretation of a design in the *Quattro libri*; the design had already been used at Wilton House in 1736 to a plan by the Earl of Pembroke and was again repeated at Prior Park by Robert Morris *c*.1755 and at Hagley Park. The practice of building such bridges passed, along with the fashion for the English garden, to the continent, where it can be seen at Tsarskoïe-Selo in Russia and again in the 20th-century French garden created by Bestegui at the château of Groussay.

The talent of Kent was to implant all these buildings in a natural landscape. According to Edward Hyams[2], this conception of a garden as being very close to the natural state of the landscape corresponded to the philosophy of Shaftesbury expressed in *The Moralists* (1709), which declared that things had to be approached 'in genuine order' to find what was pure and permanent in nature. Such an ideal of nature is reflected in the paintings of Poussin, Claude and L'Orizzonte; it is the *nature naturante* of Spinoza, the nature of the Creator, *nature naturae*, and not of the creature.

The ideal of pure nature is, however, illusory on two counts. Firstly, nature does not exist in such a state except in the oceans and deserts, the Amazon region and the Himalayas. For the forests of Italy, France or Germany, where the quest for nature in its pure state has long been pursued, are the product of human intervention on a monumental scale.

Once again we are faced with the theme of origins, the eternal inspiration of the gardener's art. The guiding principles of English garden design in the 18th century may seem paradoxical: although preoccupied with naturalism, the nation's architecture was to achieve its greatest refinement in Palladianism. The contradiction is, however, only apparent, since both garden design and architecture were drawing on the same source of inspiration. An ancient temple located on the fringes of a wood at Stowe must to some extent evoke the same impression as that felt by a Greek confronted by such a temple before entering a sacred wood. Here, too, is an expression of that search for an Arcadia

[1]The 'Victory' was added after the Seven Years War.

[2]Edward Hyams, *The English Garden*, London, 1964.

*R*ousham Park: the
pool of Venus.

which was also the concern of the Roman painters of the 17th century.

Nature and the antique are even more closely allied in the garden of Rousham House, which Kent was commissioned by Colonel Robert Dorset to redesign in 1737. Kent deliberately created groups of sculpture to act as 'eye-catchers'; one of these is of Venus about to take her bath, while two Cupids mounted on swans safeguard the modesty of the goddess by chasing away a bird. The fauns, gods and goddesses and animals seem to be the true proprietors of these meadows and woods. The demarcation between the park and the surrounding countryside has been left imprecise and one of the 'eye-catchers' is a specially constructed Gothic ruin on a neighbouring hillside.

Perhaps Rousham is a little too self-consciously 'natural' and the profusion of marble figures a little too intrusive. At Stourhead, however, nothing disturbs the noble silence of a carefully arranged landscape which, more than any other, evokes the historical painting of the 17th century. The garden at Stourhead is the work of an amateur, its owner Henry Hoare (1705–85). A Temple of the Sun, inspired by the architecture of Baalbek, sits gracefully on top of a wooded hill. The focal point of the whole design is a lake with a Pantheon, designed by Henry Flitcroft, on its bank. Opposite, a branch of the lake is crossed by a four-arched bridge of a type which is found repeatedly in Flemish or Italian painting and which here serves as a connecting element between the two parts of the garden.

Not far from the Pantheon, but invisible from it, is a Gothic hermitage. Water, the source of all life, is commemorated within the design in the form of two grottoes. One shelters a river god, while the other contains a reclining nymph representing Ariadne asleep. The lack of deliberate planting in the garden gives it an air of austerity, of silent majesty.

The colonnade of the Pantheon is flanked by two niches containing figures of Dionysos and a Muse. The interior is full of statues, including a Hercules (1756) and a Flora by Michael Rysbrook, a Livia Augusta dressed as Ceres from Herculaneum, and a Meleager and a Diana by John Cheere from antique casts. Far from being excluded by the taste for the natural in the landscape garden, the antique continued to play a dominant role, although this had to be shared with other elements.

The term 'landscape' seems first to have been applied to a garden by William Shenstone (1714–63) in his *Unconnected Thoughts on Gardening*, published posthumously in 1764. The term is perhaps more suitable for

The grotto of the nymph at Stourhead, inspired by an antique statue of Cleopatra.

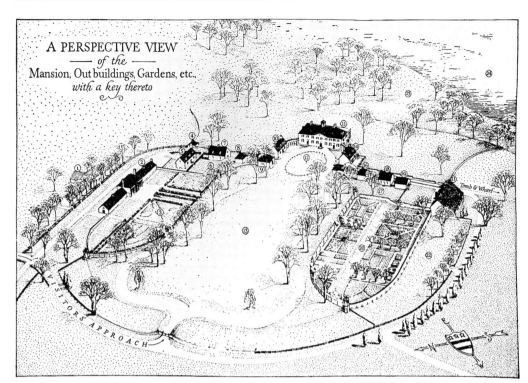

A PERSPECTIVE VIEW
of the
Mansion, Out buildings, Gardens, etc.,
with a key thereto

VISITORS APPROACH

Perspective view of George Washington's house at Mount Vernon (drawing).

the last phase of this style of garden, while 'picturesque' is a more accurate description of the first, since it was often directly inspired by painting. In its most developed form, seen at Syon House and at Kenwood, both near London, the landscape garden was really not much more than a carefully cultivated stretch of natural land; and the main residence would be situated on the edge and not, as formerly, in the centre, as focal point of the entire design. Man clearly no longer felt himself to be monarch of the whole universe. The mansion now looked out on what was in effect a vast field which could best be mown by allowing cattle to graze at leisure – a true spectacle of rural peace and contentment for the master and mistress of the house, their family and guests.

One of the advantages of this type of garden was that its relatively low cost put it within reach of a much wider section of society. The most modest country squire could afford one; it was but a short step to the ornamental farm. We can gain a very accurate idea of this concept from the Mount Vernon estate in Virginia, built on the banks of the Potomac by George Washington and enlarged by him in 1787. It has been restored by the Mount Vernon Association founded by Miss Ann Pamela Cunningham in 1853.

The utility buildings, both for the farm and the workshops, are pleasantly sited around the main residence which, built partly of wood, has all the elegant simplicity of the post-colonial style. On the left side of a great lawn is a flower garden and on the right a kitchen garden. There is also a botanical garden for experimentation in new planting techniques, and a herb garden; the three elements of the medieval garden are thus reunited. Beyond the garden the general would have been able to see the vast landscape stretching out on the other side of the Potomac, a sight to provoke strong emotions in keeping with the unassuming lives of the founding fathers of the Union. The garden itself seems to breathe virtue and the joy of living; perhaps it is here, in this simple environment, that we can come closest to understanding the fundamental nature of the garden and the significance it holds for us.

The American colonists also constructed a number of gardens in the English style. At Williamsburg, the capital of Virginia between 1699 and 1781, many of the old buildings and landscapes have been restored, thanks largely to John Rockefeller Snr., including the Governor's House, the plans of which were found in the British Museum. The garden is a good example of an English garden at the beginning of the 18th century, in the French style but more relaxed than its continental counterparts, with a number of 'English' features: a bowling green, a labyrinth (in holly), and a mount for viewing built above an ice-pit, a feature mentioned by Bacon in his essay on gardens.

To relieve the occasional monotony of England's native vegetation, efforts were sometimes made to enliven it by bringing

PRECEDING PAGES

Stourhead: the bridge, with the Pantheon in the background.

George Washington's house at Mount Vernon: the pleasure garden.

other species from the continent or even from farther afield. From this need developed the botanical garden during the 18th century, notably at Edinburgh and Kew. Of these, Kew is the most famous, with its buildings by Chambers and fine 19th-century hothouses. Irreparable damage was done to some of the planting in the great storm of autumn 1987.

The extreme simplification of garden design led to the development of the flower bed. Since the garden was now no longer decorated with buildings and statuary, other means had to be found to alleviate the new austerity. The English taste for floral gardens dates from this period and English gardeners have remained unsurpassed in their skill at such arrangements. Philip Southcote mentions a 'rosary' at Woburn Farm in 1734. Batty Langley's *New Principles of Gardening* advocated scented flowers as one of the charms of the garden. Thomas Whately, in his *Observations of Modern Gardening* (1770), noted that every vacant corner should be taken up with a rose garden or bank of flowers, whereas no place had been found for floral display in the formal gardens designed by Bridgeman around 1720. Other advocates of the revival of the flower garden were Joseph Spencer, Richard Belteman and Thomas Wright. By the end of the century, a growing eclecticism seemed to herald the end of a centuries-old tradition of garden design. The Chinese pagoda became a neighbour for the Temple of Apollo, and the House of Confucius for the hermitage; believing in everything is perhaps not very far removed from believing in nothing.

The myth of Chinese wisdom was soon to be joined by that of the noble savage and a pure and simple peasant morality. The West, having rejected religious values, seemed to be seeking to fill the vacuum. The Orient satisfied this need admirably, since the imagination always sees things distant as possessing greater mystery and significance.

One man who described the marvels of China was William Chambers (1723–96), who returned to England in 1755. Scottish by birth, he had been sent to Sweden with his father and had later worked for the Swedish East India Company, under whose auspices he had visited Canton in 1745 and again in 1749. He attended the courses in architecture given by Blondel at the Academy of Architecture in Paris and completed his training by a voyage to Italy. He was appointed architectural tutor to the Prince of Wales in 1756 and caused a sensation the following year with the publication of his book *Designs of Chinese Buildings*, which he followed with other works on China. He was then commissioned to design a number of buildings by the Dowager Princess

of Wales for the botanical gardens she had established at Kew. These included the famous Chinese pagoda in the form of a tower with ten levels, each one of which was formerly decorated with figures of dragons bearing bells which rang in the breeze. The House of Confucius was designed by Chambers and decorated by Joseph Goupy.

At the same time, the Chinese influence had extended to Europe. Between 1754 and 1756, J.G. Büring built a Chinese teahouse in the garden of Frederick II at Potsdam. It was modelled on a building by Héré for King Stanislas at Lunéville (1745) and contained a number of terracotta figures.

A direct descendant of the Kew pagoda is the one at Chanteloup in the Touraine, built in 1778 by Le Camus de Mézières in honour of the friends who had accompanied him into exile. This elegant tower is now all that remains of the estate; just beside is a large pond in which the reflections of the tower can be seen from various angles as the sun moves round, thus making it a giant sundial. The tower, in its isolation, is one of the most beautiful sites in France.

The end of the century was marked by the appearance in France of a large number of books on the art of the garden; some of them paid particular attention to the new fashion for Chinese buildings, notably the *Jardins anglo-chinois à la mode*, published in instalments by the geographical engineer Le Rouge between 1776 and 1789. Numerous Chinese houses sprang up in gardens. One of the most beautiful of these was built by Désert de Retz for H. de Monville, and decorated with fine exotic sculptures in wood; still intact 30 years ago, it was then destroyed by its owner, and there are now plans to rebuild it at considerable cost. The kiosk (the word is of Chinese origin) of Tury-Harcourt has recently been restored, as has the exceptionally elegant example from the park of Cassan which belonged to de l'Isle-Adam and later to the financier Bergeret.

In France, the taste for the English garden brought with it a preference for the sinuous line at the very moment that it fell from fashion in architecture and the decorative arts. Rococo had finally had its day and the straight lines of the Louis Seize style succeeded the graceful curves of the Louis Quinze. The paradox was similar to the coexistence in England of Palladianism and the landscape garden.

After the peace treaty of 1763 between England and France, the English garden became fashionable almost overnight across the Channel. The painter Watelet, with the assistance of Boucher, designed one of the ear-

The pagoda at Chanteloup (1775–8), by Le Camus de Mézières.

liest of these in 1754 on the Ile de la Seine, and called it Moulin Joly. He later helped to spread the fashion with his *Essai sur les jardins* of 1764, republished in 1774. Other books which extolled the landscape garden were those of the Prince de Ligne, the Duc d'Harcourt and the Marquis de Girardin, and many were built, often sited at the edge of a French-style garden or around a small château, which was referred to as a 'folie', but not in the sense as understood in the Middle Ages. The term is particularly well suited to the one at Bagatelle (near Paris), which was built in three months by the Comte d'Artois after a wager with Marie-Antoinette. The impermanent nature of some of these projects ensured them of a relatively short life. Hardly any still remain, apart from Bagatelle in the Bois de Boulogne and a part of the Jardin de Monceau in Paris (both modified during the 19th century). Other examples included the Folie-Saint-James, formerly in the Bois de Boulogne and now at Neuilly, which was restored in the 19th century by the landscape architect Jean-Charles Moreux; the garden of the Marquis de Girardin at Ermenonville; the Hameau de Chantilly, one of the first of its genre (1772–3); the garden of Rambouillet and, finally, the most famous of all, that of the Petit Trianon, laid out by Richard Mique for the country pleasures of Marie-Antoinette. The garden of Bagatelle was the first to be fed by a pump, drawing water from the neighbouring Seine, a solution to many of the previous problems of gardens.

The most attractive of such gardens was, without doubt, the one made by the painter Hubert Robert, superintendent of the king's gardens, for the financier Comte de Laborde at Méréville. Laborde had bought the land in 1764 and invested seventeen million francs in it. Its crowning glory was a Temple of Sybil after Tivoli, which was sited on a hill. Robert was particularly skilful at placing ornaments along the vistas of the garden. The count commissioned a monument in honour of his two sons lost in the wreck of the *Pérouse* and a rostral column to the memory of Captain Cook, making the garden a veritable haven for the souls of the dead. This masterpiece, however, was not to survive; it was sold in 1819 and at the end of the century the Comte de Saint-Léon bought all the ornaments and had them removed to the Parc de Jeurre.

Ermenonville was eventually transformed into a romantic garden by the Marquis of Girardin, author of *De la composition des paysages et des moyens d'embellir la nature* (1770). An admirer of Jean-Jacques Rousseau, the marquis invited the already ailing philosopher to his estate; Rousseau arrived there on 22 May 1778, took up residence in a pavilion and died there of apoplexy on 11 July. He was buried for a short time on an island, before his ashes were finally laid to rest in the Panthéon. A temple of philosophy – unfinished, of course – dedicated to Montaigne was built round the island tomb. The glory of Descartes, Voltaire and Rousseau was evoked by a series of truncated columns in a gallery of the great, a precursor of Alexandre Lenoir's Elysian garden in the Musée des Monuments Français at the time of the French Revolution, known to us through a painting by Hubert Robert. In another part of the estate of Ermenonville was a 'desert' of sand, symbol of nature's inhumanity and an aid to meditation.

The name of 'Désert' which M. de Monville gave to his estate of Retz, near Saint-Germain-en-Laye, emphasized the tendency of the philosopher to withdraw from surrounding civilization. Committed to scientific speculation, the thinker would take up residence in a truncated Doric column, symbolizing the incompleteness of human knowledge.

The Prince de Condé was the first member of the royal family to create a rustic village, at Chantilly, to be followed by the queen. Marie-Antoinette's village was designed by her architect Richard Mique, assisted by the Prince de Caraman, on the site of Louis XIV's botanical gardens at Versailles. The central feature is a river that tumbles from a high rocky waterfall, opposite a music room in the form of a belvedere, the Classical architecture of which contrasts with the rocaille of the cascade. After its descent the river flows past an island on which there is a peripheral temple to Cupid (opened in 1772), with the small figure of the god being presented with a copy of 'Cupid sharpening his arrows in the

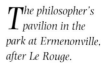

club of Hercules' by Girardon. The river then encircles a number of thatched buildings in a Norman village, which also has a main house, a watchtower and, notably, a dairy set among leafy trelliswork.

Another dairy, far prettier and more practical than the one at the Trianon, was created by Louis XVI for the queen so that she could play at being a farmer's wife. This was at Rambouillet, an unattractive estate, to which he hoped to tempt Marie-Antoinette and where he also started an experiment in raising merino sheep. Built by Thévenin, this dairy is effectively a small château with two wings, in which the salons are located and which are built around a 'temple', divided into two distinct parts. The first, a sort of vestibule, is a rotunda with a panelled cupola, lit by an oculus in the manner of the Roman Pantheon; it was used for sampling the milk, as is evident from the central table in marble surrounded by circular benches. A door gives on to the rectangular inner sanctum, also with a panelled ceiling and lit from above. The ultimate shrine of the cult is, in fact a grotto containing an exquisite statue, of almost ethereal beauty, of the nymph Amalthaea, sculpted by Pierre Julien. The chaste and other-worldly form of the nymph places her delicate foot on the flowing water, while the goat which accompanies her sniffs at it suspiciously. A table of white marble, placed there during the Empire, suggests a sacrificial altar. The group, comprising this youthful, idealized figure, venturing shyly out from the rocks, accompanied by one of the most myth-laden of animals, and all bathed in a subdued light, conveys a powerful impression of sanctity. The great mythology of gardens has thus turned full circle: for here again is the Amalthaeum, that homage to Zeus which had so delighted Cicero at the house of Atticus and which, in our time, inspired Salomon Reinach to write one of his best books on the history of religions. The statue did not remain long in place after its first appearance in 1787, but it has now been restored to its rightful position. The pails and bowls were made by the porcelain manufactury of Sèvres. A three-legged table decorated with rams' heads supports a number of bowls in the form of breasts, the moulds of which were said to have been made from those of Marie-Antoinette. The queen was to have little opportunity to enjoy her marble sanctuary, and it would not be long before the Revolution and her execution would sweep away all her dreams, pleasures and garden games.

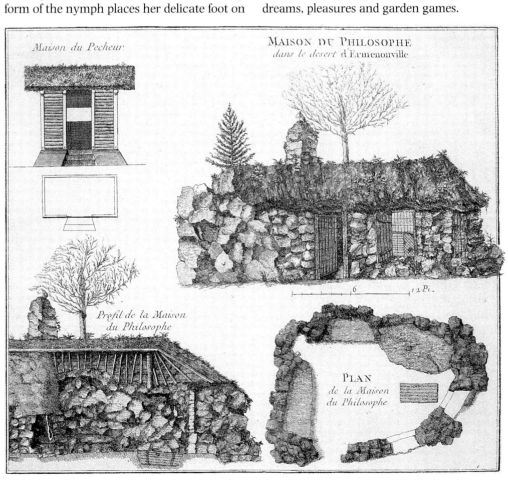

The philosopher's pavilion in the park at Ermenonville, after Le Rouge.

Coupe sur la ligne C D.

P lan for a heated conservatory; a subterranean passage in rock-work leads from a luxuriously decorated pavilion. Watercolour by Delagardette (1743–89). Private collection.

Versailles: the hamlet and the dairy of the Petit Trianon.

The houses in such specially constructed hamlets were usually as rough on the inside as on the outside. The Duc de Bourbon, however, tried to do something different at Chantilly by contrasting the crudeness of the exterior with the luxury of the interiors. Nothing remains of this attempt.

The survival of the Hermitage of Rambouillet has been of particular importance. As luxuriously appointed as the hermitage of the Margrave of Bayreuth, many of its architectural features – the niches, the columns, the capitals, the architraves, the vaulting – were made from shells and marble fragments to provide an extraordinary interior to a rustic cabin.

The period in general was notable for its extensive speculation on the art of the garden, but the grotto seems to have remained a perennially popular feature. A watercolour by Delagardette, for instance, shows a tropical hothouse with its heating room, but this is reached through a long subterranean space in the form of a grotto, entered – oddly – through an octagonal salon hung with precious fabrics.

The fashion for landscape gardens with romantic features lasted in France until about 1830. There were many evocations of the *Nouvelle-Héloïse*, temples dedicated to friendship or to the philosophers, cenotaphs and Chinese houses, even in the gardens of Parisian town houses. Very few of these ornaments still exist today.

The taste for the English garden swiftly spread towards the East as far as Russia. The garden of Tsarskoïe-Selo (Pushkin) is, in its present form, the product of the English influence. This was especially strong under Catherine II, who sent the landscape architect Vasili Neiolov to England with her son in 1770. This Russian Versailles, which was regularly inhabited for the entire summer until the fall of the Tsar Nicholas II, then underwent a series of transformations which account for its present rather eccentric appearance. The successive stages of the modifications are recounted in a rare book about the estate written in French – the international language of the time – by S. de Viltchkovsky in 1910.

Although the house (now completely restored) was burnt down by the Germans during the Second World War, the garden was mercifully spared. Nothing now remains from the period of Peter I, whose 'Dutch' (or rather 'French' on a reduced scale) garden was completely destroyed to make way for Catherine's English garden.

The Tsarina Elizabeth Petrovna left behind two monumental buildings by Rastrelli, a grotto and a hermitage. The latter is in a heavy Baroque style; the mechanism which made it possible for the main floor to be lowered into the kitchens to reappear with five fully laden tables has been preserved. This arrangement eliminated any need for domestic servants and it became a standard feature in all hermitages, including the Petit Trianon at Versailles, and permitted the owners to experience the solitude of real hermits.

Catherine left a number of more important buildings. They are grouped around a lake and include an 'Admiralty'. The most impor-

The park of Rambouillet: interior of the dairy. In the background is Julien's figure of Amalthaea.

КОЛОННАДА ДВОРЦА   LA COLONNADE DU PALAIS

ВЪ ЦАРСКОМЪ-СЕЛѢ.   А TZARSKOE-SELO.

tant of these architectural features is a Palladian bridge in granite and marble, built about 1778 and based on a design brought back from England by Neiolov. On an island Catherine commissioned a column to celebrate the success of the landing in Morea by her lover Count Orlov. To commemorate his naval victory of Cheshme over the Turks in 1771 (which Pitt described as being 'that of infantilism over decrepitude'), she commissioned a rostral column to be built in the middle of the lake. The victorious general was also celebrated by other monuments, a fashion which continued until the 19th century.

Italy, with its rich patrimony of marvellous gardens, was not particularly receptive to the English style. Its appearance at Caserta alongside the great cascade and the fountains of Actaeon and Adonis was probably due to the contacts of Ferdinand IV, king of Naples, with the English envoy Lord William Hamilton. While the rest of Europe was torn apart by war, in this corner of the Mediterranean a domestic drama was taking place between 1787 and 1798, the year when the court sought exile in Palermo under the protection of Nelson's guns. The principal characters in these escapades were the diplomat and archaeologist Lord Hamilton, then a widower, the beautiful and adorable Emma Lyon, who was to marry him, Horatio Nelson, soon to fall in love with Emma, the gardener Andrew Graefer (sent by the famous Joseph Banks, director of the Royal Botanic Gardens at Kew and in the first flush of romance over his wedding to an Englishwoman he had met in Naples), the unsuspecting King Ferdinand, whose only interest was hunting, and his impetuous wife, Maria Carolina, sister to Marie-Antoinette. It hardly seemed to matter there that the king and queen of France were going to the guillotine and that the whole of Europe was in flames. Never had the games of the garden been pursued with such passion. One exquisite creation came out of all this intrigue; Graefer was the son of a botanist and he turned the garden into an arboretum. Alongside the empty spaces of the main vista of the French-style garden is a dense, shady wood, full of rare plant species and alive with birds. The ornament consists of a *tholos*, some ancient ruins on an island, several statues, including a crouching Venus, and a false loggia in the Roman style, so carefully constructed that it too looks like an authentic ruin. Has any marriage been celebrated amid so much artifice in water, wood, ornaments and statues? We have at last returned to the *lucus*, the true sacred wood.

The park of Tsarskoïe-Selo: view of the lake, with the pavilion of the Hermitage in the right background; lithograph from a drawing by Meyer, printed by Lemercier in 1846. Bibliothèque Nationale, Paris.

THE HORTICULTURAL
GARDEN

Up to this point, we have seen how man sought to re-create the image of a primordial happiness in the garden, and how the archetypes of his very being, variously interpreted from age to age and from country to country, produced many different kinds of garden. By the 19th century, there already existed a vast repertory ready to be plundered by a society more notable for its eclecticism than for its creative spirit. By 1860, this repertory included even the gardens of the Far East, notably those of Japan.

Yet, in all the variety of guises available to the garden designer, one major type of garden continued to enjoy popularity well into the first part of the century: this was the English landscape garden. And its future seemed guaranteed if only because so many towns and cities, especially from 1850 onwards, felt the need to create public parks. The rapid growth of industrial society attracted ever greater numbers of people to urban areas where their lives often entailed physical hardship and oppression. And the garden, having reached a high point in its evolution, now had to be brought into the city centre itself to satisfy the craving of the new urban classes for the natural world, whether it consisted of a few trees around their homes or an avenue along the road leading to their place of work.

The alternative, as Alphonse Allais remarked, was that the towns had to be 'transported into the countryside'. This was to happen during the 20th century, when people increasingly developed the habit of commuting long distances morning and evening in order to live in a country atmosphere; thus began the age of the suburb, with its rows of detached and semi-detached houses, each surrounded by a small plot of vegetable garden. The introduction of the five-and-a-half day week made it possible for the more prosperous members of the new industrial society to live an appreciable distance from the city centres and to cultivate those splendid gardens which graced the English country towns and villages. And across the Atlantic, the same type of arrangement can be found in rural Maine and New Jersey, where

The Botanical Gardens of Kew: the Palm House designed by Decimus Burton, built between 1844 and 1848 with the help of the engineer Richard Turner.

the absence of any fencing between each garden gives the impression of open countryside.

The 19th-century growth of the urban population necessitated detailed planning in towns and cities. And the new concepts of urban planning, which immediately recognized the important role to be played by the garden, was nowhere applied so extensively as in London and Paris.

Early in the century, the question of municipal parks became a matter for public discussion in Loudon's *Encyclopedia of Gardening* of 1822, which includes a section significantly entitled 'Public Parks of Equestrian Promenades Are Valuable for Large Cities'. In a country such as England, where the horse was a popular form of transport, the city gentleman clearly expected to take his ride every morning.

Between 1840 and 1850, notably, more and more public parks were laid out, especially in the north of England. A number of these were designed by Joseph Paxton.

The modern city of London is built around the old royal parks, which have now become public. The oldest of these is St James's Park, acquired by Henry VIII in 1532 and formerly the garden to St James's Palace; it was opened to the public under the Stuarts. The park stretches the length of The Mall, where its magnificent mixed borders and its varied birdlife, including a sanctuary for Chinese ducks, make it the most beautiful in London. Adjoining it is the grassy expanse of Green Park. The largest and most frequented of the royal parks is Hyde Park, which is popular for boating, horse riding (along Rotten Row), band concerts and open-air political and religious oratory (Speakers' Corner). Originally forested, the park was acquired by Henry VIII for hunting and was opened to the public by Charles I. The central stretch of water known as the Serpentine extends through to the rather more exclusive Kensington Gardens, surrounded by embassies and one royal residence, at present the home of HRH Princess Margaret. Down the Thames lies Greenwich, the park of Elizabeth I, sited on a wooded hill

and arranged around the Queen's House, the work of Inigo Jones.

All London's major parks, then, owe their existence to royal initiative. Among them, Regent's Park is the most closely integrated with the surrounding architecture, notably John Nash's combinations of circuses, crescents and terraces, built during the reign of George III and the Regency. The park contains a lake, the London Zoo and Queen Mary's Rose Garden.

By 1853, Paris had become one immense building site, the birth pangs of the city as we know it today. For the most part, the new construction took place at the expense of the old: 1,500 architects and 60,000 workmen were needed to create the Paris of Baron Haussmann. The new plans did contain some provision for green spaces, all the more necessary since the spreading city had engulfed the charming villages which surrounded it – Passy, Auteuil, Belleville and the hill of Montmartre – as well as the old convent gardens.

Napoleon III had spent part of his period in exile in London and returned with the idea of introducing similar parks to his own city. Pre-

viously, the only open spaces which the people of Paris could enjoy had been such 'promenades' as the Cours-la-Reine, the Tuileries, the Luxembourg, the Jardin des Plantes and the Champs-Elysées (in all, about 220 acres). The most important boulevards which Haussmann cut through the city were lined with trees, while some of the intersections were marked by squares in the form of small gardens, usually embellished with floral displays in containers rather than in parterres; the latter arrangement would, in any case, have been unsuitable, since a parterre was designed primarily to be seen from the first storey of a great house, and in a city square the only way to display it would have been to lay it out on a slope. The rather meanly executed squares of Paris are probably the least successful aspect of the plan to introduce greenery into the capital and cannot be compared with their majestic counterparts in London, such as Bedford Square, Grosvenor Square, Portman Square and the like.

Three parks, however, were successfully created. Two of them, one to the west of Paris and the other to the east, were based on old forests where the kings of France had hunted:

St James's Park, London.

218

the Bois de Boulogne and the Bois de Vincennes. Both were the work of the architect Barillet-Deschamps and of the engineer Alphand and designed on the same principles; and they included similar features: a boating lake, paths through the undergrowth between the main avenues, rides, winding streams, a great cascade and hippodromes – one at Vincennes and two in the Bois de Boulogne. The Bois also includes the Jardin de Bagatelle, originally laid out in the 18th century and redesigned by Lord Hertford. At its foot lies the Plaine de Bagatelle, once used for equestrian sports but converted to soccer and rugby pitches after the Second World War. This transformation symbolizes well the increasingly popular nature of the Bois which, until 1914, had been the place where the Parisian upper crust showed off its horses and carriages. A magnificent avenue, 120 m wide, was built from the Place de l'Etoile to the Bois; formerly the Avenue de l'Impératrice, it is now the Avenue Foch.

To the north of Paris lies the Buttes-Chaumont in the 19th *arrondissement*; this was formerly an area of quarries which had traditionally served as a rubbish dump for the city and also accommodated a gibbet. Need-less to say, it was an evil-smelling place. An ambitious plan was drawn up to turn it into a gigantic rock garden which would far outstrip in grandeur that of Paxton at Chatsworth. A cliff, 40 m in height, looks over a lake; 22 m above the water is a bridge leading towards a belvedere, reached by climbing a staircase hewn out of rock.

Many other large cities have included green spaces in their plans, notably Lyons, Genoa and Brussels, which took the Bois de la Cambre, a part of the forest of Soignes, for this purpose.

The Parc Güell in Barcelona, built by Gaudí between 1900 and 1914, is a rock garden with many extraordinary features, including overhangs, mosaic incrustations, sometimes made up of ceramic porcelain and glass shards, and groups of tropical trees.

Rome's urban expansion was only too often achieved at the expense of the villas and their gardens, just as the growth of Paris had obliterated the convent gardens. A number of gardens, however, were brought into public use, such as the Borghese, which had been created in the 16th century and constantly modified until the 19th; this is the equivalent of the Bois de Boulogne, but in the centre of

The island with the kiosk in the lake of the Bois de Boulogne, Paris.

the city, and like its Parisian counterpart, it contains a hippodrome. Other gardens sprang up in neighbourhoods farther from the centre. Pope Pius VII had a garden built on the Pincio hill, overlooking the city, to plans by Valadier, drawn up under the auspices of the French prefect of Rome, Tournon. The main avenue is lined with busts of the great men of Italy. A number of parks also resulted from the work of Rafaele de Vico, director of gardens in Rome from 1922 to 1962, notably in the new neighbourhood of the EUR, once the site of an international exhibition.

The landscape style of garden received a new lease of life through its use in the public sector, just as it was being abandoned by private individuals. The reaction against its 'natural' approach to garden design began to appear towards 1850 and increased rapidly thereafter. In Britain, especially, the art of the garden came to assume almost the status of one of the fine arts, like architecture and painting, and was the subject of numerous controversies. During the Victorian period there was a growing tendency to hark back to earlier forms of garden design. This eclecticism, expressed in what might be called the historicist garden, was based mainly on various styles of the formal garden, described in a series of articles around 1830 by Loudon in *The Gardener's Magazine*. Due recognition was even granted to the Italian garden with its many different levels, which had never before taken hold in England. The art of topiary also underwent a renaissance, along with a taste for geometrical arrangements close to the house; more informal patterns of planting were thought appropriate in the further reaches of the park or garden. A number of books published towards the turn of the century encouraged the trend of historicism; these included *The Formal Garden in England* (1892) by Reginald Blomfield, with drawings by Inigo Thomas, *English Pleasure Gardens* (1902) by Rosa Standish Nichols, and John D. Sedding's account of the Victorian garden and its origins, *Garden-craft Old and New* (1891).

The growing recognition of the need to preserve the country's heritage of fine gardens culminated in the foundation of the National Trust in 1894 by Octavia Hill, Canon Rawnsley and Sir Robert Hunter. Three years later appeared the first issue of *Country Life*, devoted mainly to the nation's castles and stately homes.

It was in this atmosphere of innovation in English garden design that Joseph Paxton (1801–65), famous as the architect of the Crystal Palace for the Great Exhibition of 1851, was commissioned to transform the garden of Chatsworth. The original garden, begun in 1687, had been designed in the Classical style by George London for the first Duke of Devonshire. In the 18th century the fourth Duke remodelled it completely in the landscape style. By the time the sixth Duke, famous for his restoration of Chatsworth and the assembling of its marvellous art collections, had succeeded to the title, the abandoned garden had almost returned to its natural state. It was he who asked Paxton to reshape the garden entirely. Around the house, the architect reintroduced water and *broderie* parterres, fountains and new statuary. In another part of the park he established a romantic garden returning to the late 18th-century style, but on a much larger scale, with a number of huge rock structures dedicated to the glory of Prince Albert, Queen Victoria and the Duke of Wellington. Paxton's most imposing building at Chatsworth, however, was an enormous iron and glass conservatory – then the biggest in the world – to house the duke's exotic plants. This hothouse was destroyed after the First World War.

In France, the period saw a renaissance of the French-style garden, thanks mainly to Henri Duchêne and his son Achille, who undertook the restoration of Vaux-le-Vicomte, Courance, Chenonceaux, Wideville, Langeais, Champs, Breteuil, Voisins and the Marais, occasionally by inspired guesswork, when they had none of the original plans to guide them. Their reputation was widespread, and they worked for the Duke of Arenburg at Nordkirchen, Mr V. on Long Island and the Duke of Marlborough at Blenheim.

The development of garden design in the latter part of the 19th century was thus marked by deep nostalgia. At the same time, another strong influence was directing the attention of gardeners back to the essential natural constituents of the garden itself, exemplified by a growing interest in the forms and quality of the actual plants – the flowers, shrubs and trees. This was inspired not so much by a need to develop new forms of the garden as by a genuine appreciation of the scientific and technical aspects of horticulture. The results obtained from a rigorous application of botanical knowledge could only be beneficial to fundamental aspects of gardening, such as plant selection. Plants could now be chosen for their strength as well as their beauty; and rarer plants could be used since far more was now known about the problems of acclimatization, of especial importance in growing exotic plants from distant places for their shape, colour or scent.

It is worth recalling that the acclimatization of plants from abroad had been a concern of the Persians and Babylonians. It was

Ceramic Cornamentation in the Parc Güell, Barcelona, designed by Antonio Gaudí.

also one of the subjects treated in Pliny the Younger's *Historia Naturalis*. In the 15th century, the botanical research carried out by Cosimo de' Medici at Careggi aroused great interest and admiration. And as was the case with many other branches of scientific investigation, the 16th century saw enormous advances in botanical studies on an international scale. Botanical gardens, originally largely pharmaceutical in purpose, were established by the universities of Pisa (1543), Florence (1545), Padua (1545), Rome (c.1566), Bologna (1567) and Leyden (1577). The *Orto Botanico* at Padua, created by Francesco Bonafede, has retained its circular form which was conceivably inspired by the depiction of the island of Cythera in the *Hypnerotomachia Poliphili*. Meanwhile the West continually extended the range of both its medicinal and decorative flora by taking plants from the Orient where the Persians and Turks had brought horticulture to a high degree of sophistication. In 1554, the tulip was introduced from Turkey to Vienna.

Three centuries later, the attentions of flower-growers were directed primarily to the Far East, while the explorations of botanists took them from the Himalayas to Australia. One notable feature of the 19th century was the intensive cultivation of the rose. New species appeared in rapid succession, giving rise to competitions and exhibitions, and making it obligatory for every great garden to have its own rose garden.

Gaston d'Orléans, brother of Louis XIII of France, made a great contribution to the study of plants, birds and animals, which is now one of the richest treasures of the Musée d'Histoire Naturelle, formerly Louis XIV's Jardin des Plantes, in Paris.

Botanical studies were massively advanced by the work of the Swedish scholar Carolus Linnaeus (1707–78) who finally produced a satisfactory system of plant classification based on a binomial principle derived from the pistil and stamen formation.

The object of the science of botany is the definition of plants and, during the 19th century, the greatest advances were made in England; this was especially noticeable in the application of the science to the art of the garden. The Horticultural Society of London, founded in 1804, was to have its own experimental garden, first at Chiswick and then at Wisley in Surrey. The botanical gardens of Kew, Edinburgh and Glasgow undertook intensive research programmes. Botanical expeditions were made to some of the farthest corners of the globe and by private collectors who prided themselves in the pursuit of rare plants and their subsequent successful acclimatization for use in the garden. The conservatories which were constructed in a number of botanical gardens also led to considerable public interest in tropical plants and shrubs. Even the owners of private houses began to acquire them. Derived from the earlier orangeries, but unlike them (except in Russia), conservatories were now heated. Indeed, heated versions date back to the 18th century, one model being illustrated, as already mentioned, in a watercolour by Delagardette; but natural overhead lighting did not become technically possible until the end of the century. In France its application to the lighting of museums caused much stir; the

Salon of 1789 was held in the Salon Carré of the Louvre which had just been given a glass roof. In France, the Duc d'Orléans, the Comte d'Artois and the paymaster-general of the Marine Baudard, known as Saint-Jammes, were among the first owners of private conservatories. In England, too, developments in metallurgy eventually made possible the construction of buildings wholly in glass held together by an iron frame. In addition to being heated, the plants in a conservatory could now benefit from full natural light.

The finest conservatories in England are those at Kew. Some of these house entire tropical gardens (such as the Palm House), while others are used for sowing, bedding, planting and winter protection.

The gardens at Kew were served throughout the 19th century by a number of eminent directors who, through their experiments and advice, exercised considerable influence at every level over the development of the garden in England. The first Superintendent, for some 47 years, was Sir Joseph Banks, appointed by George III in the 1770s. And the first official director, when Kew was handed over to the nation in 1841, was Sir William Hooker. One man of genius with a matchless appreciation of both the aesthetic and technical aspects of gardening was John Claudius Loudun (1783–1843). His concept of the garden was based on the notions of the Scottish philosopher Archibald Alison, who treated nature as an abstraction, so that the landscape garden was as arbitrary as the formal garden or the Tudor garden. The garden was thus envisaged as a work of art, eliciting a response from the observer. As such it was to appeal to an ever growing number of enthusiasts. Once the preserve of great families, gardens were soon being created at all levels of English society; even the modest cottage garden, increasingly popular in town and country alike, formed the subject matter of specialist literature.

Loudon, from a Scottish farming family, had been drawn into the circle around Joseph Banks by the time he was twenty; there he met Jane Webb who was to become his wife and close collaborator. In his design for the garden of Mrs Lawrence, he introduced no less than 3,266 varieties of plants to produce a veritable deluge of colour. Such liberality encouraged the view that the garden should be closer to painting than to nature, as had been the case in the 18th century, or to architecture, which had characterized the traditional French garden. So the 'picture garden' evolved; and this explosive use of colour in the English garden coincided with a similar phenomenon in French painting.

It was during this period that extensive experiments in plant selections, notably those conducted by the Royal Horticultural Society at Wisley, brought into being that central, glorious feature of the modern English garden: the mixed border. This consists essentially of the careful arrangement of both shrubs and herbaceous plants along a banked border to achieve the maximum display of colour. Needless to say, a considerable skill is necessary to prevent such a border from dissolving into a mass of disparate elements.

Other experiments at Wisley concerned themselves with the 'woodland garden', the 'rock garden', a miniature version of the alpine garden, and the 'wild garden'.

At the end of the century, the Irishman William Robinson, curator of the Botanic Gardens in Regent's Park, London, designed a number of gardens throughout Britain, notably at Mount Usher, Castlewellan, Caerhays, Lochinch, Bodnant, Knightshayes, Garinish

Island and Trengwainton. He also founded two journals: *The Garden* (1871) and *The Garden Illustrated* (1879). The latter was particularly intended for the owners of small gardens and devoted many articles to the cottage garden. Gertrude Jekyll (1838–1932) worked with Robinson from 1875, subsequently writing numerous books on garden design, and strongly advocating the native rural tradition, especially the cottage garden. Indeed, Robinson, Jekyll and Lutyens were all strong advocates of the wild garden. In 1896 she had a house built at Munstead in Surrey, where she was to work so extensively (on more than 300 gardens) that it seems almost appropriate to talk of a Surrey School in gardening.

Another interesting development during the Victorian period was that of the domestic conservatory or verandah, which was usually built against the back of the house on the level of the ground floor. Heated by a stove in cold weather, this structure had a dual purpose: it

The verandah of the house built by the author's father before 1870; he is seen here surrounded by his family, while his wife sits in a buggy drawn by an Anglo-Norman crossbreed.

allowed the occupants of the house to enjoy the garden throughout the year and it served as a sitting room in winter. Its connection with the garden was reinforced by covering the wall parts with wooden trellis. Blinds were installed over all parts of the verandah, including the glass roof, to filter the light. It was used to accommodate tropical plants and, around the middle of the century, cacti. An early advocate of this architectural feature was Humphrey Repton, and examples could be found as early as the 1820s. A whole category of plants and flowers began to appear in florists specifically for use in the verandah. But although pleasant in winter, it could be insufferably hot in summer and difficult to maintain. Moreover, it often prevented light getting through the windows of the rooms behind it.

Such winter gardens had become obligatory for all substantial houses by the end of the 19th century; they frequently provided the settings for love scenes in contemporary romantic novels. The problems of the winter garden have been largely resolved nowadays by constructing entire buildings of glass, so that people actually seem to be working or living inside a greenhouse.

The art of the garden has seen numerous exciting developments during the 20th century, notably in the British Isles, the United States (California and South Carolina), on the Côte d'Azur in France and on the Ligurian Riviera in Italy. The greatest innovations, however, have been in England and the United States.

In Britain, a change in the tax laws, involving the introduction of inheritance tax, sounded the knell of the great estates and many of these immense properties were eventually ceded to the National Trust. In such circumstances, creating large gardens was virtually impossible; and although a number of important gardens were established by wealthy individuals, they obviously could not rival the great parks of the aristocracy. The most promising work in this area was done in the United States during the 1930s.

The increase of home ownership, promoted in all the western democracies, coupled with the wish to live in the country, led to the development of the mini-garden in the 20th century and the growth of garden centres and nurseries. An early example of this was the firm of Vilmorin et Andrieux, established in the 18th century on the Quai de le Mégisserie in Paris and, until very recently, still in the ownership of the founding family.

In the modern English garden, seasonal plants, as determined by flowering times, took on a new importance. March would see the appearance of the crocus, to be followed by the narcissi and the hyacinths, then the tulips and, finally, magnolias, rhododendrons and hydrangeas. A large part of English weekend life was now given over to the cultivation and arrangement of flowers – the garden had almost become a way of life.

There is, then, a strongly botanical aspect to the modern garden; the actual layout is secondary to its role as a collection of plants and is conditioned by the primacy of display. This conception is sufficiently elastic to allow even small collections of plants to be made into effective gardens. Many books have been written about small gardens, beginning with Gertrude Jekyll's *Gardens for Small Country Houses* of 1912 and continuing in her *Flower Garden*, in which she recounts her experiences with her own garden at Munstead. Remarkable results can be achieved, even in a restricted space, with a little patience and imagination.

One of the oldest and strangest private botanical gardens is the garden on Tresco in the Scilly Isles, about 40 km to the west of Cornwall. It was established in 1834 by Augustus Smith on the site of an ancient abbey. Tresco was a barren, windswept place but the warming influence of the waters of the Gulf Stream provided a favourable environment, on the windward side of a hill, for a riot of tropical plant life, unequalled anywhere else in Britain. The making of the gardens is described in minute detail in Smith's own journal.

The garden of Powerscourt, not far from Dublin, was started in the same year as that of Tresco, although the house dated from 1743. But whereas Smith had wanted to indulge a taste for dramatic and innovatory effects, Viscount Powerscourt apparently longed for a return to an aristocratic past. The result is a magnificent historicist garden. A superb vista in the Classical style stretches from the southern façade of the house; this is arranged as a series of terraces in the Italian manner and leads down to a majestic round pool. Beyond this strictly controlled design stretches an informal countryside of meadows and woods, so that the garden seems almost unfinished, despite the imposing barrier of the Wicklow Mountains in the background. Both antique and modern ornaments are positioned here and there in the park; these include nymphs, superb grilles and urns copied from Bagatelle and Versailles. The English taste for heraldic beasts manifests itself in the two figures of Pegasus on either side of the grille which leads to the great round pool.

The garden of Bodnant in Wales, famous for its hundreds of hybrid rhododendrons, is also

*P*owerscourt: the
central vista.

arranged in Italian-style terraces. It was begun in 1875 by Lady Aberconway and continued by her son and grandson, who both in turn became presidents of the Royal Horticultural Society. The surface of a canal provides a mirror for the very pretty Pin Mill, built around 1730 but only transported to Bodnant just before the First World War. Often positioned amidst banks of flowers, other features include statues, Baroque rocaille, balusters and sphinxes. Here, the historicist garden has been blended with the floral garden.

Hidcote Manor, established on virgin land in 1907 by the American Lawrence Johnston, could be described as a 'mixed garden'. It is, in effect, a succession of gardens, each one enclosed in hedges of different species – copper beech, silver spindle-tree and yew, alone or combined with holly and other plants. In one enclosure are some fine modern examples of the topiarist's art, including two figures of birds.

Enclosure is one way of bringing an element of discipline to an informal collection of plants; at the garden established by Harold Nicolson and Vita Sackville-West at Sissinghurst in Kent, this framework is provided by the ruins of a Tudor castle. It would be hard to define the particular style either of Sissinghurst or Hidcote, since they both seem to hover between the traditional and the modern.

Sir Robert Lorimer's plans for the restoration of Earlshall in Scotland were continued by the Purvis family, which acquired the estate in 1925. This is one of the greatest topiary gardens in the country, the peacocks appearing particularly lifelike.

It is unusual for the gardens of the United States to display characteristics from more than one culture or period, and a modern garden rooted in a French-style garden and dating from the colonial period is rare indeed. But such a garden does exist in South Carolina, close to the old city of Charleston, at Middleton Place, which takes its name from the first president of the Federal Congress, who was also governor of the state, Henry Middleton. He commissioned a formal garden to be laid out along the west side of his Georgian house, a mark of his high standing in the colony. The president's son, who was one of the signatories of the Declaration of Independence, continued his father's horticultural work; the garden now contains masses of camellias, another historical reminder, since the first camellia was introduced to the United States in 1783 by the Frenchman André Michaux, a friend of Henry Middleton's grandson. During the following century, the tradition of the gardens was continued by William Middleton, Henry's great grandson, who inherited the estate in 1846 and planted it with a profusion of azaleas. A lawn, terraced

like an amphitheatre, as at Chiswick, stretches along one of the vistas and may be a remnant of the first garden. A large lake is crossed by a Chinese bridge.

Cypress Gardens, also in the neighbourhood of Charleston, is a strange water garden which has to be visited by boat; despite its rather primeval appearance, it too evokes memories of a more immediate past. It had been, in fact, an immense estate of rice plantations, worked by 500 slaves, known as Deam Hall. Abandoned after the Civil War, the rice fields rapidly reverted to virgin marsh, until what was left of the estate was acquired by Mr and Mrs Kittredge, who planted beds of azaleas beneath the cypress trees, so that the flowers were reflected in the dark water.

South Carolina has a warm, semi-tropical climate and many of the gardens around Charleston are bright with flowers in early spring. Magnolia Gardens is aptly named; and above the fields of magnolias is a tangled world of vegetation clinging to the marsh cypresses: lianas, epiphytes, Spanish mosses,

succulents and climbers, all running riot in the warm, wet environment, suffused by the heady scent of the magnolias. This extraordinary garden was begun by the Reverend Grimke Dayton, who had been advised by his doctor to take up some form of exercise; so a clergyman, by indulging his hobby, laid the foundations of one of the most astonishing botanical parks in the world.

Old Westbury on Long Island was built by an Englishman in a pastiche of the early 18th-century Georgian style. The gardens, however, are unabashedly modern and designed to give the visitor a series of surprises. Wooded areas planted with pine or beech lead to floral enclosures and pergolas. One avenue, known as the Alley of the Phantoms, is lined by sombre eastern hemlocks. This garden of rare species was created by John S. Phipps and became a charitable foundation in 1958.

The house and garden of Huntington House in California together constitute a museum. The house, built in colonial style between 1906 and 1914 by Henry Edwards

Sissinghurst: the remains of the Tudor castle.

The garden of San Simeon, Los Angeles: the swimming pool with antique temple.

PRECEDING PAGES

Magnolia Gardens, near Charleston.

Huntington, contains a valuable library and a famous collection of English portraits, including Gainsborough's *Blue Boy*. The garden, too, is a 'collection' for it includes a Japanese garden, a tropical garden, a water-lily garden and a Shakespeare garden based on the originals at Stratford-upon-Avon, with all the species of trees and flowers mentioned in the playwright's works. (In 1957, at the instigation of the French cultural attaché in London, a similar garden was planted in the old green theatre of the Pré-Catalan in the Bois de Boulogne in Paris.)

The most famous of the Huntington gardens is a dazzling collection of cacti which occupies no less than ten acres and includes 25,000 plants.

Amidst this variety of styles, there are reminders of the ancient civilizations of Europe. The figures of Cupid and Venus shelter under a *tholus*; antique ornaments, urns and grilles are arranged here and there; and Classical statues are interspersed, somewhat incongruously, between the individual trees in a long avenue of palms.

The newspaper magnate William Hearst showed no hesitation in opting for the past rather than the present when he built his California home. The colossal ensemble of his Casa Grande and the gardens of San Simeon would have graced a film epic by Cecil B. de Mille, except that here the marble and bronze were genuine. Like a latter-day Louis XIV, the American press baron was intent on making his palace and garden of San Simeon a place of high festivity and drama. Here, accompanied either by his wife or the film star Marion Davies, Hearst received hundreds of guests who were flown in to his private airport. The mixture of Classical and Baroque décor must have suited his purpose admirably. Hundreds of lamps, illuminating the nightly revels, were borne on herms which lined all the staircases and terraces up to the Casa Grande. The centrepiece, however, was an immense swimming pool in blue mosaic flanked by the façade of an antique temple specially transported to the estate and complete with its original statuary. Now frequented only by informally dressed tourists, this strangely eclectic garden, part of which is completely abandoned, looks as sad as a theatre after the show has closed and the actors and spectators long departed.

More or less contemporary with the Hearst estate was the series of gardens built on a 20–acre site at Boulogne-sur-Seine near Paris by Albert Kahn. Kahn, who came from a humble background in Alsace, had emigrated to France after the 1870 war and had there made a fortune in banking, only to be ruined by the crash of 1929. The gardens were then bought by the local *département* which sold part of the estate to developers in order to pay for the maintenance of the rest. This consists of a very attractive ensemble, including a French garden, an English garden, a mountain garden (inspired by Kahn's native Vosges), a delightful Japanese garden designed by specialists brought in from Japan, and several others. All the trees are now superb and it is a pleasant surprise to come across these gardens so near to the park of Saint-Cloud.

How closely does the Western-style tropical garden, which has enjoyed such a vogue in modern times, resemble the real thing? One genuine tropical garden, the park of Boa Vista on a hill overlooking Rio de Janeiro, was actually built by a French engineer, François-Marie Glaziou. Arriving in Rio in 1858, Glaziou became Director General of Forests and Gardens under the Emperor Pedro II; he also made a number of botanical discoveries and catalogued 25,000 specimens. In our own day, the architect Roberto Burle-Marx has devoted himself entirely to landscape design. A pupil of Lucio Costa, the original planner of Brasilia, Burle-Marx trained himself by visiting the older parks and botanical gardens throughout Europe. He established his own

Herms in the role of lamp standards in the gardens of San Simeon.

experimental garden at Campo Grande, where he raised hybrids. When the residential neighbourhood of Pampulha, near Belo Horizonte, was built, it was the first distinctly modernist architectural project in Brazil after Le Corbusier; Burle-Marx was commissioned to carry out the natural landscaping. His gardens are frequently embellished with arrangements of rocks or structures, often in a Cubist style. The various elements of his plans are always beautifully balanced, although they lack the luxuriance of the North American gardens.

The most perfect example of the horticultural garden is undoubtedly the Savill Garden in Windsor Great Park, named after its creator, Sir Eric Savill. The garden, begun in 1932, now covers 60 acres of the wooded park of Windsor Castle. It seems rather appropriate that the only great new garden created in England in the 20th century should stem from royal initiative, for it was the idea of King George V and Queen Mary. The plan of the garden, though simple, is a perfect expression of the 'paradise garden style', a category of garden design which has developed recently in England. It consists essentially of masses of flowers arranged informally in the clearings or in the shade of trees. Once again we seem to have gone back to the beginning and rediscovered the garden in its simplest and purest state before the concept of paradise was gradually elaborated and modified over the centuries. Perhaps this garden represents most closely the inner vision of the blind Milton, its sensual delights a nostalgic reminder of the dreamlike world we have lost.

*P*etropolis: the summer palace.

The Kahn gardens at Boulogne-sur-Seine: the Japanese garden.

THE CHINESE AND JAPANESE GARDEN

From its very beginnings until the present day, the art of the garden in the West, as we have seen, has been characterized by a central tradition which has remained constant in every successive civilization: the search for another, better world born from a longing for the lost paradise or some vanished Golden Age. The Oriental or Far Eastern garden has been subject to a quite different set of values. The key concepts and figures of Western garden mythology are conspicuously lacking: no paradise lost, no Adam and Eve banished, no Adam-Prometheus figure punished for discovering the secret of fire, and no Eve-Pandora responsible for the dissemination of Evil on earth.

However, vestiges of the concept of a Golden Age are evident in some of the profounder reaches of Chinese religious thought. Confucianism, for instance, ascribes certain lost virtues to dead ancestors, which may be rediscovered through the honouring and imitation of the dead. According to Hsun-Tzu, one of the disciples of Confucius, the kings of ancient times had drawn up a number of moral principles to make conflict impossible. Even before Confucianism, the theologians of the Zhou Dynasty, in their search for arguments to overthrow the Shang, created a model of the ideal leader based on the figures of Yao, Chouem and Yu, the legendary founders of Chinese civilization. The Shang, according to the Zhou, had lost the attributes of 'Son of Heaven' by their excesses, extortion and crime: the mandate to govern, awarded to the founder of the dynasty, had now been withdrawn by the heavenly powers.

Elements of the myth of the gentle sovereign would seem to have existed in the pre-Confucian era, although it was Confucius (551–479 BC) who made of *yen*, the tendency to love one's neighbour, the basis of a balanced society. This belief in the original goodwill of man, corrupted by institutions, grew even stronger after Confucius. His successor, Meng-Tzu, venerated the sovereigns of antiquity as being the creators of the institutions and of a morality to which the people should return under his guidance.

The Chinese scholars of the Confucian era believed that a harmonious society had existed at the very beginnings of their civilization; there was also a belief in an earthly paradise, but one which was still in existence and which it was the task of the emperors to find. During the reigns of the princes Wei (378–342 BC) and Hsuan (342–324 BC) and of the king Chao (311–279 BC), maritime expeditions were sent out to search for the Isles of the Immortals, which were described by historians as a range of three mountains. Some of the expeditions had succeeded in approaching them, without actually exploring them fully yet near enough to observe that the palaces and the gates were of the purest gold and silver. A text by Mich-Tzu dating from the era of Liu-ch'ao (AD 420–588) elaborates on this description and speaks of five island-mountains, where all the waters of the Earth and the rivers of Milky Way flow together, where the birds and animals are of a dazzling whiteness and all the palaces are built of gold and precious stones; all the flowers give off a wonderful scent and the succulent fruits protect the eater from old age and death. The position of the islands was not, however, very secure, since the Lord had decreed that they should rest on the backs of tortoises, of which only three remained after a giant made off with the other two. The last unsuccessful expeditions were despatched by the emperor Wu-Ti (141–7), who was then driven to building his own isles in a large pond to gain favour with the ancestral spirits. These legends continued to exercise an appeal, and gardens were designed with their own Isles of the Immortals positioned in the middle of ponds.

Such paradise gardens can also be found in Japanese civilization; the concept of the 'happy isles' occurs in Zen Buddhism, and such legends were also part of the metaphysical system of belief known as the Tao which, with Confucianism pragmatism, helped to formulate the Chinese system of thought. Sin is recognized by Buddhism in the sense that it is only by demonstrating his capacity for good that an individual can climb the ladder of being and thus know the deliverance from the

The Zen garden of contemplation at Ryōan-ji, Kyoto.

evil which is life. Among the Buddhist sects in China, the concept of the great vehicle (Mahayana), with its promise of a much happier salvation than that of the small vehicle (Hinayana), was by far the most current and contributed therefore to the concept of a paradise within the culture.

The various currents of thought and belief which influenced the art of the garden in China were, then, as metaphysically complex as those which had informed the various stages of the same art in the West. Constantly under threat of invasion from the north and, apart from the period of the Tang, never enjoying the kind of peace and unity which Rome succeeded in imposing on its empire, the troubled history of ancient China must also have provided another strong motivation for its scholars, poets and philosophers to dream of an ideal world which could be expressed in the garden.

In spite of such similarities, however, there is no doubt that the Oriental garden differs enormously from the Western, and this is due to two widely differing attitudes towards the natural world. Western man does not consider himself so much a part of nature as a vehicle for its understanding; the natural world is something to be studied and known, but in an objective fashion. After all, did not God ask Adam to give names to all the animals he had created? Adam's sin consisted not in his efforts to *know* but in his efforts to *do*, to put himself on equal footing with God by desiring knowledge which could only belong to God (that of good and evil), the same sin as that committed by the Archangel Lucifer.

The philosophy of the Tao condemns all discursive knowledge, since this leads to multiplicity in the soul, when its only concern should be the unity of things. In the same spirit as the prohibition on seeking to know nature, the Tao also forbids any intervention in the passage of events. Power is thus as strongly condemned as knowledge, which explains the long indifference of the Chinese towards technological progress.

Man, therefore, is expected to feel himself at one with nature, having accepted that the ultimate Being is a single unity in which all differences and contradictions are contained and resolved. Once this state of recognition has been achieved and all the artifice of civilization has been renounced, the seeker after knowledge can hope for purification which will permit him finally to achieve complete illumination and perfect at-oneness with the world.

It is hardly surprising, then, that the Chinese gardens should look so unfamiliar to Western eyes. They are not a reproduction, an imitation or even an evocation of nature, they are nature itself. Such a garden could be created simply by choosing a site and then organizing it for human use. Only two basic elements were necessary for a setting to be suitable: the *yang* (the notion of movement, and therefore male) and the *yin* (the notion of stillness, and therefore female); the two concepts were represented respectively by the mountains and the water. If an entire area cannot just be taken over to create such a garden, then one can be made artificially; in the last resort, a spade can be used to dig a hole, the earth removed to make the mountain, and the hole refilled with water. Thus the *yin* and the *yang* will be present and the meditation on the principles of nature may then commence. The location of the garden, therefore, should ideally consist of the most varied terrain, including mountains, valleys, hills, rivers, brooks, ponds and lakes. Among these features are pavilions which vary according to the purpose of the part of the garden in which they are situated, whether destined for social use or for solitary reflection. There are residential pavilions, pavilions for meeting, others serving as music rooms, libraries, tea rooms, meditation rooms, hermitages, grottoes, kiosks and special vantage points from which to view the most dramatic parts of the site. There are even pavilions to observe the rising moon. The various parts of the garden are linked by tracks, paths and footbridges; if a pathway has to cross a stretch of water, then the bridge is given a semi-circular form so that it forms a complete circle when joined with its reflection in the water, as the symbol of perfection. Vegetation must be chosen for its beauty in every season, flowers for their scent and effect (blue being the colour preferred) and fruits for their taste.

The flower has a basic, primeval importance, since it affects both sight and smell; it is also a great aid to meditation. China's geographical location in a semi-tropical zone of the northern hemisphere has given it an exceptional abundance of flowering species, which have been sought for Western gardens since the 16th century. The Chinese have traditionally increased this natural wealth through horticulture; their favourite flowers were the chrysanthemum and the peony, a token of love. Red lilies were supposed to aid the birth of male children and pregnant women would carry them in their belts. Of course, the climate favoured the cultivation of countless species of orchid, lilac, water lily, hydrangea, hollyhock and finally the lotus, emblem of the Buddhist religion. Bamboo and willow grew in profusion on the banks of the lakes, while the mountains provided a home

The palace of Yuen Ming Yuen, part of the Summer Palace in Peking, painting from a collection of forty paintings on silk from the Ming period. Bibliothèque Nationale, Cabinet des Estampes, Paris.

for the windswept pine.

The first Chinese gardens, like those of Persia and Babylon, were probably hunting reserves, but carefully planned gardens were created by the emperor Zhou around 2000 BC. We have detailed descriptions of gardens from the time of the Qin Dynasty (221–216 BC) and the Han (206 BC-AD 201). The gardens of the emperor Wu-Di (140–87 BC) were spread over 130 square kilometres around his capital of Chang-an, in western China. The ideal of love had already been associated with the concept of the garden as a 'paradise', and the emperor dedicated one to his beloved Fei Yan, whose beauty was celebrated by contemporary poets and, in this country devoted to tradition, still an inspiration to writers 800 years later.

Even more than Muslims, the Chinese see the world through a veil of poetry. Everything they create seems to exist in an imaginary world; even their naming of places is couched in poetic terms and metaphor: gold, jade, silver, coral or other precious stones. At the Summer Palace in Peking, for instance, we encounter successively the hill of a thousand-year life, the garden of golden waters, the temple of perfect tranquillity, the garden of marvellous hills, the palace of the spring in bloom, the garden of perfect charity, the palace of the calm sea, the palace of delights and harmony, the view of the distant lake, and so on.

When Buddhism spread through China, a new type of monastery garden began to appear, known as Lu Shan, which was intended solely for meditation. This type also appeared in Japan.

The Chinese garden is one of the great absentees from the history of garden design; its disappearance is as complete as that of Greek painting. However, numerous descriptions of the garden of the past exist, either by Western visitors or by the Chinese themselves. Paintings of such gardens can be misleading, partly because the subjects may not be representative and partly because the vertical and horizontal scales of such works are not the same, to accentuate the hilly effect of the garden. The most accurate depictions are to be found in engravings made by Westerners, often secular priests or Jesuits. The best of these was the Italian Father Castiglione, a painter who worked in the Chinese style and was resident at the court of the emperors Yong-Cheng and K'ien-Long. With a Father Benedict, he was also called upon to act as architect when one of the emperors decided to extend the Summer Palace, complete with

The poet Li Po receives his friends in the garden of flowers and peach trees, painting by Ch'iu Ying, 16th century. Private collection, Paris.

*T*he lake of the Summer Palace in Peking. In the distance is the Hill of the Jade Fountain.

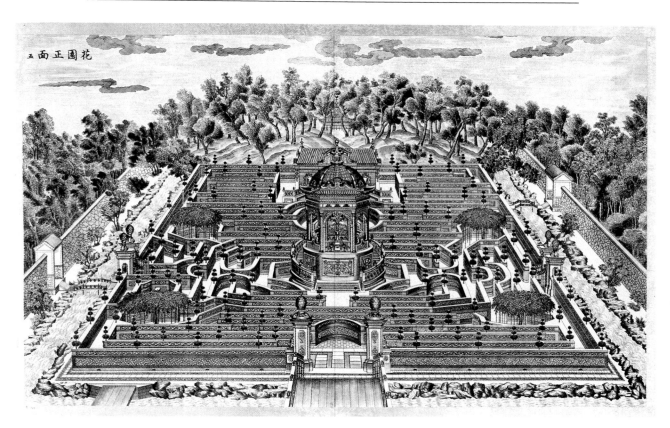

French-style gardens and fountains, to form the ensemble known as Wancheou-yuan (the garden of the thousand-year life). Even a labyrinth was included. There remain a number of ruins of this palace and it is possible that it may be restored under the present Chinese government. Perhaps more than any other country, the artistic patrimony of China has suffered terrible periods of destruction, including the recent Cultural Revolution, when the Summer Palace was devastated, or rather what remained of it after it had been pillaged by Anglo-French troops in 1860 and again sacked and burnt in 1900 by troops from the Western legations.

The Summer Palace is a collection of pavilions and gardens about 10 km north-west of Peking. There the emperor Wan Yung Leang built a pleasure residence in 1153. This habit was continued to the present century, since the house of the deceased could not be occupied by his successor, and so a whole series of pavilions and gardens came into being, housing fine collections from the great periods of Chinese art, mainly of paintings. These collections were removed in 1949 by Chiang Kai-chek on his withdrawal to Formosa and are now in the museum of Taipeh.

Contrary to the situation in China, a large number of older Japanese gardens have survived. Some of these are very ancient indeed (in fact, the oldest in the world), but have been maintained and renewed through successive periods. Japan considers the creation of gardens to be a major art form, reflecting the importance of nature in its culture. The claims of spring and autumn as the best seasons for appreciating the beauty of gardens are a constant theme of conversation among garden lovers, although even winter and its snow has its partisans.

One great Japanese scholar, Osamu Mori, has devoted 50 years of research to the art; he has restored several gardens, even excavating for traces of prehistoric gardens. Garden specialists are certainly not new to Japan but there, more than anywhere else, they tended to be scholars and members of the nobility or the clergy. The latter became great experts in the art from the Kamakura period (1185–1333) onwards. Especially famous was one monk who played a major role in the spiritual life of Japan, Musō–Sōseki (1275–1351). In the 17th century, Kobori Enshū (1579–

A labyrinth (showing European influence) in the palace of Yuen Ming Yuen, part of the Summer Palace; engraving from a painting brought back by Jesuit missionaries in the 18th century. Bibliothèque Nationale, Cabinet des Estampes, Paris.

The Bridge of the Jade Belt in the Summer Palace in Peking.

1647), a functionary of the *shōgunat*, was a noted architect and gardener.

The essential materials of the Japanese garden, which is almost always asymmetrical, are stone, sand, water, moss, trees and flowers, although they may represent other things. For instance, sand may stand in for water when its surface has been given a wave-like configuration with a rake, or it may represent a mountain when it has been formed into a conical heap. Stones can be used in various functions; their most obvious role is to represent mountains, but they can also symbolize, with varying degrees of abstraction, other natural elements. In the dry garden or *karesansuï* of Zen Buddhism, the stone can be water or even water in movement, such as a cascade. A large number of written works with illustrations exist on the various uses of stones, such as the *Chōsetsudō teizumaki*, an illustrated scroll showing gallery gardens opening on to a snow scene, dating from the Momoyama period (16th century). Many different types of stone can be used in the garden: granite, red jasper, white and yellow limestone, green or grey slate in slabs, schist and volcanic rocks. They must be chosen with great care, since their degree of erosion will have a bearing on their symbolic significance. Very high sums can be paid for stones suitable for garden use and their price was actually subject to control during the Tempo period (1830–44).

During the period of the horticultural garden in the West, flowers were massed together to create a startling effect of colour; their use in the Japanese garden is quite different, where each flower is an essential part of the composition, the better to bring out its individual quality.

Another fundamental feature is the pond, without which the garden would literally be devoid of structure, since it would lack one of the two basic natural elements, the *yin*. The *chitei* pond is a garden formed of a stretch of water with winding banks and bordered by a path which goes all the way round the water's edge, thus permitting the garden to be viewed from all angles.

The contemplation garden, in contrast, is not intended for promenades; it is designed to be observed from the residence of the scholar, noble or monastery superior. Such gardens often take take the form of *karesansuï* or 'dry garden', in which various 'islands' would carry different meanings. The *roji* (tea garden) was specifically designed for the ritual tea drinking ceremony.

Plant life flourishes in the subtropical climate of the country. Among trees, the pine is dominant. The Japanese gardeners are past masters in the art of shaping vegetation to the forms and even the sizes they require. The pines are often grown to give an effect of twisted branches, while the technique of reducing trees to produce dwarf varieties (*bonsai*) is a Japanese speciality which is known the world over, making the concept of the 'pocket garden' a reality.

Moss is not used in its natural habitat, but cultivated as an ornament, principally of stones.

The bridges of the Japanese gardens are very different from those of the Chinese; they either take the form of a segmented arch or have a graceful, arrow-like trajectory. Sometimes, the stretches of water in the Japanese gardens are provided with fords in the form of piles of stepping stones resting on the water's bed. In some landscape gardens, the water is represented by sand or pine needles.

The greatest number of sanctuaries and gardens is to be found at Kyoto, the capital of Japan from 794 to 1603. The form of the Japanese garden came originally from China by way of Korea and proved easily acceptable there, partly because the indigenous *shintō* religion embraced a certain number of animist beliefs. This assimilation was reinforced by the arrival of Buddhism in its Chan form, becoming Zen in Japanese, which observed a close relationship with the natural world without such intermediary devices as statues of the Buddha or of Kwanon. A further impetus was given to its spread by the fall of the southern Sung Dynasty (1127–1279), which caused many scholars and monks to emigrate to Japan.

There is another type of garden in Japan, known as the 'paradise garden'. We find it, for

Ryōan-ji, Kyoto: the Oshidori lake.

instance, at the end of the Heian Period (794–1185). The sense of nostalgia, which is so potent a force in the creation of gardens, is very apparent in this form; here, in a supreme refinement of the courtly arts, it is informed by a feeling of melancholy provoked by political strife and unrest, a foreboding of the end of things. Some solace for this sense of regret and yearning was provided by the doctrine of paradise or *Jōdokyō*, which came to Japan from Korea. This maintained that all who led an ascetic life and indulged in good works could be brought to rebirth in the 'Western Paradise', the realm of the Buddha Amitabha. Certain theologians believed that intense prayer, coupled with the contemplation of paradise on earth, was sufficient to achieve redemption. One priest, Genshin (942–1017), wrote: 'Pray with compunction to obtain redemption through Amitabha, and so you will be reborn.... The flowers of many pleasures are spread out on the pond of grace.... And all the flowers shift in the light breeze....'; water 'flows calmly, neither too quickly, nor too slowly, with a faint, magical murmur'. The reborn would find themselves in the midst of palaces, pavilions, precious stones, scented trees and celestial musicians surrounding Amitabha and his *bodhisattvas* (Buddhist saints).

The Japanese nobility began to build these paradise gardens, which were then turned into temples. One example of this is the famous residence of Byōdō'in, which is on the river Uji near Kyoto. This was the country estate of the Fujiwara family, which one of its members, Yorimichi (991–1074), converted into a temple in 1053. The garden of the residence still exists, although very much changed, and the temple still stands on an island amidst pine trees, reflected in a stretch of calm water. Inside, in the Amida gallery, are the same charming musicians floating in the air around a statue of Amida (Amitabha), the angels of Mahayana Buddhism. On the crest of the roof is the figure of a phoenix, the symbol of redemption. A sense of poetry is conveyed by the mirage effect of the temple in the lake, with its coloured woods and white walls, crowned by the elegant curves of the roof, reflected in the lake. A similar *jōdoshiki* garden, dating from the middle of the 12th century and belonging to the temple of Enjōji near Nara, was restored by Osamu Mori in 1976.

The famous Golden Pavilion (Kinkakuji) was begun in 1394 and finished in 1408 by a member of the Ashikaga clan, prince Yoshimitsu, who gave up his position of *shōgun* in favour of his son to devote himself entirely to the building of his retirement home, the Kit-

Kyoto: the garden of the Silver Pavilion (Ginkakuji).

Byōdō'in, Kyoto: the Temple of the Phoenix.

243

The monastery of Ryōan-ji, Kyoto: garden of the chitei *pond.*

ayamadono to the north of Kyoto. It was originally planned that the interior should be decorated with gold, but it is somehow in keeping with the spirit of Japanese culture that this decoration was never actually carried out. Yet the intention to decorate the residence in such a luxurious manner has somehow contributed to its magical atmosphere; such lightness and immaterial grace give the impression that it is floating above the surrounding waters. Unfortunately, the building we see today is a reconstruction after the destruction of the original by fire in 1955.

Another example of the paradise garden, this time intact, is that of the Silver Pavilion (Ginkakuji). This was begun in 1482 as a retreat for Ashikaga Yoshimasa and is one of the most poetic gardens of Kyoto. It benefits enormously from its site, which is on the west slope of the hills to the east of the city. The prince originally intended it to be a mountain villa. The garden suffered damage during the civil wars, after which it was abandoned, to be restored in 1615.

Once through the entrance portico, the visitor follows a wide avenue lined with camellias and clipped pines; a bend in the avenue preserves a sense of expectation. In fact, the garden proper is still to come. First there is an enclosed floral garden with geometrical paving stones (very rare) which leads to a second portico, and from here, suddenly, we see the mystical dry garden, nestling like a jewel amidst stones, pavilions and pines. A cone of white sand, its point flattened, stands out from an expanse of grey sand arranged in bands of contrasting tones; this is the *seko*, symbolizing the beauty of a Chinese lake. According to legend, the master of the house for whom the garden was created discovered this pile of sand which had been left behind by the workmen. It looked so beautiful in the moonlight that he gave orders for it to be preserved in its original form and for flakes of mica to be added to make it sparkle. There may, in fact, be a more esoteric explanation for the popularity of this form. It evokes, for instance, the form of Mount Fuji, which is one of the key images associated with the empire of the Rising Sun; and there are also other sacred mountains in Buddhist mythology, such as Mount Meru. Yet whatever mountain is represented by this heap of sand, it forms the centre of the world, which is the garden; and a circle marked on its surface formerly indicated the best position for contemplating the moon.

At the far end of the neighbouring lake are the three storeys of the Pavilion of the Temple, on an island surrounded by rocks. The phoenix, symbol of immortality, rises proudly from the crest of the roof. There are several islands in the immense lake, dominated by a steep hill covered with pines and maple trees, which turn red in autumn. A massive cascade runs down the hill, a rarity in Japan. This natural backdrop prevents one's thoughts straying to the world beyond and encourages mental and spiritual concentration on the heart of the garden.

Ryōan-ji, also at Kyoto, is the most famous example of the contemplative garden; it adjoins a sanctuary which dates from the end of the 15th century. There are two quite distinct parts to the garden. First, the visitor passes through an entry gate to find a *chitei* pond, which boasts an island and a platform-shaped peninsula. This serves as a landing stage and also provides a view of the entire pond and its tangled water plants which seem to express the quintessential exuberance of nature. When I visited the garden, a dead tree was pinned against the bank by two pieces of wood. The monastery itself stands on a terrace; there is a water basin outside for ritual cleansing before entering.

Inside, the dragon paintings on the partitions have been preserved and, most importantly, so has the enigmatic dry garden. On an expanse of carefully raked white sand are arranged five groups of stones according to odd-number sequence, seven-five-three. The meaning of this scheme has been lost over the ages and it is therefore now open to different interpretations. It has been taken to represent the Confucianist story of the tigress crossing the ocean with her cubs, as the islands in the great sea, or as the summits of the mountains in the sea of clouds, and so on.

There is no such confusion about the interpretation of the dry garden of Daisen in the temple of Daitokuji, built between 1509 and 1513 by the Zen priest Daisho. Arranged in the form of a square, it expresses the vicissitudes of the soul during the course of earthly life. The symbolism of the garden is expressed in stone and moss, with a few shrubs, and includes an evocation of the tortoise (material life) and the footsteps of the Buddha. The representation of Mount Horai in a corner of the square forms an unusual element of landscaping in a dry garden, between the rock of Permanence and a cascade (in stone, of course). Then comes the Sea of the Ocean, crossed by the Bridge of Existence, symbolized by a stone tile attached to a rock, itself the head of a dragon. On one side of the bridge lie the stone-mirror and the Island of the Crane; on the other are the Head of the Hermit, the boat loaded with the Treasures of Experience, the Sea of Eternity, Mount Miei, the Island of the Pearl and the Sleeping Animal. The garden adjoined the quarters of the Superior who

M onk in contemplation before a dry garden (karesansuï). Daisen monastery, Kyoto.

248

could concentrate on one or other of the motifs simply by moving screens. A balcony opposite these quarters gave on to the 'without hand or foot' garden and on to the Ocean of the Morning, an expanse of raked sand embellished with two conical piles of sand and the *sara-soju* tree. These themes can also be found in the Chinese ink painting of the Sung Dynasty, which had considerable influence both on the *karesansuï* garden and, elsewhere, on the landscape garden.

Westerners have always found the idea of the purely symbolic dry garden peculiarly attractive and have detected in it certain resemblances to modern abstract art, as though the designers of such gardens were going through the same process as Kandinsky in reducing the outside world to its essentials. This seems to me to be a misreading of the intentions of the Zen Buddhists who remain for hours, days and even years in contemplation of a *karesansuï* to achieve a state of ecstasy; theirs is a metaphysical search, while Kandinsky's is anchored in the realm of forms. It seems to demand that we lose the consciousness of self in the changing yet timeless world of nature, to go beyond mere appearance – an approach to life with which Plato would have concurred.

The transformation of many aristocratic country residences into temples has rather tended to obscure the importance of the garden in the life of the Japanese upper classes. The gardens of the princes and of the court were the scene of festivities and celebrations, described by countless writers and poets; the lakes of the great gardens were also used for nautical sports as was to happen later in the West.

For the Buddhist monk, the maintenance of the gardens was an act of piety. It is also interesting to note that many of these gardens were inspired by Chinese or indigenous paintings, just as the designers of the landscape gardens were to be inspired by certain French and Italian artists of the 17th century. A number of gardens reproduced famous landscapes, while others took up themes from literature, adding interest and complexity to the art of Japanese garden design. The fact that so many gardens from this classical period have survived makes it possible to observe their development, which also reflects the evolution of a whole civilization.

The secular Japanese gardens which have been preserved are fewer and more recent. One famous example is that of the palace of

Katsura, near Kyoto, designed by Kobori Enshū and built for the Imperial Prince Toshihito between 1625 and 1650. Although the design of the gardens looks confused at first sight, it is in fact carefully planned for the pleasure of the visitor who is offered a fresh view at every step, an aspect which the first Westerners in the 18th century misunderstood. There is another example at the palace of Hamarikvū in Tokyo, which extends over no less than 60 acres. It was last redesigned in 1773–1841 and became a public park in 1945. Designed on three levels, it contains a number of islands and thick woods; the ponds were formerly used for duck shooting, but this is now forbidden.

The use of infusions (*Camelia sinensis* or *Camelia japonica*), which is practised by Buddhists to remain awake during their meditations, goes back to the third millennium BC and the time of the mythical emperor Chennong. The stimulating properties of the beverage give it special status, and thus its consumption was the occasion for a complete ritual. The rules were laid down during the 15th century; by the 16th century, there were several different schools, some of which derived their practices from Zen. The art of taking tea (*chanoyu*) requires a tea master and a chosen location. This location is the tea garden or *roji*, which may be quite separate, but is more often joined to another garden, secular or religious. Traditionally, the garden was divided into several sectors, for welcome, waiting, making the tea, consumption, meditation, and finally the ceremony of leavetaking. This particular sequence of activities was intended to uplift the spirit. The tea gardens were always decorated with stone lanterns, which are found elsewhere but only in ornamental roles. It is this ritualization of an act or gesture which carries us into the realm of the sacred – something not understood by the Catholic church, for in curtailing its ritual, it has compromised the very structure to which faith clings. The rituals of etiquette in Japan, even those of daily life, have allowed the Japanese to retain their distinct identity, while still holding a prominent position in the modern industrial world.

In conclusion, let us think of the monk in contemplation of his dry garden at all seasons and in all weathers, at every hour of the day and, when appropriate, by moonlight, always in the hope of arriving at the ultimate illumination.

A Zen Buddhist monk contemplating a landscape with cascade, by Monotobu. National Museum, Tokyo.

Glossary

A

Aiola Italian word for a parterre.

Alley/allée A narrow walk, lined with hedges or trees, within a garden; the French *allée* was often used in a wider sense, as at Versailles, to denote an avenue.

Amalthaeum (Latin), **Amaltheion** (Greek) Sanctuary, generally in the form of a nymphaeum or grotto, designated as a shrine to the nymph Amalthaea, nurse of the infant Zeus.

Ambulatio Latin word for a promenade under a portico or in the open air.

Antique Dating from an early period, specifically an art style, usually Greek or Roman.

Arboretum Place for growing a variety of rare tree species.

Avenue A road or walk, lined on either side by trees, usually through grounds as an approach to a house, but also, given its breadth and the size of the trees, within a garden.

Azulejo Portuguese word for a faience tile with a decorative surface, usually in blue but sometimes polychrome.

B

Balustrade A row of balusters (short, pillar-like supports) for a coping or railing, sometimes broken by piers supporting garden ornaments.

Banqueting house In Elizabethan times, a building, specifically designed for dining, usually in keeping with the style of the main house and located inside a walled garden.

Barchetto Diminutive of *barco*.

Barco Antique Italian word for park.

Baroque A florid style of art and architecture, originating in early 17th-century Italy, notable for its bold, flowing lines and curves and its exaggerated ornamental effects.

Belvedere An ornamental garden structure designed for admiring a view.

Bonsai Japanese word for a miniature tree or garden grown by special methods in a porcelain dish; the art of growing such plants.

Boulingrin French phonetic translation of English *bowling green* to describe a parterre of sunken lawn for playing bowls.

Broderie French word for a parterre, the design of which, in box, shrubs or flowers, resembles embroidery.

C

Cabinet An enclosed space in a French garden containing greenery and, as a rule, status.

Cascade A larger water theatre on several levels with a variety of jets and fountains.

Casino Italian word for a small summer house or country house.

Catena d'acqua Italian garden feature comprising a sloping, ornamented channel down which water flows.

Chabutra Moghul word for a stone platform, surrounded by flowers, on which the emperor sat.

Chandelier French word for a jet of water falling into a basin at ground level, resembling a candle of a chandelier.

Charbah Moghul word for a garden divided into four quarters by canals; also a large garden containing a palace or pavilion.

Classical Style of Greek or Roman antiquity, applicable to art, architecture, literature and philosophy, distinguished by balance, clarity and simplicity.

Conservatory A glass-covered room or house for growing and displaying plants.

Cottage garden A garden of a small house or cottage.

Cupola A small dome surmounting a roof or tower.

D

Delizia Italian word for a country house dating from 15th century onward.

E

Exedra A semi-circular or rectangular recess with raised seats or benches, originating in ancient Roman or Greek porticoed room for conversation.

F

Formal garden A garden laid out on formal lines, with plantings symmetrically arranged in rows or geometrical figures.

G

Gazebo An ornamental garden building in the form of a pavilion or summer house, comparable to a belvedere, affording a fine view.

Grotto An artificial recess or structure, usually arched and rocky, resembling a natural cave.

H

Haha A wall or fence, set in a ditch as a boundary to the garden, without interrupting the view over the landscape.

Herm A square stone pillar surmounted by a bust or head, originally of Hermes.

Hortus conclusus Latin name for a garden enclosed by walls.

K

Kiosk An open summer house or pavilion with pillars of stone or wood.

L

Labyrinth A garden maze consisting of paths flanked by tall, dense hedges, all communicating and leading to a central point but designed to lead walkers in wrong directions or to bring them to a dead end.

Landscape garden A garden laid out on informal lines, with a mixture of natural and artificial features arranged for visual effect.

Loggia A gallery or arcade, forming part of a building, open to the air on at least one side.

M

Maze A complex of hedge-bordered paths in a park or garden; a labyrinth.

Mixed garden A garden containing borders and banks of mixed herbaceous plants and shrubs.

N

Nymphaeum A building or room, originally Roman, containing a spring or fountain, plants, sculptures, etc.

O

Orangery A greenhouse or similar protected place where orange trees are cultivated in cool climates.

P

Pagoda An ornamental, many-storeyed, pyramid-shaped building, based on the Indian or Chinese sacred tower or temple.

Palissade French word for a wall of greenery formed by pruned trees.

Palladian An architectural style derived from the designs and works of the 16th-century Italian Andrea Palladio, used for many 18th-century English garden buildings.

Palm house A large tropical greenhouse.

Paradeisos Greek word, derived from the Persian, for an enclosed place, hence a 'garden of delights'.

Parterre A section of garden with a varied and ornamental arrangement of beds or plots, especially of flowers.

Patio A court or courtyard of a building, usually paved and open to the sky.

Pavilion A light ornamental structure or projection to a house, usually with oriental features, designed for leisure, shelter, etc.

Pergola An openwork arbour or arch, supported by columns, over which plants are trailed; a small architectural structure in this form.

Peschiera Italian word for a fishpond or vivarium.

Pomario Italian word for an orchard.

Portico A roofed structure, open or partially enclosed, supported by columns, often forming the entrance to a temple, church or house.

R

Riadh Arabic word for an enclosed garden.

Rocaille Style of 18th-century ornmentation based on the forms of rocks and shells.

Rock garden A garden on rocky terrain or with rock features in which alpines and similar plants are grown.

Rococo A highly ornamental 18th-century architectural style, originally from France, evolved from the Baroque, but lighter and more elegant.

Roji Japanese word for a tea garden.

S

Stoa Greek word for a portico.

Summer house A simple garden building designed for relaxation and shade from summer heat.

T

Telamon A male figure used as a supporting column.

Term A pillar or boundary post surmounted by a bust or head, originally of the god Terminus.

Tholos A circular building of ancient Greek origin.

Topiary The art of pruning and trimming plants, e.g. box and yew, into ornamental shapes.

Turf maze A spiral labyrinth, associated with folklore, cut into the turf or lawn.

V

Villa A country residence with a garden.

Villa rustica Latin term for an agricultural estate.

Viridarium An area planted with clumps of trees; a tree nursery.

W

Wild garden A garden containing colonies of naturalized hardy wild and garden plants.

Woodland garden A garden with trees and plants that reproduce the natural effect of a wood.

INDEX OF NAMES OF PERSONS AND PLACES

Bibliography

ACTON H., *The Villas of Tuscany*, London 1973. 2nd edition 1984.

BERRALL J., *Illustrated History of Gardens*, London, 1966.

BEURDELEY C. et M., *Castiglione, peintre jésuite à la cour de Chine*, Fribourg, 1971.

BLOMFIELD R. and THOMAS F.I., *The Formal Garden in England*, 1892.

BOITARD P., *Traité de la composition et de l'ornement des jardins*, Paris, 1825.

BORD J. et CLARENCE-LAMBERT J., *Labyrinthes et Dédales du monde*, Les Presses de la Renaissance, Paris, 1977.

BOYCEAU DE LA BARAUDIÈRE J., *Traité de jardinage selon la raison de la nature et de l'art*, Paris, 1638.

BRIÈRE G., *Le Parc de Versailles*, Paris, 1910.

CASA VALDES, *Jardines di Espana Aguilar*, Madrid, 1973.

CECIL E., *A History of Gardening in England*, London, 1910.

CHARAGEAT M., *L'Art des jardins*, P.U.F., Paris, 1962.

CLIFFORD D., *History of Garden Design*, London, 1962.

COATS P., *Great Gardens of the Western World*, London, 2nd edition 1968.

COFFIN D.R., *The Villa d'Este at Tivoli*, Princeton, 1960.
— *The Villa in the Life of Renaissance Rome*, Princeton, 1979.

CORPECHOT L., *Les Jardins de l'intelligence*, Paris, 1910.
— *Parcs et Jardins de France*, Plon, Paris, 1937.

COX E.H.M., *The Modern English Garden*, London, 1927.

DAMI L., *Il Giardino italiano*, Turin, 1924.

DELILLE J., *Les Jardins ou l'Art d'embellir les paysages*, Paris, 1782.

FITCH J.M. and ROCKWELL F.F., *Treasury of American Gardens*, Harper, New York, 1956.

FOUQUIER et DUCHÊNE, *Des divers styles de jardins*, Paris, 1914.

GANAY E. DE, *Les Jardins à la française en France au xviiie siècle*, Paris, 1943.
— *Les Jardins de France et leur décor*, Larousse, Paris, 1949.
— *Beaux Jardins de France*, Plon, Paris, 1950.
— *André Le Nostre*, Paris, 1950.

GEBELIN F., *Les Châteaux de la Renaissance*, Paris, 1927.

GIRARDIN R.-L., *De la composition des paysages ou des moyens d'embellir la nature autour des habitations en joignant l'agréable à l'utile*, 1775; éd. du Champ urbain, Paris, 1979 (reprint of 1777 edition).

GOKYONOKO Y., *Sakutei-ki ou le livre secret des jardins japonais*, version of P. and S. Rambach, A. Skira, Geneva, 1973.

GOTHEIN M.-L., *Geschichte der Gartenkunst*, Jena, 1914.
— *Indische Gärten*, Munich, 1926.

GRIMAL P., *Les Jardins romains à la fin de la République et aux deux premiers siècles de l'Empire*, Paris, 1943.
— *L'Art des jardins*, P.U.F., Paris, 1954.

GROMORT G., *Jardins d'Italie*, Paris, 1922.
— *Jardins d'Espagne*, Paris, 1926.
— *L'Art des jardins*, Paris, Massin, 1934.

HAUTECŒUR L., *Les Jardins des dieux et des hommes*, Hachette, Paris, 1959.

HAZLEHURST F.H., *Gardens of Illusions. The Genius of André Le Nostre*, Vanderbilt University Press, Nashville, 1986.

HYAMS E., *The English Garden*, London, 1964.
Il Giardino Storico Italiano. Problemi di Indagine, Fonte litterarie e storiche, Atti del convegno di Studi Sierra, San Quirico d'Orcia, 1978, Florence, 1981.

JEKYLL G. and WEAVER L., *Gardens for Small Country Houses*, London, 1912.

KING R., *Les Paradis terrestres, Une histoire mondiale des jardins*, Albin Michel, Paris, 1980.

KRETZULESCO-QUARANTA E., *Les Jardins du Songe et la Mystique de la Renaissance*, Paris, 1970.

LABORDE A. DE, *Description des nouveaux jardins de la France et de ses anciens châteaux*, Paris, 1908.

LE DANTEC D. et J.-P., *Le Roman des jardins de France, leur histoire*, Plon, 1987.

LEHRMAN, *Earthly Paradise Garden and Courtyard in Islam*, London, 1980.

LE ROUGE, *Le Jardin anglo-chinois à la mode*, 1776, 1789.

McCLUNG W.A., *Dimore celesti. L'Architettura del Paradiso. The Architecture of Paradise, Survivals of Eden and Jerusalem*, University of California, 1983.

MARIETTE-BEY A., *Dier-el-Bahari*, Leipzig, 1877.

MAURICHEAU-BEAUPRÉ Ch, *Palais et Jardins du Grand Siècle*. F. Nathan, Paris, 1950.

MOREL J.-M., *Théorie des jardins, ou l'Art des jardins de la nature*, Paris, 1776.

NERAUDAU J.-P., *L'Olympe du roi Soleil*, Paris, 1986.

NOLHAC P. DE, *Les Jardins de Versailles*, ed. Manzi-Noyant, Paris, 1906.
— *La Création de Versailles*, Paris, 1st ed. 1906, 2nd ed. 1925.

PECHÈRE R., *Parcs et Jardins de Belgique*, Brussels, 1976.

POPE A.U. and ACKERMAN, 'Persian Gardens' in *A Survey of Persian Art*, Oxford, 1939.

PRIETO-MORENO F., *Los Jardines de Granada*, Madrid, 1952.
— *Quatre Siècles de jardins à la française*, Hachette, Paris, 1910.

RAMBACH P. and S., *Gardens of Longevity in China and Japan*, Rizzoli International, 1987.

RUTTEN A. et LACAM J., 'Les Jardins suspendus de Babylone', *Revue horticole*, Paris, 1949.

SANTARCANGELI P., *Le Livre des labyrinthes*, Gallimard, Paris, 1974.

SAUBAN M. et SAUDA-SKIRA S., *De folie en folies. La découverte du monde des jardins*, Paris, 1986.

SCHAARSCHMIDT-RICHTER I., *Le Jardin japonais*. Fribourg-Paris, 1979.

SHEPHERD J.C. and JELLICOE G.A., *Italian Gardens of the Renaissance*, London, 1925 (2nd ed. 1953).

SIBTHORP J., *Flora Graeca*, ed. J.E. Smith, Oxford Univ., 1806–1840.

SIREN O., *China and Gardens in Europe in the xviiith Century*, New York, 1950.

STEIN H., *Les Jardins de France des origines à la fin du xviiie siècle*, D.A. Longuet, Paris, 1913.
— 'Jardins en miniature d'Extrême-Orient', *Bull Soc. franç. d'Extrême-Orient*, XLII, 1942.

STRONG R. *The Renaissance Garden in England*, London, 1979.
— *The Garden. A Celebration of One Thousand Years of British Gardening*. Exhibition at Victoria and Albert Museum, 1979.
— *The Oxford Companion to Gardens*. Consultant editors: George Jellicoe, Susan Jellicoe. Executive editors: Patrick Gooke, Michael Lancaster, Oxford University Press, Oxford, 1986.

TRIGGS H.I., *Formal Gardens in England and Scotland*, London, 1902.

WATELET Cl. H., *Essai sur les jardins*, Paris, 1774.

CREDITS FOR ILLUSTRATIONS

110, Pratolino, Villa Demidoff/Ph. Alinari.
112, Florence, Museo Topografico 'Firenze com'era'/Ph. G. Dagli Orti.
113, Maser, Villa Barbaro/Ph. Alinari.
115, Paris, Bibliothèque Nationale/Ph. B.N.
116, Paris, Bibliothèque Nationale/Ph. B.N.
117, Paris, Bibliothèque Nationale/Ph. B.N.
118–119, Paris, Bibliothèque Nationale/Ph. B.N.
118 b, Woburn Abbey/by kind permission of the Marquess of Tavistock and the trustees of Bedford Estate.
119 tr and b, Paris, Bibliothèque Nationale/Ph. B.N.
120, Salzburg, Hellbrunn/Ph. G. Bazin.
121, Salzburg, Hellbunn/Ph. J.-Ch. Pratt-Diaf.
123, Paris, Bibliothèque Nationale/Ph. B.N.
124, Versailles, château/Ph. J.-P. Pratt-Diaf.
127, Vaux-le-Vicomte/Ph. J.-Ch. Pratt-Diaf.
128, Paris, Bibliothèque Nationale/Ph. B.N.
130, Vaux-le-Vicomte/Ph. J.-Ch. Pratt-Diaf.
131, Versailles, Grand Trianon/Ph. J. Gabanou-Diaf.
132, Versailles, Musée National du château/Ph. G. Dagli Orti.
133, Versailles, château/Ph. J.-P. Langeland-Diaf.
134, Versailles, château/Ph. J.-P. Langeland-Diaf.
135, Versailles, château/Ph. J.-P. Langeland-Diaf.
136–137, Versailles, château/Ph. J.-P. Langeland-Diaf.
138, Versailles, Musée National du château/Ph. G. Dagli Orti.
139, Versailles, château/Ph. J.-Ch. Pratt-Diaf.
140, Versailles, château/Ph. J.-P. Langeland-Diaf.
141, Versailles, Musée National du château/Ph. G. Dagli Orti.
142, Versailles, Musée National du château/Ph. G. Dagli Orti.
143, Versailles, Musée National du château/Ph. G. Dagli Orti.
144, Paris, Bibliothèque Nationale/Ph. B.N.
145, Montreal, Museum of Fine Arts/Ph. Museum.
147 t, Versailles, Musée National du château/Ph. G. Dagli Orti.
147 b, Paris, Musée des Arts Decoratifs/Ph. G. Dagli Orti.
148, Chantilly, château/Ph. D.R.
149, Chantilly, Musée Condé/Ph. G. Dagli Orti.
150–151, Chantilly, château/Ph. B. Régent-Diaf.
152, Nîmes, Jardins de la Fontaine/Ph. G. Biollay-Diaf.
153 t, Paris, Bibliothèque Nationale/Ph. B.N.
153 b, Marburg, Hessisches Staatsarchiv/Ph. Staatsarchiv.
154 t, Schwetzingen, castle/Ph. J.-P. Langeland-Diaf.
154 b, Paris, Fondation Wildenstein/Ph. G. Dagli Orti.
155, Schwetzingen, castle/Ph. J.-P. Langeland-Diaf.
156 t and b, Peterhof, castle/Ph. J.-P. Garcin-Diaf.
158–59, Schönbrunn, castle/Ph. B. Régent-Diaf.
161, Budapest, Hungarian Historical Monuments Service/Ph. H.H.M.S.
162, Collodi, Villa Garzoni/Ph. B. Belly-Diaf.
163, Frascati, Villa, Aldobrandini/Ph. Alinari.
164, Frascati, Villa Aldobrandini/Ph. Anderson-Alinari.
165, Paris, Bibliothèque Nationale/Ph. B.N.
166 t, Florence, Boboli Gardens/Ph. Alinari.
166 b, Rome, Villa Albani/Ph. Alinari.
168–169, Florence, Boboli Gardens/Ph. Brogi-Alinari.
170, Florence, Boboli Gardens/Ph. G. Dagli Orti.
171 t, Collodi, Villa Garzoni/Ph. Lamontagne-Diaf.
171 b, Collodi, Villa Garzoni/Ph. Alinari.
172, Isola Bella, Palazzo Borromeo/Ph. Alinari.
173, Paris, Bibliothèque Nationale/Ph. B.N.
174, Caserta, palace/Ph. Brogi-Alinari.
175, Valsanzibio, Villa Barbarigo/Ph. G. Dagli Orti.
176–77, Valsanzibio, Villa Barbarigo/Ph. G. Dagli Orti.
178, Stra, Villa Pisani/Ph. G. Bazin.
179, Stra, Villa Pisani/Ph. G. Dagli Orti.
180, La Granja, San Ildefonso/Ph. Ch. Bouret-Diaf.

181, La Granja, San Ildefonso/Ph. Ch. Bouret-Diaf.
182–183, Benfica, La Fronteira/Ph. G. Dagli Orti.
184, Paris, Bibliothèque Nationale/Ph. B.N.
185, Paris, Bibliothèque Nationale/Ph. B.N.
186 t, Bayreuth, hermitage/Ph. G. Bazin.
186 b, Bayreuth, hermitage/Ph. D.R. coll. G. Bazin.
187, Vertshöchheim, castle/Ph. Schapowalow-Sperber-Diaf.
188, Paris, Bibliothèque Nationale/Ph. B.N.
189, Melk, abbey/Ph. Th. Jullien-Diaf.
190 t, Braga, Bom Jesus/Ph. G. Bazin.
190 b, Braga, Bom Jesus/Ph. Confraria do Bom Jesus do Monte.
191 t and b, Braga, Bom Jesus/Ph. G. Bazin.
191 c, Ancaiano, Villa Cetinale/Ph. G. Bazin.
192, Kew Gardens/Ph. J. Foley-Diaf.
193, Stowe Gardens/Ph. J. Foley-Diaf.
195 t, Paris, Bibliothèque Nationale/Ph. B.N.
195 bl, Paris, Bibliothèque Nationale/Ph. B.N.
195 br, Stowe Gardens/Ph. J. Foley-Diaf.
196, Woodstock, Blenheim Palace/© Helen Gibson, with kind permission of Blenheim Palace Estate Office.
197, Woodstock, Blenheim Palace/Ph. J. Foley-Diaf.
198, Woodstock, Blenheim Palace/Ph. J. Foley-Diaf.
199, Paris, Bibliothèque Nationale/Ph. B.N.
200, Rousham House/Ph. J. Foley-Diaf.
201, Rousham House/Ph. J. Foley-Diaf.
202, Stourhead/Ph. J. Foley-Diaf.
204–205, Stourhead/Ph. J. Foley-Diaf.
206, Mount Vernon/c The Mount Vernon Ladies' Association of the Union.
207, Mount Vernon/Ph. Lamontagne-Diaf.
208, Chanteloup/Ph. R. Rozencwajg-Diaf.
210, Paris, private coll./Ph. D.R.
211, Paris, Fondation Wildenstein/Ph. G. Dagli Orti.
212, Paris, private coll./Ph. D.R.
213 l, Versailles, Petit Trianon/Ph. J. Loiseau-Diaf.
213 r, Rambouillet, château/Ph. J.-Ch. Pratt-Diaf.
214, Paris, Bibliothèque Nationale/Ph. B.N.
216, Kew Gardens/Ph. Lamontagne-Diaf.
218, London, St James's Park/Ph. J. Foley-Diaf.
219, Paris, Bois de Boulogne/Ph. J. Foley-Diaf.
221, Barcelona, Parc Güell/Ph. Pratt-Pries-Diaf.
223, Coll. G. Bazin/Ph. D.R.
225, Wicklow, Powerscourt/Ph. Lamontagne-Diaf.
226 t, Gwynedd, Bodnant Gardens/Ph. Pratt-Pries-Diaf.
226 b, Hidcote Manor Gardens/Ph. Lamontagne-Diaf.
227, Sissinghurst Castle/Ph. Lamontagne-Diaf.
228–229, Charleston, Magnolia Gardens/Ph. Magnolia Gardens-Diaf.
230, San Simeon, Hearst Castle/Ph. B. Régent-Diaf.
231. San Simeon, Hearst Castle/Ph. B. Régent-Diaf.
232, Petropolis, Summer Palace/Ph. J.-P. Langeland-Diaf.
233, Boulogne-sur-Seine, Albert Kahn Garden Ph. Lamontagne-Diaf.
234, Kyoto, Ryōan-ji/Ph. S.H.-Diaf.
237, Paris, Bibliothèque Nationale/Ph. B.N.
238, Paris, private coll./Ph. G. Dagli Orti.
239, Peking, Summer Palace/Ph. A. McKenzie-Diaf.
240 t, Paris, Bibliothèque Nationale/Ph. B.N.
240 b, Peking, Summer Palace/Ph. A. McKenzie-Diaf.
241, Kyoto, Ryōan-ji/Ph. S.H.-Diaf.
243 t, Kyoto, Ginkakuji/Ph. Katsuhisa Otsuka-Sekai Bunka Photo.
243 b, Kyoto, Byōdō'in/Ph. S.H.-Diaf.
244, Kyoto, Ryōan-ji/Ph. S.H.-Diaf.
246–247, Kyoto, Daisen/Ph. S.H.-Diaf.
248, Paris, private coll./Ph. G. Dagli Orti.